Being Christian

Being Christian in Education

*Reflecting on Christian professional
practice in a secular world*

Edited by

Hazel Bryan and Howard Worsley

Canterbury
Christ Church
University

CANTERBURY
PRESS

Norwich

First published in 2015 by the Canterbury Press Norwich
Editorial office
3rd Floor, Invicta House,
108–114 Golden Lane,
London EC1Y 0TG

Canterbury Press is an imprint of Hymns Ancient and Modern Ltd
(a registered charity)
13A Hellesdon Park Road, Norwich,
Norfolk, NR6 5DR, UK

www.canterburypress.co.uk

British Library Cataloguing in Publication data

A catalogue record for this book is available
from the British Library

978 1-84825-752-8

Typeset by Manila Typesetting Company
Printed and bound in Great Britain
by 4edge Limited

Contents

Contributors

Clare Andrews is a senior lecturer in diagnostic radiography at Canterbury Christ Church University. Prior to that she was a teacher of religious education at secondary level and has a degree in theology. Her teaching responsibilities are focused primarily on collaborative practice and radiography in complex environments. Clare's academic interests include the nature and development of professionalism in student radiographers, and the relationship between theology and education in the higher education sector.

Martin Bedford: born on the last day of 1959 into a loving family, Martin was proficient in the arts but studied politics at university. Finding his vocation (and future wife) in nursing, Martin worked with people with cancer and later became a clinical nurse specialist in haemophilia and HIV disease, then a senior lecturer in nursing at Canterbury Christ Church University. Happily married with two sons and living in a rural Kent community, he became a Christian 12 years ago and is active in his local church.

Trevor Gerhardt was born in South Africa. He trained and worked as a Baptist Church minister and served as a staff member of Youth With A Mission. He has lived and worked in the UK since 2002. He is married and has two children. He is the assistant director of Formation and Ministry for the Diocese of Rochester (Church of England) with specific responsibility as the programme director for curacy and adviser for continuing ministerial development. In his spare time he enjoys surfing.

Tom German is a qualified teacher who taught for two years in a further education college before changing careers. He began in higher education by taking an undergraduate degree in religious studies and a masters degree in applied theology that focused on the purpose of religious education. Tom's academic areas of interest include modern theology, continental philosophy and their possible applications to education.

Joan Gibson qualified as a teacher in 1980 and has worked in a range of primary schools in the Midlands, latterly as head-teacher. From an early stage of her career she became interested in children who did not conform to expectations within school. The Church of England school that Joan led over the last 12 years developed a strong reputation for inclusivity and had specialist provision for children with moderate and severe learning difficulties and autistic spectrum disorders.

Aidan Gillespie: originally from County Mayo in Ireland, Aidan came to the UK in 1999. After studying with the Open University for a degree in religious studies and linguistics, Aidan completed his teacher training and embarked on a career in education which has seen him teach in faith and non-faith primary schools. Aidan is now lecturing in initial teacher training at Canterbury Christ Church University and is currently researching teachers' understanding and expressions of spirituality in their professional practice.

Andrea Haith is a teacher of religious education and English. She is currently working in a secondary school in Derbyshire. Her interests include the teaching of values, controversial issues and philosophy for children. She has a particular interest in the teaching of religiously inspired violence.

Robert Jackson: 'I've always rebelled . . . or is it simply a case of wanting to be myself? As a vicar's son, I became an atheist during confirmation classes, only to be brought back into the fold, mid-Atlantic, after a disastrous seven-year exploration of life as I wanted it to be. Ordination after another seven years clearly meant following the family tradition and running a parish but no . . . I found myself working in boarding schools for 19 years. I needed to justify myself so had to work out a Christian rationale for what I was doing. One of my key concerns was how might I serve, as a Christian, within the confines of a classroom, not ashamed of my faith, and prepared to give it epistemological status in a secular education system that is resistant to alternative world-views'.

Martin Jamieson: Martin's involvement in educational development work began in 2003 while teaching trainee teachers in South Africa and Zambia. Contact with Malawians in Zambia led to small-scale projects in both countries. In 2007 he worked with Voluntary Service Overseas at the Ministry of Education in Ethiopia, guiding the country's teacher-trainers training programme. This provided invaluable insights to 'development' work. He is currently working with a Malawian NGO, building a teacher centre where inclusive practice and spiritual values are encouraged.

Marion Khan is a Christian, a nurse and a clinical educator working in the NHS at York Teaching Hospital's NHS Foundation Trust. She currently leads the clinical development team within the organization and facilitates the clinical skills, education, and professional development of non-medical staff. She has a particular interest in spirituality issues in health care, especially in the education and training of nurses.

Nana Kyei-Baffour is a Pentecostal minister with Assemblies of God, UK. He has been in church ministry since 1992; an educator in Pentecostal theological institutions and a Pentecostal/generic health care chaplain at Guy's and St Thomas' NHS Foundation Trust, London since 2004. His current roles include: senior pastor at Victory-City Assemblies of God Church, London; spirituality and disability advisor/chaplain at Guy's and St Thomas NHS Foundation Trust; an adjunct faculty with Global University (USA); and a distance learning tutor with Assemblies of God Bible College in Mattersey, Doncaster.

Janet Northing has been a Church Army evangelist and non-stipendiary licensed lay worker in the Church of England since 1987. Qualifying as a primary school teacher in 1998, she gained a first class B.Ed (honours) degree from Cheltenham and Gloucester College of Higher Education, and subsequently taught in a range of community and church primary schools. In 2002, following two years' part-time study at King's College London, she gained a masters in religious education (distinction). Janet's career in primary education culminated in her becoming head of a Church of England primary school in 2007, a post she held until her retirement from primary headship in 2013. Janet now works part time as a diocesan schools support consultant for Peterborough Diocese and carries out SIAMS inspections for several dioceses. She is currently leading a project with eight primary schools linked to 'What if Learning' for Peterborough Diocese.

Phillip O'Connor was born in Birmingham, England but brought up in Jamaica by Evangelical Christian parents. In 1982, at the age of 18, he embarked on teacher training at the University of the West Indies, through Mico Teachers' College. Phillip taught for eight years in Jamaica before emigrating to the Cayman Islands where he taught in a private church school for six years, concurrently serving three years as youth minister at his affiliated local Evangelical church. Phillip returned to the United Kingdom in 2001 and has continued in the teaching profession to date. Although he has taught many subjects over the last 30 years at both primary and secondary levels, he is now teaching advanced level sociology and personal social health and citizenship education (PSHCE) in a grammar school while also pursuing a doctorate in education part time. Phillip has been facilitating and continues to facilitate faith-based youth and men's seminars and serves as lay-speaker in Jamaica, Cayman Islands, USA and five churches in the UK.

Susan Thompson's current role focuses on supporting or leading schools to secure rapid school improvement as an interim school leader. In this capacity she has worked as a deputy head in voluntary controlled Church of England primary schools and as the acting head of a community infant school. Previously she was a diocesan schools officer working to support church schools, a Local Authority religious education adviser, and held leadership roles in a comprehensive secondary school. Susan attends a local Anglican church.

Tatiana Wilson works as a diocesan education officer for the Church of England supporting schools to be the best they can be. Previously she worked as a lecturer in primary education at Exeter and Plymouth universities as well as teaching and leading in primary and middle schools and working as an advisory teacher in London and Devon. Current projects include improving church school leadership at all levels, developing pathways for initial teacher education and supporting the improvement of religious education in schools through the Learn Teach Lead RE project www.ltlre.org. Her doctoral thesis intends to explore the Renovaré Movement's approach to spiritual development and how this might be helpful to church school leaders.

Foreword

As a Christian entering teaching at Banbury Comprehensive School in the mid-1970s, I was truly energized at the prospect of being able to live out my faith in the context of my new professional role. At university I had experienced the excitement of thinking Christianly about education and I had even managed to publish an article about that called *From the Changing Room,* which I co-authored with my lifelong friend and colleague, John Shortt (now professorial fellow in Christian education at Liverpool Hope University). But I had a bit of a shock. Apart from the writings of Philip May, a lecturer at Durham University, there was little to read that emanated from the UK; most of what I could find came from North America and Australia where the education systems were very different. The prevailing assumption seemed to be that the only way to be Christian in education was to work in an independent, explicitly Christian school. Those of us working in the state system were considered 'compromisers'. But on the other hand to seek a conversation about Christian approaches in the state-funded system was considered suspiciously fanatical. After all education is, we were told, a neutral activity governed by the tenets of reason alone. Faith had nothing to do with it. The one alternative voice that I could find came from the other side of the world in the writings of Brian Hill, a professor of education in Perth (Australia, not Scotland!). Thankfully things are different now. Across the UK, church schools are asking what it means to offer a distinctively Christian education that is an inclusive experience for all their pupils.

Now at the end of my career, I am deeply privileged to be employed as a professor of Christian education but, even so, probably only the second person to ever hold that title in an English university. I work in an institution that is proud of its foundation in 1962 as a Church of England teacher training college and is committed enough to the concept of thinking Christianly about education to have created a unique centre called the National Institute for Christian Education Research. In 2012, we celebrated our Jubilee at Canterbury Christ Church and an invitation was issued by our vice-chancellor for ideas as to how that could be marked. In one of those casual conversations that later turn out to be highly significant, my colleagues Lynn Revell, Hazel Bryan and Nigel Genders (then a governor of the University but now the chief education officer for the Church of England) came up with the idea of setting up a Jubilee cohort on our newly launched professional doctorate programme. We were joined later by Howard Worsley, and our idea was to create a learning fellowship (what some now call a community of practice) of education professionals who would commit to working each on their own thesis, but supporting each other in the shared endeavour of thinking Christianly about our different professional roles. It was a great delight to recruit 15 students; and even more of a delight for all 15 to complete the seven modules and for each to contribute a chapter to this book.

The exciting thing about this class of 15 is their diversity in the midst of shared purpose. Although all education professionals, they range across classroom teachers, headteachers, health professional educators, teacher educators, clergy educators, librarians, school chaplains, advisers, mission entrepreneurs and pastors. They also reflect a range of theological positions more diverse than anything I have experienced in any other Christian setting. There was no cosy consensus that some associate with the concept of fellowship. No one in their right mind would have brought together such a theologically diverse group. But the shared experience of struggling together with challenging ideas about education, of being side-by-side when work was failed and of trying to write at level 8, the highest level of writing required of any university student, created a spiritual bond of fellowship that transcended our theological differences. A symbol of this unity was that at each of the taught module weekends, we celebrated a Eucharist together usually led by one of the university's Anglican chaplains, but occasionally by one of our ordained course members. This celebration in the tradition of the Church of England was a powerful reminder of unity in Christ and of the saving power of the cross offered to all. For me, celebrating the Eucharist in this way was a powerful realization of that desire I had as a newly qualified teacher, namely that I might find a way for my Christian faith to be enacted in the context of the public classroom and not marginalized as a private matter, being deemed to be religious clutter in the rational task of education.[1] But it was also a symbol of how even deeply held differences of belief and experience need not be barriers to fellowship. As a group I think we learned to love each other and discovered how to be friends and encouragers to each other. Without that experience I doubt very much that there would be 15 chapters in this book. It has certainly convinced me that universities ought to think more about how to make the student experience one of love and fellowship; and indeed worship.

This book is made up of 15 tales from Canterbury. Each tale is the story from one of our students, the story of how their Christian faith and their professional role have interacted. The newly qualified teacher that I was in 1974 would have been thrilled to have had such a book to read, although no doubt nonplussed that the Christian world is not the uniform phenomenon that I, at that time, assumed it to be.

Trevor Cooling
Canterbury, April 2015

---

1 Trevor Cooling, 2010, *Doing God in Education*, London: Theos

Preface

The world seems more religious than ever and the religious has never been more controversial. News is dominated by reports of religious-inspired violence, and conflict and interventions by religious leaders are often treated with suspicion or as anachronistic. As a teacher of religious education and then as a lecturer in initial teacher education I understood that my subject was not like other subjects, it was more sensitive, more likely to cause offence, and it was harder to justify its place in the curriculum than other subjects. The backdrop to my job as a specialist in RE and then as programme director of the Ed. D has been characterized by ongoing debates about the nature of the education provided by church schools, or the legitimacy of faith perspectives on education. I have always wondered why these discussions are often so acrimonious and defined by caricatures and stereotypes of what religious people think or how Christian teachers behave. The frenzied and often comical polemics of the new atheists seem to have set the tone for much of the current debates and I have been entertained but never challenged: they seem to protest too much.

Teaching in a Christian university and often teaching Christian students it was impossible not to realize that the hostility and fear of the religious and the hysterical tone of much of the debates about religion and education often had the effect of closing down discussions. In an educational system that is supposedly liberal and one that reflects a plural and diverse society, Christian voices, indeed all religious voices, seemed to be marginalized and even censored. There are many areas of education that are informed and underpinned by Christianity that are rarely the subject of research. The experiences and insights of many Christian teachers and headteachers are often ghettoized and therefore lost to mainstream discussions about education.

Shortly after launching the Ed. D at Canterbury Christ Church University, I asked my head of department, Hazel Bryan, whether it would be possible to develop a cohort that was designed to welcome Christian teachers and educators so that we could create a community of learners that shared a desire to discuss and research in Christianity and education. With her support we developed the idea. Trevor Cooling helped us translate the ideas into a plan and the authors of the chapters in this book became the Jubilee cohort.

The idea for a book written by students came out of a desire to capture the spirit and camaraderie generated by the Jubilee cohort but also to share the insights and experiences of students who had worked to understand the relationship between faith and education in so many different ways. The stories are particular and personally inspired by faith but they are also universal.

Every teacher and everyone involved in education struggles in some way to reconcile or comprehend their personal beliefs in the context of the bigger education picture. The expectations of curriculum and institutions, Ofsted or professional codes means that we must all find ways of being true to our beliefs while upholding the highest professional standards. The chapters in this book provide a glimpse of how difficult that juggling between faith, belief and professionalism can be, but also how valuable and how rewarding.

Lynn Revell
Programme director, Ed. D
Canterbury, April 2015

Introduction

Canterbury Christ Church University celebrated its Diamond Jubilee in 2012. As part of a suite of celebratory initiatives, we designed and welcomed a Christian cohort onto our professional doctorate, the Ed. D. The outcome of this venture was a critical mass of thinkers and research that began to debate the Christian contribution to public education. As the group of 15 students began their journey, it was clear that they were beginning to bring their lived experience and researched perspectives to shape new thinking in education. This book is the published reflections of that cohort.

The experience of the Jubilee research cohort

From the outset, it was clear that this cohort of students was special, evidenced in the energy that was felt when the group convened for the residential conferences that focused upon philosophical, political, sociological and methodological dimensions of education alongside the insights of Christian thinking. In this group we had students who were headteachers and teachers in both the primary and secondary sectors studying alongside church ministers and chaplains. To complete the cohort there were also staff from the university, educationalists from the health sector and people in early retirement. Together we formed a temporary community, committed together for the duration of the taught programme. At the end of the initial 18-month period of face-to-face teaching, before the students progressed to conduct their field research under supervision, they agreed to write an article for publication. It is this you now hold in your hands. The writing is creative, reflective and above all, earthed, arising from the lived context of practitioners who are developing as reflective researchers that feed back into their praxis. They all comment on the experience of what it is to be Christian in a changing landscape.

What being Christian feels like in Britain today

There has been significant shift in public thinking in the UK in recent years. It seems as if the historic confidence of religious faith is no longer available in public discourse. Maybe religious thinking has lost its privileged position as occupying the moral high ground and must now compete for a humbler place. In this competed space the measured, gentle voice of historic faith is not often heard, since it is drowned out by the more extreme voices of either religious fundamentalisms or confident humanisms. As well as an increasing secularist confidence, another factor impacting on Christian experience and the lived reality of all engaged in public schooling is the influence of political intervention. The educational policy landscape in the UK has been characterized by high levels of government intervention since the Education Reform Act (ERA 1988). This period coincides with the wider public reforms that Conservative, New Labour and then the Coalition governments initiated. At the heart of these reforms was a view that the public sector could not be left to the professional groups that traditionally ran them. New policies for education saw the introduction of an internal market where schools were encouraged to compete for pupils and resources allocated on the basis of need. The reforms were based on the idea that the public sector could learn from the private sector and were characterized by high levels of managerialism where the focus was on the 'delivery' of public services that were efficient, effective and economic. This has led to what can be termed 'the commodification of education' where education has been subjected to high levels of marketization. The resulting educational sphere has been referred to as a 'quasi market'. The essence of this shift has been that education is moving from a social to an economic good, where 'particular versions of events' are generated as policy discourse. This has been a rich vein of research for our Jubilee cohort of doctoral students who have reflected this shift in their discussions, research and writings.

A Christian response to education?

In parallel with the education policy backdrop sketched above, the Church has traditionally worked in three particular ways in education: mission, nurture and service. Seen in broadest terms these might be described as:

- Mission: viewed as a broad concept, yet both explicit (such as mentioning Jesus, prayer) and implicit (such as doing things in a Christian manner, relying on God's Holy Spirit);
- Nurture: nurturing people in faith or simply as human beings and nurturing the developing child;
- Service: serving the nation. This is an inclusive understanding of education, often attached to government agendas.

To paraphrase Jeff Astley, honorary professor in the Department of Theology and Religion at the University of Durham, these concepts might also be described in three distinct styles of seeing Christian involvement in education. These are:

- Education into Christianity;
- Education about Christianity;
- Education in a Christian manner.

The Jubilee cohort were students who could relate to these various aspects of traditional Christian involvement in education while looking for fresh engagement in an increasingly secularist and yet religiously and spiritually pluralistic society.

Structure of the book

This book is structured in two parts:

Part One: 'Travelling with Faith: reflections upon Christian professional practice in a secular world'.

Part Two: 'Living with Faith: making sense of faith in professional contexts'.

In Part One the chapters reflect the ways in which Christian professionals seek to navigate their personal beliefs within secular, public sector contexts. Martin Bedford's Chapter 1 takes the reader by the hand into the lived experience of a Christian nurse trainer as he considers the impact of his faith on his professional identity and practice. Martin proposes love-centred virtue ethics as a basis for nurse training in this particularly personal chapter.

In Chapter 2 Clare Andrews explores the notion of Christian hospitality as a paradigm for inter-professional learning. In this, Clare proposes the concept of teacher as host, and situates practice within the context of professional requirements. Do these, Clare asks, act as boundaries to learning and what part might the notion of teacher as host play in addressing this?

Chapter 3 opens with a morning car journey to work, listening to the *Today* programme on Radio 4; who among us hasn't made such a journey? In this chapter Marion Khan explains how one such journey changed her perspective on her professional practice, enabling her to fuse her Christian faith with her nursing practice. Marion's image of the aviator is particularly imaginative, and plays with concepts of control, autopilot and, of course, flying.

Aidan Gillespie's Chapter 4 invites us into the world of Quakerism, illuminating in a deeply personal fashion what living to the educational ideals of Quakerism means for a teacher-educator. In this chapter, Aidan brings to the fore the ways in which his professional practice, shaped by his Quaker belief, is rooted in relationships. Aidan's faith influences the way he enacts and interprets his professional role, as one where he seeks to help students to find their unique gifts.

In Chapter 5, Phillip O'Connor asks what sustains a life in professional practice. Phillip's work as a teacher of PSHCE, now in a grammar school in England but previously in the Caribbean, is explored in relation to his faith.

The final chapter in Part One has been written by Andrea Haith, a teacher in a secondary school in England. Chapter 6 takes a deeply political stance, considering the concept and construct of 'Fundamental British Values' as set out in the Teachers' Standards of 2012. Andrea grapples with faith, values, education policy and notions of 'British-ness' in this chapter.

Part Two explores the ways in which professionals who work in Christian contexts interpret and enact their roles, and illuminates challenges they face in the daily life of their work in the public, private and third sectors.

In Chapter 7, Martin Jamieson takes us into faith-based development work. As a founder and director of a Christian non-governmental organization in Malawi, Martin sets out the complex ethical and cultural dilemmas he navigates as he enacts his Christian mission. In his work Martin explains the guest house and its integral and essential place in the project. The notion of host resonates here with Clare Andrew's considerations of hospitality in Chapter 2.

The African Pentecostal Church (APC) is the subject of Chapter 8. Nana Kyei-Baffour provides the reader with a highly detailed and colourful picture of the African Pentecostal Church, considering the structural ingredients needed for effective ministry as well as for the healthy and holistic growth of congregation. Adult education within the APC is of particular focus in this chapter.

Trevor Gerhardt takes us into the world of curate training in Chapter 9. Trevor proposes a theology of learning and formation as he sets out a range of scenarios to provide the reader with insights and challenges in the professional development of the curate.

Chapter 10 considers the competing voices of church, state and church schools in education in Britain today. Tatiana Wilson calls for schools to be supported through the Church in developing a language to articulate more explicitly a vision for the 'good life'. Tatiana's experiences as a headteacher and diocesan education officer ground this chapter in lived experiences.

The Christian school theme continues into Chapter 11 where Janet Northing proposes the notion of the church school as a pilgrim community. In this, Janet draws upon her experiences as a former headteacher, and explores pilgrim identity and pilgrim community as a means by which the church school can interpret and enact its mission.

Joan Gibson is also a former headteacher. In Chapter 12 Joan grapples with the dilemma of leading a school, the philosophy of which is based upon inclusive practice, when faced with the 'performative' consequences of admitting a child whose profile would compromise the overall school performance grades. In this Joan asks 'Which of you, if your son asks for bread, will give him a stone?' This is a deeply challenging position that Joan navigates with dexterity.

The role of the headteacher is also explored by Susan Thompson in Chapter 13. Susan takes the image of the good shepherd and explores leadership in relation to shepherding, managing one's flock, considering rare breeds and standardized practices when faced with particular needs in a specified geographical area. The biblical image of the good shepherd infuses this chapter with a Christian focus.

Chapter 14 introduces the reader to the way in which Robert Jackson teaches spiritual and moral education to secondary pupils. Robert makes an impassioned case for storytelling as an essential pedagogy in speaking to young people. Robert's mission as a school chaplain was to educate the character and in this he draws upon Alasdair MacIntyre's *After Virtue* to situate his philosophy and practice.

Tom German's chapter on the use of Michel Foucault completes Part Two of this book. Tom introduces the reader to key elements of Foucault's writing, in particular *Discipline and Punish* and *Madness and Civilization*. Tom draws out key images and concepts from both texts that 'speak' to education in Britain today. Chapter 15 sets out the ways in which Foucault's work can illuminate current challenges in Christian education.

We hope you enjoy our tales from Canterbury and find them illuminating, challenging and thought-provoking.

Part One

'Travelling with Faith: reflections upon Christian professional practice in a secular world'

I

Engaging love: A teacher of nurses' tale

MARTIN BEDFORD

Christ has no body now but yours, no hand, no feet on Earth but yours.
Yours are the eyes with which He looks with compassion on the world.
Yours are the feet with which He walks to do good.
Yours are the hands with which He blesses all the world.

Teresa of Avila (attributed)

Abstract

This chapter considers (with a nod to Chaucer's *Canterbury Tales*) a journey of faith for a nurse teacher and the impact of faith on nurse preparation. It explores the state of nurse education today and offers a commentary upon the educational reforms in nursing over the past 30 years. Discerning an identity crisis in nursing, the chapter undertakes a reappraisal of nursing's roots including Florence Nightingale and her virtue ethics. The synthesis of Aristotelian virtue ethics with the early Christian care ethos is examined and contextualized with the current dialogue on the foundations for moral philosophy.

Love-centred virtue ethics is proposed as the basis for nurse preparation, concluding with a sketch of some of what this might look like.

Keywords

Love; faith journey; nurse education; Christian nursing; virtue ethics

Introduction

One of features of Chaucer's *Canterbury Tales* is the pervasive social stratification and the way in which each pilgrim is defined by their occupation, set within a functional divide of estates (status) of those who fight (*bellatores*), those who contemplate and preach (*oratores*) and those who work (*laborares*) (Knox, 1999). Although Chaucer's satire often hints at the decline of chivalry and of worldly corruption in the Church, his is a world where each knows their place. When they challenge this order, like the crude miller changing the prescribed order of storytelling, it is more Saturnalia than threat to the status quo.

Our Canterbury tales at this university is comprised of *oratores* – teachers, lecturers and clergy with the common purpose of exploring what it means to profess and live their faith in a range of different educational settings and contexts. In our commonwealth of equals there may be no social ordering, but each of us in our work will be affected in some way by it.

Although there are many religious references within Chaucer's *Canterbury Tales*, most of the pilgrims (including the clerical characters) are markedly worldly (Br Anthony, 1994). Unlike these largely secular tales in the God-centric medieval world of Chaucer's *Canterbury Tales*, our tales are of faith in a seemingly secular world (Armstrong, 2004) coming from rather than going to Canterbury.

Prologue

My journey into faith was an unusual one. My mother, born into a devoutly Catholic Irish/Manx family was the daughter marked to become a nun. She was happy with this pathway until she met my father, from a non-practising, nominally Anglican background. They married before World War Two, during which my father served in the Italian campaign and was shocked at the wealth of the Church in the midst of the poverty and near starvation of wartime Italians. This removed any vestiges of faith he had in churches but he retained a belief in a Supreme Being.

My family upbringing was in a house filled by the love of my parents for each other and for us children. My mother was able to convince each of us into believing that we were her favourites – we were.

I was not brought up in the church other than family weddings, baptisms and funerals and largely accepted my father's disbelief in organized religion. By my late teen years I identified with the peace and love of the hippy movement and later, at university studying politics, became a radical socialist taking a Marxian materialist view of man making God, and of religion being 'the sigh of the oppressed creature, the heart of a heartless world, and the soul of soulless conditions ... the opium of the people' (Marx, 1844).

I was happy in my unexamined atheist certainty, but I was becoming aware of the contradiction between my core ideals of peace and love and the aggression of much radical politics and increasingly disillusioned with sectarian infighting between different socialist groups, and the dogmatic interpretations of Marx's writings as credo. Looking back, I had evolved into Graham Greene's socialist lieutenant from *The Power and the Glory*, a 'little dapper figure of hate carrying his secret of love' (Greene, 2001, p. 55). After university I remained politically oriented but this became a private belief rather than an organized activity.

Entering nursing and enjoying caring for people removed any vestiges of belief in heroic revolutionary violence. Here I would love to be able to say that I had an incredible epiphany during which I had personal experience of Christ – but this did not happen. Instead, I learned my trade, became good at it and felt it allowed me to express who I am. My conversion came later in a more subtle manner, following discussion with my wife about whether we should have our children christened.

On a superficial level we wanted a family celebration, but this raised the question of why would we wish the endorsement of an institution as faulty as the Church, and a naming of our children for a superstition? This led me to consider the evidence for my atheism and the conclusion that ironically, atheism is actually a belief that cannot be proven or refuted by systematic enquiry. As such it is no more 'scientific' than belief in God. This was quite challenging for me as it undermined the foundation of many of my premises. At the same time it was a liberating paradigm shift. If there was no irrefutable evidence either way, individuals must choose atheism, God or being an agnostic. As someone who has never sat on the fence, the last of these did not seem an option so I felt I had to consider the former two. Ultimately my decision rested upon the question of whether I would prefer to live in a world with or without God. Having never really considered the possibility of God, the ripples from this *what if?* pebble reframed my perspectives. By the time I enrolled in an Alpha course I had pretty much decided and started believing in God with Jesus as my saviour and was grappling with the challenge of living *as if*.

This change was by any reckoning a fundamental shift, but in relation to my core ideals there was actually a much better fit than with Marxism. Reading the Gospels, their message of social justice and inclusion founded on a love of neighbour and fellowship (Acts 2.42) was as radical and uncompromising as anything written by socialists – arguably, with the injunction to love our enemies (Matthew 5.44), more so. Any attempts to avoid this interpretation of the Gospels seems especially wilful in the face of the clear dichotomy drawn between God and money (Matthew 6.24–26).

Although there is an abundance of very clever theology, the activity that has most deepened my knowledge of Christ has been preparing junior church lessons, and from this has grown the understanding that love is the central organizing principle of Christianity.

For me the most important moment was when I decided to look for God, rather than attempt to disprove his existence. I may not have seen my God with my physical eyes, but have perceived him with the eyes of my heart (Ephesians 1.18)

The nurse teacher's tale

This tale is that of the teacher of nurses. I have chosen the term teacher over the job description 'university lecturer' as teacher, from the Old English *tæcan*, is a broader description of the role than is lecturer with its emphasis on the act of reading.

Similarly, although the preparation of nurses is most commonly called nurse education, I shall refer to nurse training (the older term) as this is most inclusive of the breadth and physicality of this preparation and also hints at the broader socialization and inculcation of students into nursing that largely happens in the workplace.

The combination of nurse and teacher engenders a degree of identity challenge: for years I considered myself a nurse who happens to be working in education, but reflecting on my osmotic move from practice to university as a lecturer practitioner then as a full-time lecturer, I am, at the moment, despite continued engagement with practice, more of an educationalist than a practitioner.

As a vocational teacher, I focus more on the development of nurses than on excellence in a particular subject. While it is wonderful to come across a student nurse who is also a scholar, my goal in teaching is to facilitate the development of excellent and resilient nurses. This may to some degree alleviate accusations of living in an ivory tower isolated from the real world that is sometimes levelled at subject-based lecturers.

The dualistic model implicit in this perspective owes much, as Arendt (1998) reminds us, to classical Greek thought and the division between necessity and freedom where the greatest good is to be able to choose how you wish to spend your time (the *mores* of a slave economy): as she terms it the *vita activa* in contrast to the *vita contemplativa*. The Platonic take on this in the *Republic* proposes the tripartite division of function between the Guardians, subdivided into philosopher rulers and soldiers, and the remainder of the people, that is, those who work (Plato, 2001), although distorted to the needs of feudal hierarchy, this principle is the logic of the estates.

Arendt's innovation was to further subdivide the *vita activa* into labour, work, and action with each containing greater degrees of autonomy and engagement (Arendt, 1998). Arendt also points out that there is no scriptural foundation for superiority of the *vita contemplativa*; indeed she proposes that the Gospels indicate that Jesus embodies action (ibid., p. 318).

These divisions have been further altered by the development of the information age, specifically with the notion of 'information is physical' (Gleick, 2001, p. 355) in a digital economy and where thought itself has become a category of labour.

The challenge for freedom is therefore no longer the move from physical activity to mental, but rather the degree of autonomy and purposefulness that is experienced in activity, mental or physical.

As I choose to believe in Christ and that he wants us to act in the interests of our fellows, what consequence has this for nursing preparation and nursing generally?

Nurse education now

Properly conceived, teaching nurses is a challenging task. The knowledge and competency demanded of nurses has increased exponentially in recent years. This is in part due to improvements in medical technology combined with increased demand (WHO, 2003), but also due to the role-shifts in nursing practice to fill the gap left by the incremental reduction in junior doctors' hours (Ewens, 2003). This, coinciding with the move of nurse preparation from hospital-based schools of nursing to university as recommended by the UK Royal College of Nursing (RCN) Judge report on nurse education (Rye, 1985) and enacted by the United Kingdom Central Council for Nursing, Midwifery and Health Visiting (UKCC) in the 1990s as Project 2000 (P2K) (UKCC, 1986), has changed the face of nursing and health care dramatically. The confluence of these three aspects is often ignored by detractors of present-day nursing who blame academia for all of nursing's ills.

In the change from a hospital-based apprenticeship model to a formal academic one, the underpinning theoretical bases of nursing are now examined in much greater depth than previously. If nursing is the magpie profession because of its overlap with all other health-care professions, there is much that needs to be gleaned to understand the complexity of health care. P2K was long on structure and process but short on content and essence. It instituted a move from a medical model of training focused on disease and interventions to nursing models with sociological and psychological bases (Roxburgh et al., 2008) and a shift from traditional teacher-led teaching methods (Casey, 1996). Some commentators (Bradshaw, 1995) see this as an unwelcome implant of American nursing theory, diluting traditional British nursing values and vocation.

More recently there has been a greater emphasis on inclusion and diversity training with an attendant application of critical social theory (Duchscher, 2000). This has led to some conflict with calls for a greater attention to spiritual support (Nardi et al., 2011) for patients, as witnessed by such incidents as the suspension of a nurse without pay for offering to pray for a patient on the basis of breaching the NMC code of conduct by not demonstrating a personal and professional commitment to equality and diversity (editorial, *Nursing Times*, 1997). This is not to imply that critical social theory is not compatible with spirituality; it is more about conflict with a secularized bureaucratic vision of how diversity should be managed, as part of what Timmons and Narayanasamy (2011) see as *militant atheism*.

Concerns about the degree of preparedness of third-year student nurses for the staff nurse role led to a revision of the original vision of P2K with the UKCC (1999) Fitness to Practice curriculum and its greater emphasis on clinical science (Jordan et al., 1999) together with management and leadership models, and to a reorientation to practice. To some extent this represents a return to a behavioural model of training with its emphasis on practice competences.

Although there is no longer a national curriculum for nursing, external stakeholders in the form of the EU, central government, local commissioning authorities and the Nursing and Midwifery Council (NMC), all hold sway over the content and delivery of the nurse training programme. In responding to these often conflicting demands, the original intention of the proposed curriculum may be challenged, and the skill of the programme writers is to make the necessary compromises while still keeping sight of core ideals. At best these compromises and additions create an object that has the appearance and illogic of a Heath Robinson mechanism, which somehow works. At worst, they create a programme that is overcomplex, that overassesses students and follows no logical progression. Without a clear unifying concept teaching may be atomized into a modular rather than programme focus. Students may see each module as a hoop to leap through and relevance to practice may not be recognized: one of the effects of the so-called *Mcdonaldization of Higher Education* (Hayes and Wynyard, 2002).

In both, once the unifying purpose of the curriculum is obscured, there may be a reduction in engagement and an increase in both strategic learning and teaching – the students are taught, and learn what they require, to pass module assignments, rather than what they need to be effective and caring nurses.

Some analysts bemoan the manner in which nursing curricula change so rapidly in response to external demands (Roxburgh et al., 2008) and compare it unfavourably with the more self-confident and self-referring medical curriculum. While this willingness to adapt to the external context is central to its role of responding to the needs of the world, perhaps nursing should be more evaluative about which and whose needs it is responding to. This would require a greater consensus on what nursing's core values are; perhaps the P2K experiment was ended too quickly.

For a few decades there has also been an ongoing debate regarding what advanced practice actually looks like, with some arguing for greater clinical overlap with medicine and others proposing greater nursing-based expertise, together with muddled distinctions between advanced and specialist nursing (Mantzoukas and Watkinson, 2007). This has led nursing theorists to question what nursing actually is. The RCN (2003) found it necessary to define nursing in order to distinguish it from other professions and from nursing carried out by non-professional carers, and suggested, cryptically, that nursing is a paradox and that 'part of the paradox is that the more skilful a nurse is in what they do, the less likely will be the observer, or even the patient, to recognize exactly what has been done' (ibid. p. 4).

At times it seems that nurse training is a profession with an identity crisis, a rudderless ship blown hither and thither by prevailing social winds and economic undercurrents, without even the safety of an anchoring agreed identity and mission.

In the wake of concerns around institutional abuse identified in inquiries of Winterbourne View (Flynn, 2012) and the unacceptably low levels of care in Mid Staffordshire, highlighted in the Francis Report (DOH, 2013), the Department of Health endorsed as policy chief nurse Jane Cummings' vision for nursing *Compassion in Practice* (DoH, 2012). This strategic call for action aims to embed six values – care, compassion, courage, communication, competence and commitment (the 6 Cs of nursing) in all settings and aspects of nursing, including recruitment, education and practice. The NMC has responded to the Francis report in a number of ways including a (current) revision of its *Standards of conduct, performance and ethics for nurse and midwives* – the Code of Conduct (NMC, 2013) with the express purpose of underlining the principle of always putting patients first.

Implicit within these initiatives is the recognition that the ethos of nursing has been threatened. Judgement on whether this is due to nurse education, workload, organization of care or some deterioration in the quality of nurses is an ideological acid test, but there is broad agreement that something has gone wrong.

Both the 6 Cs and the draft revision to the Code of Conduct give focus to moral behaviour as an aspect of practice competence, rather than something distinct from it. For both, health care without compassion is not health care, this being mirrored in the findings of the Willis commission on nurse education (2013).

Arendt (1978) looking to the etymology of morality (Latin *mores* – custom) and ethics (Greek – habit) makes a useful distinction between morality as pertaining to the rules and ethics as our actual behaviour.

Where there have previously been calls for the need to place ethics at the centre of nurse education, including P2K (Sellman, 1997), these have usually been interpreted by HEIs in the more abstract sense of ethical theory as curriculum content rather than the actual ethical actions of nurses, with the behavioural aspects poorly covered by the *unwritten curriculum* (ibid. p. 9).

Instead Sellman calls for a re-evaluation of Nightingale's notion of training nurses in *the virtues* (ibid.), and their basis in virtue ethics originating from a merger of early Christianity and Aristotelian ethics apparent in monastic nursing: a return to mission.

Health care and early Christianity

Centrality of care for the sick in Christianity is supported scripturally by Christ's healing mission, which is indicated in all the Gospels (Matthew 12.1–14; Mark 2.23–3.6; Luke 6.1–11 and John 5.1–18) as being more important than formal religious observation. It is also significant that Luke, who recounts the parable of the Good Samaritan, is himself a physician.

Many authors have charted the origins of nursing as an organized activity from within early Christianity. The Christian emphasis on care of strangers moved nursing outside the informal domestic milieu (Nelson, 1995), and internalization of the notion of caring for Christ through caring for those in need (Matthew 25.45) made nursing a holy duty and a form of worship in its own right.

By the sixth century St Benedict's rules (Benedict, 1949) gave primacy to this holy duty, 'Before and above all things, care must be taken of the sick, that they be served in very truth as Christ is served; because He hath said, "I was sick and you visited Me"' (Matthew 25.36).

This duty to those in need rather than those who could pay or those who were family and friends provided the founding principles of many monastic orders and the medieval hospital. Ferngren (2009) considers the development of this charitable health care for all a uniquely Christian contribution. Elsewhere Ferngren (cited in Koenig et al., 2012) also charts the emergence of the concept of *care* rather than *cure* as being a novel development and the chief motive for early Christian health practices.

The site of the world's first hospital may be disputed, but there is consensus that hospitals in the modern sense of in-patient care from physicians and nurses originated with the development of the hospital at Caesarea under the orders of St Basil, later modelled throughout the Christian world (Koenig et al., 2012).

The very words hospital, hospice and hospitality all derive from the Latin *hospes* which has multiple meanings – foreigner, stranger, guest and host. This, more than the noun *infirmary* (from the Latin, *infirmus* – weak), indicates the primacy of relationship and reciprocity between carer and patient.

Modern nursing and Christianity

With the dissolution of monasteries in Britain, and despite ongoing Protestant philanthropy, much of the ecclesiastical basis of nursing was lost and for many reverted to being an aspect of woman's domestic labour. In part this was due to the generally less *hands-on* approach of Protestant charity (Kahl, 2005) in contrast to the direct health care of Catholic nursing orders at this time.

By the early Victorian age the stereotypical nurse and midwife was represented by Dickens' grotesque Sarah Gamp – dishonest, lazy and gin sodden. Despite being a caricature, there is broad agreement that there is historical accuracy in the portrayal (Summers, 1989). Gamp was very much a servant, albeit one who was able to exercise her resentful power over her patients.

It was from continental nursing, where the monastic principles had been retained, that Florence Nightingale took her inspiration for reform. A devout Christian, Nightingale was directly influenced by Catholic nursing orders and the unmarried Protestant deaconess sisterhood of Kaiserwerth *Mutterhaus* (motherhouse). Despite considering conversion to Catholicism (Nelson, 1995), largely because of the opportunities it afforded to women, Nightingale was not attracted towards churches and saw dogma and ritual as barriers to true Christianity. Instead she opted for a Christ-inspired secular basis for nursing care, and opposed religious testing for applicants to nursing (Selanders and Crane, 2010).

Retaining much from her Unitarian roots, Nightingale's faith was in the Western mystical tradition of luminaries such as St Francis of Assisi and St Theresa of Avila (Dossey, 2010), seeking God from within and through Christ-inspired calling and action.

Virtue ethics

Nightingale insisted that a woman cannot be a good and intelligent nurse without being a good and intelligent woman (1882 cited in Bradshaw, 1999). This seemingly simplistic statement draws upon Aristotle's sub classification of virtues of the character and those of the intellect (Aristotle, 1908 translation) that informed the ethos of monastic nursing orders.

Aristotle highlights wisdom (*sophia*) and practical wisdom (*phronesis*) as key virtues of the intellect, and temperance as chief virtue of character (ibid., book 1.13).The choice of temperance may seem an odd one, but this linked to Aristotle's notion of virtue representing the ideal balance (golden mean) between excess and deficiency (both vices) in a particular trait (ibid., book 2.8). Both character and intellect come together to determine thoughtful action (*poiesis* and *praxis*) that, for Aristotle, was essential in order to be virtuous (ibid., book 1.8). Although he conceded that there was some variance in potentiality for virtue, he believed that some might win it by a certain kind of study and care (ibid., book 1.9).

Benner (1997) notes the distinction between the Greek virtue tradition focused upon the virtues of the individual and the Judaeo–Christian tradition of care centred upon the relational aspects of lived virtues (ibid., p. 47). She proposes that the two combined in dialogue may produce the first steps towards a more comprehensive moral philosophy (ibid.).

Until the middle of the twentieth century, virtue ethics was seldom explored other than from a historical perspective, then a revival in interest in virtue ethics occurred so increasingly it is seen as a valid basis for making judgements on moral actions (Oakley and Cocking, 2001). In part this might be due to some degree of disenchantment with both Utilitarianism and Kantian Rationalism and their failure to prevent the two world wars, totalitarianism and the holocaust (Beadle and Moore, 2006), and distrust of the fragmentation of post-modernist deconstructionist approaches (Pellegrino, 1995).

In his highly influential paper 'Toward a Virtue-Based Normative Ethics for the Health Professions', Pellegrino (1995) argues that restoration of virtue ethics as the basis for a moral philosophy is only possible within the health professions (at present), owing to the retention of the prima facie grounding principles of the healing relationship (ibid.). Scripturally justified by Matthew 7.16–20, a classical–medieval synthesis was presented by Aquinas in his *Summa Theologica* (Bouma-Prediger, 1998). Here, in a structurally similar pattern to Aristotle, Aquinas proposes four classically inspired cardinal/natural virtues – prudence, temperance, justice, and fortitude, and three theological/spiritual virtues – faith, hope, and charity, the exercise of these virtues bringing the virtuous to union with God (Pellegrino, 1995). Of these, 1 Corinthians 13 indicates both the primacy of charity or, as more accurate translations (for example the New International Version) have it, love, and how the other virtues are ultimately reducible to love.

Summary

Before considering how this might relate to nurse training it would be useful to summarize some of the findings of this thought journey.

From my prologue I became aware that I could not reconcile hate-full actions with love-filled results and believe that not only do the ends *not* justify the means, but the means invariably contaminate and sometimes destroy the ends. Congruence between means and ends is essential.

The seeds of my conversion were not theological but relational, first in my family home, then in nursing and finally with my children and wife. It was suspension of disbelief which created the space for considering faith: atheism is just another belief system.

I have a complex relationship with the Church. Despite being an active member of my church, I have, like Nightingale, little faith in the Church as an organization, and despair of some church politics (macro and micro).

As a PCC member I recognize the need for the stewardship required to maintain an ancient monument but would rather give more focus to mission. As a junior church leader, I am challenged by some of the resistance to family-inclusive worship, on behalf of the comfort blanket of learned ritual.

However, I do believe that all human organizations are as imperfect as us, and recognize the Church as our best hope of building transformative communities of faith. I value the love I have experienced within the Church and the reassurance of the continuity of worship that might be afforded by our church buildings.

Fortunately, I do not have to take an oath of allegiance to the Church, or to whatever part of the worship spectrum sits most closely with my views. Ultimately I see myself as someone who loves Christ, not someone who loves the Church. My choice of church is more about its locality and role in the community I live in than any doctrinal preference.

If we would walk Jesus' path we would put care before ritual; further, following Benedict, acknowledge that care of the vulnerable is a holy duty and is itself a form of worship.

After more than 30 years of ongoing changes, nursing is in turmoil, with its ethos and role being questioned from both within and without. Nursing preparation, having discarded its traditional basis, has found it difficult to avoid being manipulated by competing perspectives and interests. Nursing needs an anchor and a rudder.

More recently there has been a restatement of the characteristics required of nurses, demonstrating some parallels with Nightingale's Aristotelian–medieval synthesis of virtue ethics, with love being the prime and central virtue.

A love-inspired school of nursing: some notes

Congruence

As a Christian nurse teacher, I try to act in accordance with my beliefs and try to treat my colleagues and students with love. A Christ-inspired organization would do this through its individual members, but also in the way the organization works. This would require our processes and structures to be transparent, caring and responsive to individual needs.

None of us is perfect; the organization should not expect perfection of its students, and students should not expect it of their teachers nor of the organization. There may be times to question a student's fitness to practice; this should be undertaken in a just and compassionate manner.

Relational

If students are to become more loving, we need them to feel loved. Here the personal tutor role might be expanded to recognize properly its pastoral potential, and more attention given to promote students' cohesion and engagement with each other.

Similarly, the organization should promote excellent practice in working with other agencies and organizations and make its watchword cooperation not competition.

Care before ritual

Although there should be protected places of worship, it is important to consider the impact of the organization and its individual members on the external world. What are the fruits of the organization by which it is known?

It is not necessary to be Christian to do Christ's work, but it is necessary to do Christ's work in order to be Christian.

If the organization does justify and display its Christian credentials and clarify how its loving service to the community is part of its worship, it is more likely to lead others to Christ.

Love-centred virtue ethics: an anchor and a rudder

Although it might be criticized as idealistic, it is difficult from any perspective, theological or theoretical to oppose love as foundation, aim and objective. It also forms a sound fit with the current calls for a renewed focus on compassion (DoH, 2012), and can be used as the measure of the value of curricula content and process to teach the 6 Cs.

Conclusion

The purpose of this chapter was to explore the lived experience of a Christian nurse teacher and the impact of faith on education. It proposes love-centred virtue ethics as the basis for nurse training, and sketches some of the consequences of this project.

The ideal nurse will be learned in the discipline of nursing, and demonstrate the virtues required to provide loving care. This returns us to Chaucer, who democratizes the notion of nobility by virtuous conduct in, among other places, the Wife of Bath's Tale.

> Loke who that is most vertuous alway
> Prive and apert, and most entendeth ay
> To do the gentil dedes that he can
> And take him for the gretest gentilman

What this paper has not done is to examine the concept of love properly. But that, best beloved, is another tale.

Discussion Questions

1. How might faith best impact upon our occupational role?
2. Is nursing lessened by erasing its Christian roots?
3. Can good work occur without love?
4. What might love-based nurse training look like?
5. How should candidates for nursing be selected?

References

Arendt, H., 1978, *The life of the mind*, London: Harvest

Arendt, H., 1998, *The human condition*, Chicago: University of Chicago Press

Armstrong, K., 2004, 'Resisting modernity: the backlash against secularism', in *Harvard International Review*, 25.4, p. 40. www.questia.com/read/1G1-112984258/resisting-modernity-the-backlash-against-secularism

Aristotle, *Nicomachean Ethics Book 1*, 350 BCE, trans. Ross, W. D., 1908 http://classics.mit.edu/Aristotle/nicomachaen.1.i.html [accessed July 2014]

Beadle, R., and Moore G., 2006, 'MacIntyre on virtue and organization', in *Organization Studies* 27.3, pp. 323–340

Benedict, 1949, trans. Verheyen, *The Holy Rule of St. Benedict*, www.holyrule.com/index.htm

Benner, P., 1997, 'A Dialogue between Virtue Ethics and Care Ethics', in Thomasma, David C. (ed.), 1997, 'The Influence of Edmund D. Pellegrino's Philosophy of Medicine', in *Theoretical Medicine*, 18.1–2 pp. 47–61

Bouma-Prediger S., 1998, 'Creation care and character: the nature and necessity of the ecological virtues', in *Perspectives on Science and Christian Faith*, 1998, www.asa3.org/ASA/PSCF/1998/PSCF3-98Bouma.html

Bradshaw, A., 1995, 'Has nursing lost its way? Nursing and medicine: cooperation or conflict?', in *BMJ: British Medical Journal*, 311.7000, p. 304

Bradshaw A., 1999, 'The virtue of nursing: the covenant of care', in *Journal of Medical Ethics*, 1999; 25, pp. 477–481

Br Anthony of Taizé, 1994, *Chaucer and Religion*, Seoul: Sogang University www.scribd.com/doc/161255715/Marx-Karl-Critique-of-Hegel-s-Philosophy-of-Right

Casey G., 1996, 'The curriculum revolution and project 2000: a critical examination', in *Nurse Education Today*, 16, pp. 115–120

Department of Health UK (DoH), 2012, *Compassion in Practice*, www.england.nhs.uk/wp-content/uploads/2012/12/compassion-in-practice.pdf

Department of Health, 2013, *Patients first and foremost: The Initial Government Response to the Report of the Mid Staffordshire NHS Foundation Trust Public Inquiry*, vol. 8576, The Stationery Office

Dossey B., 2010, 'Florence Nightingale A 19th-Century Mystic', in *Journal of Holistic Nursing*, pp. 10–35

Duchscher, J., 2000, 'Bending a habit: critical social theory as a framework for humanistic nursing education', in *Nurse Education Today*, 20.6, pp. 453–462

Etymology online, www.etymonline.com/index.php?term=teach [accessed June 2014]

Ewens, A., 2003, 'Changes in nursing identities: supporting a successful transition', in *Journal of Nursing Management*, 11, pp. 224–228

Ferngren G., 2009, *Medicine and Health Care in Early Christianity*, Baltimore, MD: John Hopkins University Press

Flynn, M. 2012, *Winterbourne View Hospital. A Serious Case Review*, Gloucestershire, UK: South Gloucestershire Council

Gleick, J., 2001, *The Information*, London: Fourth Estate

Greene, G., 2001, *The Power and the Glory*, London: Vintage

Hayes D. and Wynyard R. (eds), 2002, *Mcdonaldization of Higher Education*, London: Sage

Jordan S., Davies S. and Green B., 1999, 'The biosciences in the pre-registration nursing curriculum: staff and students' perceptions of difficulties and relevance', in *Nurse Education Today*, 19.3, pp. 215–226

Kahl, S., 2005, 'The religious roots of modern poverty policy: Catholic, Lutheran, and Reformed Protestant traditions compared', in *Archives Européennes de Sociologie/European Journal of Sociology/Europäisches Archiv für Soziologie*, pp. 91–126

Knox E., 1999, 'Medieval Society', in *The Orb Online Reference book for Medieval Studies*, www.the-orb.net/textbooks/westciv/medievalsoc.html [accessed June 2014]

Koenig H., King D. and Carson V., 2012, *Handbook of Religion and Health*, New York: Oxford University Press

Mantzoukas S. and Watkinson, S., 2007, 'Review of advanced nursing practice: the international literature and developing the generic features', in *Journal of Clinical Nursing* 16, pp. 28–37

Marx K., 1844, *A Contribution to the Critique of Hegel's Philosophy of Right* www.marxists.org/archive/marx/works/1843/critique-hpr/intro.htm

Nardi D., Rooda F. and Rooda L., 2011, 'Spirituality based Nursing Practice by nursing students: An Exploratory Study', in *Journal of Professional Nursing*, 27.4, pp. 225–263

Nelson, S., 1995, 'Humanism in nursing: the emergence of the light', in *Nursing inquiry*, 2.1, pp. 36–43

Nursing and Midwifery Council (NMC), 2013, *Response to the Francis report* www.nmcuk.org/Documents/Francis%20report/NMC%20response%20to%20the%20Francis%20report%2018%20July.pdf

Nursing Times editorial, 1997, www.nursingtimes.net/a-christian-nurse-suspended-for-offering-to-pray-has-sparked-health-care-and-religion-debate/1997207.article [accessed June 2014]

Oakley, J. and Cocking D., 2001, *Virtue ethics and professional roles*, Cambridge: Cambridge University Press

Pellegrino E., 1995, 'Toward a virtue-based Normative Ethics for the Health Professions', in *Kennedy Institute of Ethics Journal*, 5.3, pp. 253–277

Plato, 2001, *The Republic*, London: Penguin

Royal College of Nursing, 2003, *Defining Nursing,* www.rcn.org.uk/__
data/assets/pdf_file/0008/78569/001998.pdf [accessed June 2014]

Roxburgh, M., Watson, R., Holland, K., Johnson, M., Lauder, W. and
Topping, K., 2008, 'A review of curriculum evaluation in United Kingdom
nursing education', in *Nurse Education Today,* 28.7, pp. 881–889

Rye, D. H., 1985, 'The Education of Nurses: A new dispensation. The Report
of the RCN Commission on Nursing Education', in *Journal of Advanced
Nursing,* 10, pp. 505–506

Selanders, L. C. and Crane, P., 2010, 'Florence Nightingale in Absentia:
Nursing and the 1893 Columbian Exposition', in *Journal of Holistic
Nursing,* 28.4, pp. 305–12

Sellman D., 1997, 'The Virtues in the Moral Education of Nurses: Florence
Nightingale Revisited', in *Nursing Ethics,* 4.1, pp. 3–11

Summers, A., 1989, 'The mysterious demise of Sarah Gamp: The domicil-
iary nurse and her detractors, c. 1830–1860', in *Victorian Studies,* 32.3,
pp. 365–386

Timmons, S. and Narayanasamy, A., 2011, 'How do religious people navigate
a secular organization? Religious nursing students in the British National
Health Service', in *Journal of Contemporary Religion,* 26.3, pp. 451–465

United Kingdom Central Council, 1986, *Project 2000: A newpreparation
for practice,* London: UKCC

United Kingdom Central Council, 1999, *Fitness for practice,* London:
UKCC

Willis commission, 2013, *Quality with compassion: the future of Nursing
Education. Report of the Willis Commission on Nursing Education,* 2012,
www.williscommission.org.uk/__data/assets/pdf_file/0007/495115/Willis_
commission_report_Jan_2013.pdf

World Health Organization, 2003, *Nurses and midwives: a force for
health: WHO European strategy for continuing education for nurses and
midwives,* Copenhagen: WHO Regional Office for Europe, www.euro.
who.int/__data/assets/pdf_file/0016/102238/E81549.pdf

2

Welcoming the stranger: Christian hospitality as a paradigm for interprofessional learning

CLARE ANDREWS

Abstract

There has been a proliferation of literature on the subject of Christian hospitality in recent years. This has highlighted the potential of the concept to change the ways in which Christians and the Church engage with one another, those of other faiths and those of none. An understanding of Christian hospitality enables a fresh way of exploring ethical issues and the way in which the Church and individuals may support and nurture the vulnerable in our communities. The starting point for this chapter is reflection on my role as a Christian educator in higher education, specifically my role as facilitator for interprofessional learning in health and social care education (IPL). It explores ways in which Christian hospitality might be a useful paradigm for IPL, in particular the barriers to learning that may exist as a result of professional boundaries. It asks what my teaching might look like were it to be framed within the concept of 'welcoming the stranger'.

Initially, it seemed most natural to identify myself, the teacher, as 'host' in the classroom; setting the table in such a way as to encourage and support engagement with learning. However, as I continued my reflection, I realized that this is an incomplete metaphor for my own practice. As much as I am 'host', I am also 'guest', receiving gifts of listening and the mutual sharing of experiences from my students. This complex interplay of roles has the potential to remove some of the barriers to learning that exist when different professions try to work together.

Keywords

Christian hospitality; theological reflection; professional boundaries

Introduction

I was asked recently by a colleague what I thought being a Christian meant to my teaching. Reflecting afterwards on my thoroughly inadequate answer, I realized that, in all honesty, I didn't know. I wanted to think, of course, that being a Christian made a difference, and that my view of human beings and sense of calling all contributed to a richer experience both for my students and myself. But was this really the case? Did my students have an experience that was any different for being taught by a Christian? This assignment offered me the opportunity to reflect in a structured way on the broader question of the place that the Christian faith, my faith, and its associated theology has in my working life.

My initial reflections focused quite quickly on my role in interprofessional learning (IPL), something with which I have been involved for ten years. Interprofessional education is defined as occurring *'when two or more professions learn with, from and about each other to improve collaboration and the quality of care'* (my emphasis)(Centre for the Advancement of Interprofessional Education, 2002) and it is intended to assist the fostering of positive working relationships between professional groups. This mode of learning, however, offers a number of challenges including inter-group stereotyping, different professional cultures, perceived elitism and academic siloing (Carlisle et al., 2004; Hall, 2005; Steinert, 2005; Baker et al., 2011). One particular issue with which I believe students struggle is the barriers to learning collaboratively which may arise from the development of professional identity and its associated boundaries. I wanted to know what Christian theology might contribute to the way in which I attempt to help students overcome these barriers. I decided to use practical theology as the overarching methodology within which this reflection would take place and adopted Cameron's broad definition, which states that practical theologians 'reflect on an aspect of theology in relation to practice, employing some theological knowledge deemed to be relevant to a situation' (Cameron, 2010, p. 30). While reflection is part of my practice both as an educator and practitioner, reflection within a theological paradigm is new to me and so I decided to use a model of specifically theological reflection to frame my work. I hoped that this would lead to outcomes within a defined theological framework. This reflection will be based on the model suggested by Lartey (2000), where his cycle includes Experience, Situational Analysis, Theological Analysis, Situational Analysis of Theology, and Response which links back to Experience. In this, there is a two-way flow between Situational Analysis of Theology and Theological Analysis, and a two-way flow between Theological Analysis and Situational Analysis: the 'theological knowledge' referred to in this model will be Christian hospitality.

Experience – defining the problem

Canterbury Christ Church University is an Anglican foundation university with a strong history and tradition of educating for the public sector, in particular teaching and health and social care practitioners. At the university, pre-registration health and social care programmes are delivered under the umbrella of an interprofessional learning (IPL) programme on which there are students from nine different health and social care professions. As part of this, students undertake one IPL module (known as 'collaborative practice') at each level. These modules are designed to complement the realities of practice in which students and practitioners work with a range of other professions within and beyond the health and social care sector. The modules focus, broadly speaking, on professional identity (year 1), team-working (year 2), and working within complex professional environments (year 3). Students study these modules in mixed, interprofessional groups providing the opportunity for them to explore the different ways in which professional groups view each other, their practice and the nature and challenges of collaborative working.

In collaborative practice modules most learning takes place through conversation, sharing experiences and the application of different theories/models of behaviour to help understand these better. As a tutor for year 3 my role is primarily facilitation, supporting students to access ideas and theories and then to consider how these may impact on both themselves and their practice. The module is, in essence, about understanding our relationships to the 'other', be they practitioners or those for whom we care. It is my experience that often students come into year 3 with negative preconceptions about collaborative practice – they expect to be bored and for the content to be only marginally relevant to them. This provides plenty of challenge in itself, but I believe that a further, significant issue for students' learning is the strong sense of professional identity that they bring to the classroom. This professional identity and associated culture and boundaries is known to foster barriers to interprofessional working and learning (Hall, 2005; Henley et al., 2000) and learning may be limited, not just for the individual, but for the group as a whole. In facilitating such learning environments my concern has been trying to enable students to move beyond these tight identities and see themselves as part of a greater whole. My question for reflection was focused on this specific issue and asked 'what does Christian theology offer that may help me to support an environment in which such professional barriers can be lowered?'

Situational analysis

The development of professional identity is a crucial part of students' development and its formation begins early on in the programme. This is an important process involving a number of different activities including reflection on students' educational histories, knowledge and discussion of professional standards and codes of conduct and ethics. As part of this process students are encouraged to develop an understanding of the nature and purpose of professional boundaries. Such boundaries are crucial for professional practice. They help define aspects of appropriate behaviour and the need to recognize the limits to occupational practice. But they may also feed into the interprofessional dynamic in which they are used by professions to defend and improve their perceived status, creating barriers between groups (Halpern, 1992; Nancarrow and Borthwick, 2005).

Practice placement further embeds students' identities and sense of boundaries – they are given a uniform and an identity badge which marks them out as belonging to a particular group and they begin the process of socialization. The importance of socialization, acculturation and role-modelling in developing professional identity are reported widely (Luke, 2003; Cruess and Cruess, 2006; Hodges et al., 2011). Carpenter (1995 a and b) and Hind et al. (2003) highlight the stereotyping that occurs between different groups of professionals and the barriers that this may create for interprofessional learning. I believe that these processes are crucial to the way in which students engage with each other in interprofessional learning. Professional identity seems to provide them with a safety zone to which they retreat when challenged to think differently; students use their professional identity in place of their individual one (see Slay and Smith, 2011). What this means for the classroom is that students may bring with them a sense of valuing their 'own' professional knowledge and values over other types. Set alongside this different approaches to and models of care, variety of language and terminology and vastly different workplace settings, and the chance of effective communication and engagement between students of different professional backgrounds becomes even more challenged; boundaries have become barriers.

Collaborative learning and interprofessional working are about relationships and the way in which these are sustained and nurtured. In their third-year module, students are challenged to explore the ways in which patients or service users experience care, and the ways in which individual and collective attitudes and beliefs may affect the care they receive. For example, what happens when a patient is negatively labelled? Where do these labels come from? How might such a label alter the care that a patient receives? Students explore the impact that organizational cultures and beliefs may have on themselves and their clients and identify the ways in which interprofessional practice may be promoted. These topics have the potential to cut to the very core of individual beliefs and the way in which we, as practitioners, view those in our care. By exploring the way in which individuals, both staff and service users, respect and value each other, how relationships are nurtured through effective communication and by developing self-awareness, students are enabled to have greater awareness of 'the other'. There seems to be a strong resonance between this type of learning and the idea of 'welcoming the stranger', be they someone from another professional group or a service user or carer. When we see those who are different to ourselves as 'other', how does this affect our behaviour? Often the groups I work with on this module don't have radiography students, my own professional group, in them. This means that not only are many of the students strangers to each other, but I also am a stranger, both professionally and personally.

I have been involved in this module for a number of years, long enough to have become comfortable. I feel confident in my role in the classroom and I know the module material. To start with, this seemed to be a positive aspect of this reflection; after all, surely this meant that I could focus on the students and leave myself out of the equation. However, I realized quickly that far from this being the case, my confidence and safety were potential barriers to reflexive thinking. I tend to find the position of 'authoritative teacher' (Grasha, 1996) the one in which I feel safest and this, along with my familiarity with the teaching materials, made me wonder if I was being less student-focused than I would hope to be. I like to understand, even define, the rules of the classroom and, in my experience, students often slip comfortably into 'recipient-mode'. My status is maintained and students get what they want . . . But there is always a niggle at the back of my mind, a slight sense of guilt for not pushing myself further away from my comfort zone and disappointment that this 'traditional' model of teaching practice has so many missed opportunities. Rather than being part of the 'solution' to the issue of professional barriers, I may actually be part of the problem! This meant that my approach to writing this reflection needed to shift away from viewing professional boundaries as the problem to be solved. Instead I felt that I needed to ask questions about my role in the classroom and how my responsibilities as a Christian educator might be underpinned theologically in such a way as to foster the types of positive classroom relationships which I believed lead to meaningful collaborative learning.

Theological analysis

I had been introduced to the concept of Christian hospitality through Dorothy Bass's article 'Eating' (Bass, 2011). In this she attempts to develop a 'practical theology of eating' (p. 52) and explores the relationship between food, individuals and God's people in its broadest sense. This idea resonated for me. I realized that hospitality was something that I was already trying to practice, in a small way, without really understanding that this was the case. For some time I had been aware that the opportunity to eat together altered the nature of interactions that took place between students and myself and each other. This was particularly the case when they were being challenged or when the focus of the session felt negative. So, sometimes when I was preparing for a teaching session which I anticipated would be difficult for me or particularly challenging for students, I baked! I would then make available cakes and biscuits at a point when I felt some 'defusing' might be necessary. The turning of conversation to who preferred which flavour, the discovery of mutual enjoyment and even shared hobbies, almost always made the 'post-cake' conversation more positive and fruitful. As students relaxed, as they became more open to each other and to me, the space changed. It became hospitable – 'inviting as well as open, safe and trustworthy as well as free' (Palmer, 1998, p. 74).

I particularly noted the positive effect that eating together had on students in my collaborative practice sessions. It seemed there was a need for us to get to know each other as individuals, not just as students from different professional groups; we needed no longer to be strangers. The concept of 'stranger' is central to Christian hospitality and the idea that somehow hospitality might be a paradigm within which classroom relationships between students might be nurtured and barriers broken down was something that I wanted to explore.

As a starting point, hospitality might be seen as providing the basic human needs of food and shelter, and in its most recognizable Westernized form is frequently associated with entertainment. Christian hospitality has a deeper meaning though. Certainly it is the sharing of resources, but this is combined with something of the view or orientation of the host herself; it includes meeting the social as well as the physical needs of guests. Oden (2001) notes that 'taken as a feature of Christian life, hospitality is not so much a singular act of welcome as it is a way, an orientation that attends to otherness, listening and learning, valuing and honoring' (p. 14). The biblical notion of hospitality identifies that it is essentially about the relationship between host and guest, the establishing of 'relationships of mutual welcome' (McAvoy, 1998, p. 23). This extends from the belief that humankind is the guest of God's hospitality and so each one of us has a responsibility to mediate this to others (Hagstrom, 2013). Hospitality, therefore, has a moral dimension because it involves what it means to be human and relies on our actions and orientation towards each other; it requires 'not grand gestures but open hearts' (Homan and Pratt, 2002, p. 16).

So what might hospitality look like in the classroom? Palmer (1983) suggests that hospitality is central to the art of teaching, stating 'a learning space has three major characteristics, three essential dimensions: openness, boundaries and an air of hospitality' (p. 71). In the hospitable classroom this means that each participant receives 'each other, our struggles, our newborn ideas with openness and care' (p. 73). It is fairly easy to identify the teacher as host in this paradigm. It is they who, superficially at least, occupy a position of power or authority, who hold the resources that the class want to access. They then make these resources available to the guests, their students. But Christian hospitality requires more of the host than this 'charitable' model of teaching. Hagstrom (2013) uses the metaphor of 'setting the table' as a means of expressing the role of the teacher as host. This table-setting can be seen as a mixture of practical and thoughtful processes: are the table and chairs set out in a way that promotes conversation and interaction? In what way are students welcomed to the room? Has the mode of teaching been chosen for ease for the teacher or as the best way for students to learn? But the responsibility of the teacher to engage students in particular learning suggests that there are times when limits may apply to this table-setting.

In professional education, the content of curricula is defined within tight, regulated limits and students required, rather than invited, to attend. Here, the table may need to be set in a way which reflects this; the host may not necessarily set the table at which the guests necessarily want to sit! In no way does this suggest that there are limits placed on hospitality but, as Hagstrom (2013) states, 'the guests are welcomed to the table, but the hosts are not expected to change the table setting simply because the guests are not used to these habits and customs' (p. 13). What the host *is* required to do though is to make their guests feel secure and welcome. In the classroom this is achieved through the setting of boundaries and values, and by creating a sense of confidence in their approach to teaching. As host, it is the teacher who, by words and actions, sets the tone for a hospitable classroom, one which demonstrates and promotes dialogue and openness to new and strange ideas. By demonstrating acceptance and welcome of every member of the class, the teacher helps each student to develop their own welcome towards each other and in the process create a community of learners.

The setting up of conditions to enable open and free dialogue is part of what Groome (1988) calls 'intellectual hospitality' – letting go of the control of knowledge to facilitate the thinking of students. This requires a degree of 'intellectually humility' which accepts that teachers may learn from their students (Alexander, 1996, p. 145). Nouwen (1978) states that 'teachers who can detach themselves from their need to impress and control, and who can allow themselves to become receptive for the news that their students carry with them, will find that it is in receptivity that gifts become visible' (p. 87). As the teacher models intellectual hospitality, then the possibility arises that the host and the guest tell their stories. These stories are part of the gifts to which Nouwen refers and pave the way for 'education made possible by friendship . . . the circulation of gift which is also a way of describing hospitality' (Newman, 2007, p. 141). The 'circulation of gift' requires, however, that the gift be received as well as given. Attentiveness is an integral part of this – the suspension of our own thoughts and position in order to understand the other, not on our terms but on theirs. Palmer (1983) calls this 'the discipline of displacement' (p. 115), whereby we hold our own position in abeyance as we listen intently and receptively. As we do this we acknowledge the intrinsic worth of the other and so treat her or him as potentially authoritative. Language plays a particular part in the creation of hospitable classrooms in a context in which both guests and host come from different professional cultures. For each member of the learning community to be a resource for the others there needs to be a common language or understanding that enables hospitable learning to take place. Inherited patterns of expression, use of exclusive language and profession-specific jargon may block instead of nurture hospitality. The teacher, as host, must model not only the use of appropriate vocabulary but also frame questions in such a way as to convey interest rather than presumption, 'considered possibility rather than assumed fact' (Bennett, 2003, p. 52).

It would be wrong to think that hospitality is simply about creating a 'nice place' where 'nice people' can be nice to one another! Hospitality, both in and out of the classroom, is hard work and potentially threatening. It challenges what Bennett calls our 'insistent individualism', the efforts we make to establish our own worth, and it sets values and worth away from the realm of private preference and into the public realm (Bennett, 2003,

p. 57). It means that our protective mechanisms need to be abandoned and that we can no longer insist upon our own terms; we must open ourselves to the possibility of change. We need to be aware that 'the perspective of the other could easily supplement and perhaps correct one's own work or even transform one's self-understanding' (p. 24).

Situational analysis of theology

Initially it may seem that the idea of professional boundaries is somewhat problematic in the context of Christian hospitality; after all the idea of placing limits on a practice which should be open and generous seems to undermine its fundamental tenets. But boundaries are not necessarily problematic in and of themselves. On the contrary, they may be crucial to the way in which different professional groups work together. They provide safety in terms of accountability, they are an important mechanism in the creation of solution-focused patient-centred care, they help to identify the point at which a practitioner's expertise or skills are exhausted and others' must be invited. Boundaries are not the same as barriers and they have an important place in education too. Boundaries are liminal spaces, spaces of discovery, 'places where social practices are open to negotiation and the ideas carried in established practices are informed by new insights' (Edwards, 2009, p. 5). They are important because 'the work that occurs there gives shape to the collaborations that occur as a result . . . they are sites of struggle where different meaning systems and the motives they carry vie for dominance' (pp. 13–14). Boundaries are not neutral and it is this that makes them so valuable in education. But boundary-work in education is both challenging and risky to those who engage in it since boundaries may be hidden among our day-to-day activities and interactions. This is where I believe Christian hospitality offers a means of supporting and nurturing such activity. Hospitality is 'offered for the sake of what it can allow, permit, encourage and yield' (Palmer, 1983, p. 74). If boundary-work takes place within the paradigm of hospitality then greater openness, more ideas, thoughts, insights and feelings may enter the learning that takes place. It may even be that enabling the simple acknowledgement of professional boundaries leads to greater awareness of the 'other' and their different priorities and values. Hospitality is 'the art of setting of intentionally vulnerable boundaries' (Frank, n.d., p. 2).

From a practical perspective Christian hospitality wasn't something about which I felt I could be explicit – the curriculum was set and I suspected that the majority of students would, frankly, be upset by any profession of faith from me. It wasn't something that I could get students to 'do' or explore in particular. Initially I was troubled by this; I couldn't see how a Christian paradigm could be applied to what amounted to a secular context. I realized, though, that this is a question about how I understand the nature and purpose of practical theology itself. If I believe that theology is always contextual, then it is also, by default, practical; without this characteristic it risks becoming an isolated, purely academic exercise. Practical theology should 'illuminate Christian practice in religion to life's concrete problems and issues' (Browning, 1985, p. 15). Understanding practical theology in this way opened up far more possibilities for consideration than I had initially thought. In one sense hospitality was about the relationship that I have with students, the way in which I role-model the behaviours and attitudes that I hope to see in them. In another sense it could be about the practical way in which I set up a classroom – does this in itself encourage openness or inhibit it? Hospitality could be concerned with the relationships that students develop with each other. Might it even open up new prospects for the way in which they approach their working practices and patients? I believe that hospitality has the potential to act as a metaphor for each of these.

Recently, I had a student who made it abundantly clear that she felt being in my collaborative practice class was a total waste of her time! She articulated her belief that the module could teach her nothing and refused to engage positively in any discussion or share any of her experiences. My response to this was to tolerate, try to stay calm and be thankful if she didn't turn up! At the end of the module she handed in the most negative module evaluation I've ever seen. I was tempted to throw this away, ignoring it as clearly unrepresentational since the majority were positive. Reflecting on hospitality has made me rethink my feelings about this student. I had placed the responsibility for engagement in the module firmly with the student – it was she who was required to enter my world and work within my (the module's) 'rules'. At no point had I tried to understand the module from her perspective; I had simply set the table and expected her to 'sit up and eat nicely'! In this, I had failed to welcome her as my guest. As a Christian I am required not only to welcome the stranger in my midst, but to see that person as representing Christ. The stranger does not need to have any particular qualities or, in my eyes, be especially deserving to receive hospitality. 'To be a recipient of Christian hospitality one does not have to do or be anything; one's status as guest is received as a freely given gift from Christ' (Bretherton, 2004, p. 102)

Response

It is clear, I hope, from the discussion above that I believe Christian hospitality has much to offer interprofessional learning as a paradigm for classroom relationships. In particular, its encouragement to work at the boundaries, to challenge the status quo, to cross borders and allow the outsider to become the insider (Reynolds, 2006) all speak to the challenges that exist when professional boundaries risk becoming barriers to learning. As I write this, I am preparing to meet the next group of students who I will guide through this module. I hope that as a result of my understanding of hospitality I will be able to approach their learning in a modified way. Hospitality does not exist merely through discrete acts such as the provision of food; rather it is a complete, holistic approach to teaching and learning. One of my responsibilities as a teacher is to help my students see familiar things in new ways. This may be a difficult process for them but as an educator I have the privilege of accompanying students in this process, 'through initial conflict and even denial, into reflection that leads to deeper, fuller . . . perspectives' (Marmon, 2008, p. 38).

For much of this reflective process I have seen myself very definitely as host; after all I set the structure and content of a teaching session and it is my responsibility to create the sense of security, boundaries and values without which meaningful relationships, and learning, cannot exist. But as my reflection has deepened I have realized that, for me at least, this identification of 'teacher as host; student as guest' is an incomplete expression of my role. Certainly, I do recognize myself adopting at times the role of 'expert', the person who welcomes students into a world of knowledge. What I now realize is that I experience something else as well, something more subtle. This is a sense that when I enter a classroom and join a group of students I am asking to be invited into *their* world; I have to be their guest before I can be their host. My bringing of cake might not be welcoming students to my table as much as offering a gift to my host. In this I begin to recognize that I do not hold a monopoly on knowledge and that I might learn from my students if I will let them teach me. In the process of shifting from host to guest I am enabling, even empowering, students to tell their stories and in this they become expert while am the novice (Ogletree, 1985). Finally, I wonder, if I am able to make this shift of understanding, then is there the chance that students might make a similar one in relation to those they care for? Might it be that, in learning to welcome each other, students may become practitioners who are able to welcome their patients, as strangers, into their care? And might they even be able to see themselves as guests in the worlds of their patients?

Discussion Questions

1. In what ways do you see professional boundaries as being used in your own area of practice to create 'recognizable identities and particular cultural attributes'? (Becher and Trowler, 2001, p. 44)
2. Do you agree that unless theology is always practical, it risks becoming an isolated, purely academic exercise?

3. How easy is it, do you think, for teachers/educators to adopt the position of guest and so see themselves as the novice and their students as expert?

4. What do you see as the opportunities implicit in engaging in boundary work?

5. Do you agree that practical theology should engage with the secular educational context, or should they remain separate?

References

Alexander, H. A., 1996, 'Editorial: inclusiveness and humility in religious education', in *Religious Education*, 91, pp. 142–145

Baker, L., Egan-Lee, E., Martimianakis, M. A. and Reeves, S., 2011, 'Relationships of power: Implications for interprofessional education', in *Journal of Interprofessional Care*, 25.2, pp. 98–104

Bass, D. C., 2011, 'Eating', in Miller-McLemore, B. (ed.) *The Wiley-Blackwell Companion to Practical Theology*, Malden, MA: Wiley-Blackwell, pp. 51–60

Becher, T. and Trowler, P. R., 2001, *Academic Tribes and Territories: Intellectual Enquiry and the Culture of Disciplines*, Buckingham: Open University Press

Bennett, J., 2003, *Academic Life: Hospitality, Ethics, and Spirituality*, Boston: Anker Publishing

Bretherton, L., 2004, 'Tolerance, Education and Hospitality: A Theological Proposal', in *Studies in Christian Ethics*, 17.1, pp. 80–103

Browning, D., 1985, 'Practical Theology and Political Theology', in *Theology Today*, 42.1, pp. 15–33

Cameron, H., 2010, *Talking about God in Practice*, London: SCM Press

Carlisle, C., Cooper, H. and Watkins, C., 2004, '"Do none of you talk to each other?" the challenges facing the implementation of interprofessional education', in *Medical Teacher*, 26.6, pp. 545–552

Carpenter, J., 1995a, 'Interprofessional education for medical and nursing students: evaluation of a programme', in *Medical education*, 29.4, pp. 265–272

Carpenter, J., 1995b, 'Doctors and Nurses: Stereotypes and Stereotype Change in Interprofessional Education', in *Journal of Interprofessional Care*, 9.2, pp. 151–161

Centre for the Advancement of Interprofessional Education, 2002, *Defining IPE*, at http://caipe.org.uk/about-us/defining-ipe/ [accessed 14 May 2014]

Cruess, R. L. and Cruess, S. R., 2006, 'Teaching professionalism: general principles', in *Medical Teacher*, 28. 3, pp. 205–208

Edwards, A., 2009, 'Understanding boundaries in inter-professional work', in *Scottish educational review*, 41.1, pp. 5–19

Frank, A. (no date) *Christian Hospitality as Intentional Vulnerability*, at www.practicingourfaith.org/christian-hospitality-intentional-vulnerability [accessed 10 May 2014]

Grasha, A. F., 1996, *Teaching with Style*, Pittsburgh: Alliance Publishers

Groome, T., 1988, 'The spirituality of the Christian Educator', in *Religious Education* 83.1, pp. 9–20

Hagstrom, A., 2013, 'The Role of Charism and Hospitality in the Academy', in *Integritas* 1.1

Hall, P., 2005, 'Interprofessional teamwork: Professional cultures as barriers', in *Journal of Interprofessional Care*, 19 pp. 188–196

Halpern, S. A., 1992, 'Dynamics of Professional Control: Internal Coalitions and Crossprofessional Boundaries', in *American Journal of Sociology*, 97.4, pp. 994–1021

Henley, E., Glasser, M. and May, J., 2000, 'Medical Student evaluation of nurse practitioners as teachers', in *Family Medicine*, 32, pp. 491–494

Hind, M., Norman, I., Cooper, S. et al., 2003, 'Interprofessional perceptions of health care students', in *Journal of Interprofessional Care*, 17.1, pp. 21–34

Hodges, B. D., Ginsburg, S., Cruess, R. et al., 2011, 'Assessment of professionalism: Recommendations from the Ottawa 2010 Conference', in *Medical Teacher*, 33.5, pp. 354–363

Homan, D. and Pratt L. C., 2002, *Radical Hospitality: Benedict's Way of Love*, Brewster: Paraclete Press

Lartey, E., 2000, 'Practical Theology as Theological Form', in Woodward, J. and Pattison, S. (eds) *The Blackwell Reader in Pastoral and Practical Theology*, Oxford: Blackwell

Luke, H., 2003, *Medical Education and Sociology of Medical Habitus*, Dordrecht: Klewer Academic Publishers

Marmon, Ellen L., 2008, 'Teaching as Hospitality', in *The Asbury Journal*, 63.2, p. 33–39

McAvoy, J., 1998, 'Hospitality: A Feminist Theology of Education', in *Teaching Theology and Religion*, 1.1, pp. 20–26

Nancarrow, S. A. and Borthwick, A. M., 2005, 'Dynamic professional boundaries in the healthcare workforce', in *Sociology of health and illness*, 27.7, pp. 897–919

Newman, E., 2007, *Untamed Hospitality: Welcoming God and other Strangers*, Grand Rapids: Brazos Press

Nouwen, H. M., 1978, *Creative ministry*, New York: Doubleday

Oden, A., 2001, *And You Welcomed Me: A Sourcebook on Hospitality in Early Christianity*, Nashville: Abingdon Press

Ogletree, T. W., 1985, *Hospitality to the Stranger: Dimensions of Moral Understanding*, Philadelphia: Fortress Press

Palmer, P., 1983, *To know as we are known*, San Francisco: Harper

Palmer, Parker J., 1998, *The Courage to Teach. Exploring the inner landscape of a teacher's life*, San Francisco: Jossey-Bass

Reynolds, T. E., 2006, 'Welcoming without Reserve?: A Case in Christian Hospitality', in *Theology Today*, 63.2, pp. 191–202

Slay, H. and Smith, D., 2011, 'Professional identity construction: Using narrative to understand the negotiation of professional and stigmatized cultural identities', in *Human Relations* 64.1, pp. 85–107

Steinert, Y., 2005, 'Learning together to teach together: Interprofessional education and faculty development', in *Journal of Interprofessional Care*, 19, pp. 60–75

3

Am I flying?

MARION KHAN

Abstract

As a Christian nurse working within education in the NHS, there are opportunities and challenges to be faced both personally and professionally around faith issues. An unexpected encounter with a radio programme discussing an aviation training model prompted me to consider whether my faith position, as a tutor, is really 'flying'. By using the framework of the aviation model – Aviate, Navigate and Communicate – and the construction of mind maps, I have undertaken a personal journey to explore the development and sustainability of my faith when positioned against the requirements of my professional and organizational role. I have uncovered classroom and personal issues around keeping my faith airborne, the factors to navigate my faith and avoid obstacles, and the content and mechanisms of faith communication. From this work I believe my faith position is indeed flying, but is not complacent about unseen 'turbulence' that can arise in such an educational setting.

Keywords

Personal faith; work environment; aviate; navigate; communicate

Introduction

On a cold and dark morning drive into work, I was listening to *Today* on Radio 4. To be truthful, I was only half-listening as

44

I was already thinking ahead to the teaching sessions I had that day. I became aware, however, of a news story covering a recent flying accident and, I must admit, paid attention with increasing surprise as an aviation expert spoke. The actions he suggested the pilot may have taken when the emergency became evident were, for me, totally counter-intuitive. In the event of some form of crisis, I had visions of the pilot first putting out a Mayday call: after all, is it not common sense to let others know of difficulty? And I clearly remember Tom Hanks saying, 'Houston, we have a problem.' According to the expert, however, this was not the first action – rather, the first action was to maintain flight. Once this was achieved and the immediate emergency condition addressed, he explained, it was then important to identify current position, any difficult terrain or obstacles, and how to proceed. Finally, and only then, communicate to relevant air traffic controllers the status of the flight.

As the radio discussion continued, and the applications of Aviate, Navigate, Communicate were explored, it occurred to me that much of the language and dialogue used was suggestive of my own position within my work environment. Although not an emergency situation of course, as a nurse, a clinical educator and also a Christian, I needed to keep my Christian faith 'airborne', to sustain my personal faith. Second, I felt it essential to 'navigate' my faith through the increasingly secular, yet pluralistically correct challenges of my role and profession; and third, I wished to open lines of 'communication' around my faith within the work environment. As I drove I reflected on what I had heard, arranging and linking my ideas into rapidly developing mind maps, and planning to elaborate on my thoughts further after work.

Am I flying?

Mind maps work for me. The visual experience of seeing my thoughts and ideas develop, link, and develop further is an exciting personal journey. So later, while revisiting my early morning experience, I started to scribble a mapping process around the three pilot-guidance words of Aviate, Navigate, Communicate.

A question had developed in my mind since hearing the Radio 4 programme earlier: *Am I flying?* While my job role is centred upon clinical education within a health service organization, how is my own personal faith sustained or kept airborne in that role, how do I navigate the position of holding a Christian faith when working in the NHS, and can I open lines of communication as regards my faith in such a work setting? As my mind maps progressed it became clear that I was exploring my own position as a 'pilot' to find out if I could really fly – as a Christian, as a nurse, and as an NHS educator. My initial priority then was to establish whether I was able to 'aviate'.

Aviate

The first element of the Aviate mind map was my own Christian conviction, brought about through a personal phenomenon, and held as belief and truth. And while researchers such as Bridges (1999) argue that 'in practice how we go about determining the truth of a belief, and, hence, to some extent what we mean when we claim the truth of a belief, vary considerably according to the nature of the belief' (p. 607), the personal experience that defies a proficient narrative would, I suggest, still hold validity. I own both meaning and significance from that personal experience and, as Cooling (2010) argues, have applied the understanding of it to my own world-view. While writers such as Wolterstorff (1980) question holding such a view on the grounds that it emphasizes 'cognition' (p. 14) rather than development of a Christian way of living and being, I disagree. I believe it is the understanding (as far as we are able) that enables us continuously to build our faith, through convicted belief, and thus embrace a Christian way of living. So how does my faith, arising from that world-view, through a Christian conviction, remain airborne?

I am aware that I hold values, I call them faith values, reflecting my Christian way of living, influencing my decision-making and choices, and giving my faith a deeply personal reality. Taking a biblical perspective, I can identify four markers that keep my personal faith sustained, or in flight. First, my faith is drawn from the biblical witness to the revelation of God in Christ, and accepted intellectually as a statement of truth. Through this conscious intellectualism I am, however, comfortable to challenge and critique my own perceptions of this truth, acknowledging self-questioning, self-doubt, and the limitations drawn from the frailty of my human understanding of such a truth. But I cannot deny the absolute internalized assurance I receive, that my faith is founded on this truth, through John 20.31: 'These are written that you may believe that Jesus is the Christ, the Son of God, and that believing you may have life in his name' (NIV). Second, my personal experience of that faith brings a trust in, and response to, a God who is manifest in my being, heart and mind. In *The Bible According to Peanuts*, Robert Short (1990) warns of a spiritual laziness that can take hold if we do not have regard for God's commandment: 'But as for you, continue in what you have learned and have become convinced of' (2 Timothy 3.14, NIV), and it is this direction to 'continue' that helps to maintain my faith aviation. Third, by addressing the commandment in 2 Timothy 3.14, my faith is recognized in, and expressed through, action. Throughout the New Testament, the concept of an active faith is identified – 'If faith is not seen in actions it is dead' (James 2.17), 'faith active in love' (Galatians 5.6) being just two examples. In other words, my faith has a public aspect which must be seen in activities, words and relationships (Wakefield, 1983) and such a responsibility serves to keep me committed. Fourth, there are consequences of living such a life of faith – there develops a sense of 'faithfulness' which arises from constancy in this approach, and with it an awareness of God working within. Paul, in Galatians (5.22–23), called such a working a 'fruit of the Spirit', and it is spiritual awareness of this fruit of faithfulness that makes it possible for these four markers of a Christian character to support my faith in flight.

Development of my mind map, however, pulled out a third 'aviate' element linking the previous two – personal contribution. Already discussed is the condition of an active faith, a faith that hears God's word, is uplifted by it, and answers a call to action. But God himself also takes action in 'reaching out to embrace what He has made' (Worsley, 2013) and knowledge of his action strengthens my own faith, champions my contributory actions within the NHS, and maintains my aviation.

Navigate

In a briefing note produced by the Flight Safety Foundation (FSF) entitled 'Golden Rules' (FSF, 2000), the objective of navigation is to 'Know where you are; know where you should be; and know where the terrain and obstacles are' (p. 18). I looked back to the mind map I had previously drawn and my aspiration to navigate the position of holding a Christian faith when employed in the NHS. While naturally focused on my working role, I was amazed to find a distinct synergy between my thoughts and the guidance of the FSF. Already established is my ability to keep my personal faith airborne, and recognition that such faith cannot remain in a stationary hover. To enable activity there is a need to locate my present faith position within my role as an nurse educator (that is to know where I am); then see beyond to where my faith position should sit (or should be); and have awareness of challenges (obstacles or terrain) I may face on that journey.

In 2006, the Royal College of Nursing (RCN) opened its Annual Congress with a multi-faith 'gathering' that attracted a mediocre delegate attendance (Keighley and Wright, 2007, p. 28). Previously, and indeed since its inception, a more formal service of worship preceded Congress, usually held in a local parish church and, although open to RCN members of all or no faith, distinctly Christian in its approach. Anecdotally, and from my own experience, these services were generally 'standing-room only' with in excess of 400 delegates attending. So what had happened? A lively debate followed the 2006 Congress on the letter pages of several nursing journals, reflecting on the true meaning of nursing and its historical roots, with comments ranging from 'it is worth remembering that the Christian ethos has lain at the very heart of the development of modern nursing' (Keighley and Wright, 2007, p. 28) through to 'nursing is a profession and not a Christian vocation' (Thomas, 2007, p. 32).

The original format of the Congress service of worship has since been reinstated, but the debate continues. Nurse leaders such as Vic Moffatt (2012) assert their own nursing ethic that the guidance of some of the great philosophers such as Aristotle and Pittacus to 'act towards others as we wish others to act towards us' (Moffatt, 2012, p. 5), pre-date and reflect the commandment to 'love thy neighbour as thyself', therefore this nursing premise is not distinctly Christian.

Clearly, and I would suggest inevitably, there are diverse opinions on the validity and place of personal Christian faith and the Christian perspective within nursing. While it is certainly the case (and indeed a professional requirement) that nurses should recognize the spiritual and faith needs of others, I believe there must also be a balance between private faith and professional, public service as a nurse. And that is where I would locate my present Christian faith as nurse educator – in balance – preserving my own beliefs, but also maintaining a professional approach as a public servant who recognizes and respects beliefs within others, be they patients, students or colleagues.

I feel such a balancing position contains movement however – I have a direction of travel that brings about continuous and varied encounters and meetings with students and colleagues, influencing the position of personal faith within my role as an educator and teacher: the second point on my mind map. Teaching and education, at whatever level and specialism, is a rather vexed environment containing an increasingly secular and pluralistic platform. An argument discussed by Smith and Shortt (2002) that 'basic beliefs, including Christian beliefs drawn from the Bible, can and do influence our thinking about an activity such as education, but they will do so by providing direction rather than by showing us exactly what to do' (p. 60) is, I contend, well founded.

Beck (1999) considers that a spiritual (as opposed to *religious*) crisis has arisen within post-modern society and this point of crisis is now challenging the secularization that had previously marginalized Christianity within Western civilization. Hay and Nye (1998) further state that a spirituality focus delivered in education becomes 'a more holistic model of human spirituality, which sees it as something larger than any individual religion' (Hay and Nye, 1998, p. 53).

I support these views and consider I have a part to play in developing and supporting a holistic and spiritual relationship with my students throughout their education to facilitate their delivery of compassionate patient care. And looking forward, this is where I believe my faith should be – the holistic and spiritual development of the student is broadly but slowly moving up the educational agenda as an anti-movement to aggressive positivism (Hill, 2004). As a Christian nurse educator, it is the introduction of such approaches in the classroom that I should be navigating towards. Let me move away from the 'demanding, naturalistic, rationalistic answers to all questions' (Hay and Nye, 1998, cited in Hill, 2004 pp. 69) and enable myself and my students to develop a holistic spirituality that is distinctively constructive, and embraces positive human consciousness, experiences and awareness into the classroom.

But this journey will, of course, have challenges en route and perhaps the most apparent obstacle to navigate is from nursing itself. The profession has advanced to welcome evidence-based practice and a high level of technical and clinical knowledge, but arguably the *vocational* ethos has been slowly eroded in favour of measurable competences (Bradshaw, 2011). Working in an environment that promotes a nursing model of autonomous practice could perhaps empower me to share a personal faith through a holistic, spiritual approach to teaching. However, such an approach may bring me into conflict, and open to accusations of abuse of my position or of inappropriate and unprofessional behaviour, from both profession and employer (Fawcett and Noble, 2004).

A key challenge then will be to maintain my balancing position. I have the requirements of profession, employer and my role as a nurse and educator to balance with my personal knowledge and experience of the truth about Jesus and God, my belief system and faith, my world-view and my place within it. Of course, there is no requirement on me to justify or evidence my beliefs in my working role, rather define them perhaps as 'personal pursuits which should not interfere with public policy . . . free to operate on the margins, provided that they do not try to interact in the public arena' (Hill, 2004, p. 24), but I must admit that this position does not sit comfortably.

And it is this wider scope of the public arena that, indeed, presents my third obstacle. If the public voice agrees that the prime objective and expectation of the NHS is the delivery of safe and effective health care to patients, then a question can be raised – despite nurse regulatory body requirements, why should an attempt be made to interweave a spiritual element into health care education if, potentially, delivered care is safe, appropriate and meeting the clinical needs of the patient. Basically, why bother? I would suggest that this argument is in fact my greatest challenge to navigate.

As already discussed I believe I must demonstrate and validate my own relationship with students to reflect a spiritual dimension, and enable them to seek out and develop their own personal position. We are currently travelling through a postmodern era with its 'greater tolerance of different points of view and a greater willingness to consider many paths to understanding, in addition to the path of empirical science' (Hill, 2004, p. 13). As part of this journey I hope to facilitate students to open their minds to examine personal values and moral yardsticks in order to deliver patient care that is both safe and effective, but also holistic and compassionate. I draw a line in the sand here however; I am not presuming to suggest that only Christian nurses can deliver holistic and compassionate care as I believe, and have witnessed, nurses of all faiths and of none deliver the most exceptional levels of compassion and empathy in patient care. Rather, I wish to enable my students to embrace this view, to recognize and acknowledge the many ambiguities and diversions of the greater society, and to promote a personal and expectant spiritual relationship with colleagues and patients which will, I believe, ultimately deliver a quality of compassion in nursing care that is distinctive. Navigation then, as identified on the mind map, moves through the difficult terrain and obstacles within my role, and is a continual faith challenge. My current balancing position however leads me to a clear direction of travel towards an ethos of holistic spirituality in nurse education. I will continue in my attempts to navigate this course as a Christian educator.

Communicate

As the 'pilot' of my role I am airborne and navigating, but also I need to open lines of communication as regards my faith in the work setting. Developing my mind map enabled me to explore fully the meaning of 'communicate' in the current context. There are the mechanisms of communication of course – verbal, non-verbal, written, etc. and delivery tools such as telephone, email, and television. I discarded these factors however as, in this current context of keeping my faith airborne as a clinical educator, I chose a definition to mean 'keeping myself in contact'. In other words, what are the lines of faith contact in my role?

Unsurprisingly perhaps, I feel that the first communication contact is in my personal relationship with God, expressed through prayer, contemplation, and Bible study. There are times, as a Christian educator, when my faith is bruised and battered – a difficult situation has occurred perhaps or issues with a student have arisen – and I feel the need to communicate with God specifically around my role. In his book *Confidence in the classroom: realistic encouragement for teachers*, Philip May (1988) encourages the Christian teacher to reflect the guidance of James and be 'peace-loving, considerate, submissive, full of mercy and good fruit, impartial and sincere' (James 3.17). To 'trust that my ongoing efforts to drink from those texts have had some impact on the nature of my teaching' (Smith and Shortt, 2002, p. 36) is a truly positive experience for me. It enables me to be aware of an ongoing but guiding and supporting instrument for my faith and role through a communicating contact with God.

I cannot 'drink from those texts' (ibid.) however and then be unwilling or unable to share its impact within the classroom. I must show an outward communication or contact of that impact, in faith, to my students. And this is where my mind map starts to become complex – sharing, however displayed, requires activity of some sort on my part. But activity has previously been identified as key to my 'aviation'. Looking deeper into the 'communicate' mind map however, I realize that it is not so much the 'what' of the activity that is carried out, but the 'how'.

For teachers who may be reading this chapter I am sure my assertion that every episode of teaching contact with students is different from the last, and does not reflect the future, has resonance. Taught topics, personalities, organizational directives and many other influences all serve to sustain both positive and negative momentum within the teaching environment. This momentum, however, gives me opportunities to open lines of communication in faith, and within role, by bringing holistic and spiritual approaches to my teaching – yet another link across the mind map. But what are these approaches? Clearly the imparting of clinical skill and knowledge is paramount. I believe however that the opportunity for my students to debate and discuss wider holistic and spiritual issues, and develop abilities to defend 'their own beliefs and values while engaging in constructive negotiations with others to achieve a greater consensus on the common good' (Hill, 2004 p. 204) is equally valuable, and additionally enlivens and enriches my own faith.

Which brings me to an extended element of the 'communicate' requirement. In my current position, my profession and my employer expect that I act as a role model to my students. As already discussed, I believe that as a Christian educator I should display to my students the spiritual focus necessary to support, guide and develop them in their studies. As a role model I further wish to encourage and enable my students to open their own minds in acknowledged recognition of spiritual qualities, to promote classroom relationships grounded in a supportive spiritual 'love', and to ultimately deliver patient care that is holistic, spiritual and compassionate. My own faith is then constructing a communication contact, as a role model, within my own teaching practice. Such a contact can potentially ripple outwards from myself, to my students, and bring to the patient a clinical care intervention that is effective and safe but also holistic and spiritual. And as a Christian, a nurse, and clinical educator I can think of no stronger communication of my personal faith that I would wish to achieve within an NHS education environment.

Conclusion

So, am I flying? This original question prompted my reflective mind mapping to try and determine whether, in my role as a clinical educator within the NHS, I am able to sustain my personal faith; locate, give direction and maintain its position even when facing challenges; and enable its communicating message to develop and go forward. To try and answer this question I looked back on the journey I have mind mapped and explored since hearing that radio programme in December. Keeping myself in the air, *Aviate*, was, I believe, in my hands. Enabled through my own conviction, values and activity, I look to perceive biblical guidance and truths within my role. Self-examination and application of such guidance and truth to activity opens understanding for me, strengthening and supporting my faith, and thus keeping me airborne. *Navigate*, however, was more testing. While I attempt to hold my own faith position carefully in a professional and personal balance, a vision of the horizon of where I would like to be in terms of the holistic and spiritual development of my students is more complex. I cannot overlook the potentially difficult terrain of professional and employer requirements of my role, and the immediate or long-term challenges that can arise from outside the education environment but which can impact on it so dramatically, such as the expectations and demands of society and the public arena. While I consider I am currently navigating the right course I must also recognize that there may be obstacles on the horizon ahead which may prove very challenging, requiring some form of 'tactical manoeuvre' perhaps, to keep my navigation on track.

At the present time, then, I believe I am aviating and navigating fruitfully, although not complacent about what may occur in the future. And *Communicate?* Primarily, communication through a personal relationship with God underpins my life, including my working role, and this was probably an obvious communication element for me to explore. Less obvious, however, were the open lines of communication in faith that I became aware of as a result of my reflections, and that I wished to share with my students – those of being a role model with a spiritual focus: of creating opportunities for discussion and debate on holistic and spiritual issues, and of creating an education environment that truly supports the student to aim to deliver patient care that is holistic, spiritual and compassionate. My awareness of these lines

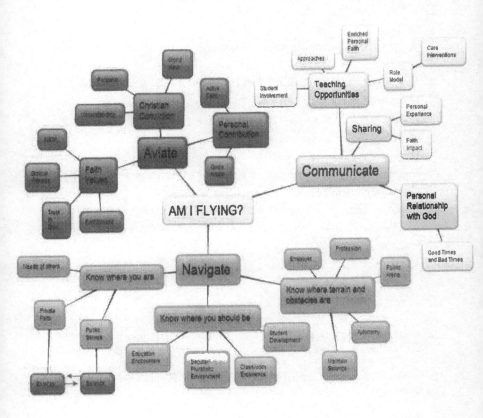

of communication running from my own personal faith, through my teaching practice to the student, and then potentially to the bedside is a very humbling experience, but one that absolutely supports my personal faith as an educator.

I believe that the answer to my original question then is 'Yes, I am flying'. It will not always be a gentle journey, however: there may be turbulence and obstacles, and perhaps even an emergency landing now and again. However, I now know what resources and approaches I need to keep myself in the air and I am confident that, as a Christian, a nurse and a clinical educator, I will be flying for a long time to come.

Discussion Questions

1. What are the issues around considering a faith position in health care?
2. For the Christian educator working in the NHS, what are the personal challenges that can arise?
3. Is it necessary for the Christian message to be brought to the classroom?
4. How would the alternative faith/no faith views of students impact on, or influence, the educational experience delivered by a Christian educator?
5. Can the faith of a clinical educator really make a difference to patient care? If yes, then what are the potential negative or positive consequences?

References

Beck, J., 1999, 'Spiritual and Moral Development, and Religious Education', in Thatcher, A. (ed.), *Spirituality and the Curriculum*, London: Cassell, pp. 153–180

Bradshaw, A., 2011, 'Compassion: What History Teaches Us', in *Nursing Times*, 107, 19/20, pp. 12–14

Bridges, D., 1999, 'Educational Research: pursuit of truth or flight into fancy?', in *British Educational Research Journal*, 25.5, pp. 597–616

Cooling, T., 2010, *Doing God in Education*, London: Theos

Fawcett, T. N. and Noble, A., 2004, 'The challenge of spiritual care in a multi-faith society experienced as a Christian nurse', in *Journal of Clinical Nursing*, 13, pp. 136–142

Flight Safety Foundation (FSF), 2000, *FSF ALAR Briefing Note 1.3 – Golden Rules* [Online] at flightsafety.org/files/alar_bn1-3-goldrules.pdf [accessed 9 January 2014]

Hay, D. and Nye, R., 1998, *The Spirit of the Child*, London: HarperCollins

Hill, B. V., 2004, *Exploring religion in school: a national priority*, Adelaide: Openbook Publishers

Keighley, T. and Wright, S., 2007, 'Nurses need an act of worship', in *Nursing Standard*, 21.30, pp. 28–29

May, P., 1988, *Confidence in the classroom: realistic encouragement for teachers*, Leicester: InterVaristy Press

Moffatt, V., 2012, 'Letter Offends Nurse's Ethical Code', in *Kai Tiaki Nursing New Zealand*, [Letters Page], 18.1, p. 5

Short, R. L., 1990, *The Bible according to Peanuts*, London: Fount Paperbacks

Smith, D. I. and Shortt, J., 2002, *The Bible and the task of teaching*, Nottingham: The Stapleford Centre

Thomas, J., 2007, 'Nursing is a Profession, not a Christian Vocation', in *Nursing Standard*, 21.32, [letters page], p. 32

Wakefield, G. S. (ed.), 1983, *A Dictionary of Christian Spirituality*, London: SCM Press

Wolterstorff, N., 1980, *Educating for responsible action*, Grand Rapids, MI: Eerdmans

Worsley, H. J., 2013, 'What motivates Christian Educational Practitioners? (Theology as Resource in the School)', in *Grove Booklets, Grove Education Series*, 17

4

'How shall we sing the Lord's song in a strange land?' (Psalm 137.4) A Quaker understanding of education

AIDAN GILLESPIE

Abstract

In this chapter I scrutinize the tensions experienced in the transition from primary school teacher to university lecturer and identify what I believe are the main tensions within this new role. From a personal faith perspective that is rooted in Quaker thinking, I question the role of education in developing individuals and as a method of societal transformation and emancipation. I examine what it means to be an educational professional with an opening and questioning faith among a student body that perhaps has needs which challenge my personal educational philosophy. The chapter examines how, as a lecturer, identifying and meeting the students' needs is juxtaposed with the vocational call to live out the values of my faith within a culture of educational consumerism.

Keywords

Divine; product; constructivist; light; collaboration; consumer and spirituality

Introduction

Through my career in education I have become aware of the ways in which someone's spirituality can become defined by what they do. I entered teaching, like so many working-class people, because it was viewed as a career with a certain amount of respectability and opportunity for advancement. Education has not only been rewarding in the sense of the satisfaction and challenge it brings as a career, but also in assisting me to find the language through which my spirituality can be defined and expressed. Recently I have made the move from primary school teaching in both faith and maintained schools to lecturing at Canterbury Christ Church University. I have found the transition to be exciting and challenging for a variety of reasons. Above all, I have found my new role as a university lecturer to be one where, in facilitating journeys of discovery, I have been forced to acknowledge the tensions between education as a vehicle for understanding, and my faith. This applies not only for myself but more importantly for the students alongside whom I have the privilege to work.

From teacher to lecturer

Having taught for several years in primary schools I had always intended to pursue a career in education which was not part of the management structure within schools, as I always felt that I wanted to develop myself through an academic rather than a managerial route. I began the doctorate in education at Canterbury Christ Church University as the cohort offered me the chance to study education from a Christian/faith perspective and this was something I was really keen to do. In the last school at which I taught, I was the religious education co-ordinator and this became so interesting that I felt I wanted to engage in further study in this area. What I hadn't anticipated was that early on in my doctoral studies I would become a lecturer at Canterbury Christ Church University in primary religious education. My new role was to deliver sessions on primary RE at both under- and post-graduate levels across a range of pathways and modules. This sudden change in the direction of my career was something that I relished and has brought vast amounts of both challenge and satisfaction as I attempt to live out my ideals as a professional educator and also to understand the past that my spirituality plays in making sense of the opportunities of my new role. The immediate task, I felt, was defining what I, my colleagues and my students perceived the role of the lecturer to be and how I, as a new lecturer and person of faith, attempted to make sense of these potentially contrasting perspectives while building relationships and teaching opportunities that nurtured a sense of community and collaboration.

Education as an exercise in uncertainty

For me education is a sacred exercise. It is an interaction which takes place in countless differing contexts and through a multitude of cultures. I believe the unifying characteristic of all educational endeavours is that they are essentially meaning making. What I mean by this is that I see education as the place in which participants come to know a little more about themselves, each other and the world. Through education we will gain a brighter, sharper perspective of reality rather than a panoramic, all-encompassing view.

My view on education is not dissimilar to my view on God or more accurately to my concept of the divine, the Light. My spirituality is Quaker and I have come to Quakerism during my doctoral studies, having commenced my spiritual and religious exploration of Quakerism several years before. I was brought up as a Catholic in the west of Ireland, but my family were not attenders at church. It could be said that as a family we were culturally rather than actively Catholic. During my early teaching career I taught at two Catholic primary schools, but this was an uneasy professional relationship as there were aspects of the Catholic faith which did not sit comfortably with me. One of these was certainty of the concept of the divine or, more accurately, the hierarchical nature of the divine within Catholicism, which I understood to be at the expense of other religions and faiths.

Quakerism offered a different perspective, one rooted in uncertainty and that is comfortable with questioning. This was far more acceptable to me as someone who had a relationship with Jesus but did not understand him to be the only route through which to encounter the Light. It was the non-creedal nature of Quakerism that allowed me to have my beliefs and to sit comfortably among other Friends, content in supporting each others' relationship, understanding and journey in the Light (Quaker Faith and Practice, 2011). Alongside that, Quakerism actively sought to meet other faiths and religions on an equal footing, without an evangelical motive and willing to accept all as having an equally valid understanding and relationship with the Light. The uncertainty of Quakerism allowed me to begin to understand my concept of the Light as an ongoing process, but also to define my understanding of education as a sacred act and one which leads to deeper understanding.

Quakerism allows for a comfortable uncertainty which leads not only to an ongoing questioning of a priori beliefs and ways of understanding the world, but also to an acknowledgement of the past that every faith plays in understanding the divine and the role of every field of education in helping to understand the world and our place in it. Quakers have traditionally held all subjects and areas within both schools and universities as offering specific perspectives on parts which contribute to the whole. This whole could be understood as the ultimate reality, God or the Light, but also the whole of a student's journey through education and the contribution each discipline makes to forming a fuller understanding of self and the world (*Quaker Faith and Practice*, 2011, 23.79). This is also a way of viewing the sacred in the everydayness of education. From a Quaker perspective the role of education is no less sacred whether students are explicitly studying religion or religious education, as they do in my sessions, or whether they are studying a subject where there is no obvious link to spirituality or faith. All are relevant to an individual's relationship to the world around them and to the people with whom they are involved. A Quaker understanding of education aims to foster an awareness of the interconnectedness of all things and our roles and responsibilities towards society and creation.

I have been heavily influenced by the writings of Simone Weil. Weil as a philosopher was concerned with the interconnectedness of all things and how this could serve as a vehicle for self-realization and growth. In her views on education she outlines how the very act of learning is a way in which an individual can journey towards the divine (Weil, 2009).

One of the aspects of this educational enterprise is the fostering of a sense of 'attention' towards all things. That is to say that a learner should strive to be aware not only of what they are attempting to learn then and there, but also to be attentive to what they have previously learned and how this may be influencing their thinking. This attentiveness should not be a forceful appropriation of knowledge. It should be an openness and emptying of pride and prejudice in the hope of attaining knowledge, rather than the active appropriation of it as one would a commodity. Seeing education, and particular disciplines within education, in this way sets the learner free from the everyday constraints of targets and grades, although Weil does acknowledge that these are necessary in formal education. Subjects and disciplines examined in this way become friends from which we can learn stories and traditions, which in turn nourish both teacher and the learner.

Weil outlines how this may be thought of in a particular learning episode. She describes learning as a demanding calculation that pushes the learner to their limits. Whether or not the learner is able to solve the problem is of little importance, but what is of importance is the energy and attentiveness that the learner directs towards it. This desire to understand, to the exclusion of all other stimuli at that particular point in time, is the essence of her thought on education. The suspension of all thought and energy in passive pursuit of understanding with willingness to accept and explore is the ultimate act of piety (Weil, 2009).

Implicit in this view of education is that its ultimate goal is understanding. Understanding of the ultimate reality or truth, whatever one's understanding of it: my own is that of the Light, for Christians it is the Trinity, and so on. Education provides a road map to guide our journey together, all of us choosing different routes and stopping to sightsee at various points but all ultimately seeking the destination of complete understanding and immersion in the Light.

How this understanding of the role of education manifests itself in my own understanding of my role of lecturer is still being defined. Education from within the Quaker tradition is a vehicle for personal and social transformation. As Quakers, we have a respectful disregard for reputation and hierarchy and this is something which is evident in my understanding of the role of lecturer, which I see as being that of a facilitator of dialogue and an adjudicator of competing views. Respect for a student's opinions and a willingness to be open to new ideas and perspectives is necessary for dialogue, particularly within religious education. Students should feel comfortable and encouraged to explore ideas and concepts that may be challenging and occasionally uncomfortable. One of the main reasons for this is to foster a sense of openness in students and to acknowledge conflict as a necessary catalyst for the germination and growth of new ideas. Not conflict in the sense of physical or moral domination of other, but the unsettling of established truths in pursuit of new, alternative perspectives, leading to deeper understanding (*Quaker Faith and Practice*, 2003, 23.85). This is a very optimistic view of education but one which I feel is not only possible but evident in my role.

What is the role of the lecturer?

How I understand the role and vocation of those involved in teaching and lecturing can at times be juxtaposed with the views held not only by my colleagues but, I would say more importantly, by my students. There are many reasons for this but an examination of some of the key tensions will highlight how I understand and live out my faith through my profession. The majority of students with whom I regularly come into contact are undergraduates who are usually in their late teens or early twenties. For the most part, they have either come straight from school or have had a gap year. In general they have come from a culture of education which does not place too many personal demands on them but none the less expects a high level of commitment and academic achievement.

Arriving at university can be daunting and this is often manifested in the demands that students make of their lecturers in both an academic and pastoral sense. First-year students in particular often grapple with the new-found freedom that they experience at university and the way in which they are encouraged to study independently through exercises, at least in teacher training courses, where reflection and self-criticality is a feature. It is often a culture shock to find that lecturers (myself included) will not hold their hands through assignments but will encourage independence and risk taking in the hope that students will learn for themselves. Students who see the lecturer as having the same role as their school teacher find this frustrating. Their expectation is that the lecturer will 'give' them the answers to the questions that they have, rather than act as a facilitator for independent study and learning.

How my understanding of education and of my role as an educator is influenced by my faith and vice versa does in some ways help to address these issues. On an educational level, I encourage students to work in a constructivist pedagogical paradigm so that they will build upon their existing attributes, knowledge and skills through dialogue and interaction with others (Wilson and Kendall-Seatter, 2010). This exploratory way of working alleviates some of their fears, in that they are not alone but working in a collegiate way. The journey of learning is as important as the destination of learning, if not more so.

There is however, an element of tension between a social constructivist epistemology, where it could be assumed that there is no objective reality but simply a view of reality which is fluid and socially constructed (as is common in education theory and classroom practice), and that of the faith position outlined above. This, however, is to misunderstand the epistemological position taken in my view of education. How one understands and names one's concept of reality is open to debate but the notion that reality is objective and mind independent is to be found in a Critical Realist ontology as described by Brad Shipway: 'At its broadest level the term "critical realist" has been used to indicate the general idea of the belief in the mind-independent reality, and the notion that this perception of reality is not direct, but is mediated by means of our perception' (Shipway, 2011).

What are the implications of this Critical Realist approach for my students' learning and for my practice? While I do think that my role is that of facilitator and companion of a student's educational journey, perhaps I would be meeting the needs of the student better if I were to acquiesce to their desire for a more direct route through education rather than an exploratory one. I do believe that students may have a desire to learn in this way as it is the educational culture that they are used to from school and compulsory education. But I also believe that there are other tensions which give rise to the student wanting to appropriate their education as they would any other service or product. Where this may be the case, the call to live out my Quaker values of equality and truth are challenged as the commercialization of education and the possible views of students regarding the role of the educator as a service provider can come in to conflict (Ritzer, 2004).

Students come to university with high expectations. Traditionally this may have meant that they expected to be challenged in an academic way, to encounter demanding ideas that would equip them with the critical ability needed for whatever profession or direction in life that they took after university. While this is still the case, students now have high expectations of their universities and in particular of their lecturers and personal tutors in other domains also. These are often manifested at panel meetings between students and teaching representatives to discuss overall concerns of an academic and managerial nature. One reason for this shift in the relationship between the student and the university is the introduction of fees to attend university. Students now have to think carefully about applying for university as they have to be mindful of the financial burden or investment that will affect them, both while at university and for many years after (Johnston, 2013).

Some of these expectations are targeted at lecturers and personal tutors in the sense that the student simply wants the lecturer or tutor to provide them with a product for which they have paid. They may not want all the extra nurturing which a good university and lecturer will provide through stimulation and prompting. Working in a collegiate and exploratory way takes a lot more time and effort than getting your answers directly from the tutor.

Alongside this, some students now see university as not only a rite of passage but as a commercial venture, an investment in their future earnings (Anchor et al., 2011). For vocational subjects, such as teaching and education, the very act of entering into this discipline would hint at the desire to make a positive contribution to society. Academic disciplines may suffer, as studying for the love of a subject may not be feasible financially as there may be no monetary return after the years of study. Teaching in the UK now is in a state of change, with private ventures encouraged to set up their own academies and free schools. The commercialization of education is taking the focus away from the idea of making a difference in society and turning it to concerns with making money. From this point of view the choice of degree or subject can mean poverty or prosperity and is governed by financial motives rather than viewed as a means to develop the person and their place and role in society.

For me as a lecturer this brings certain tensions. Of course I want to do my best for my students and this applies both to their academic development and their personal development. How do I live out my Quaker ideals while attempting to nurture my students but also meet their demands? As a lecturer and a person of faith and given that I perceive education to be a sacred encounter, I must at times acknowledge the demands of my students but also occasionally ignore certain demands and pressures with the hope of broadening their experience and guiding them along the path of discovery and truth.

The lecturer as an agent of subversion

The product-purveyor concept of education does provide opportunities for growth for both the student and the teacher/lecturer. As I said previously, I feel that education is a journey towards understanding and an unending desire for relatedness to the Light of God. The lecturer is ideally placed to assist students in coming to this realization and taking from education lessons that will be relived throughout their personal and professional lives rather than providing them with a qualification that is used for economic advancement.

One way of doing this is to direct students' attention to the political nature of education, to questions (which they should explore and answer for themselves) on the role of the lecturer, of education and of teaching. These questions should be addressed in a constructivist, collaborative manner, with the lecturer standing on an equal footing with the students and seeking to meet them wherever they are in their journey. From a Quaker standpoint, it is of prime importance to pose the question 'what are the roles, responsibilities and hierarchies involved in the practice of education?' Seeing the lecturer as an equal, albeit with a different role, is far more empowering that placing the label of 'expert' upon an individual (Pelikar, 1992). This, for me, sees 'That of God in everyone' (Fox, 1656) and recognizes the responsibility of all involved to be active participants in the teaching and learning that is taking place.

This is quite a subversive message. It turns on its head the current trend of provider–consumer relations in society and particularly in education. With this model, in which all are equal but with differing roles, a positive imperative is placed on each individual to be proactive and responsible in all their undertakings, and a brighter light shines than the neon of consumerism.

But perhaps the lecturer can be seen as expert and still serve others. The lecturer should not only be foregrounding to students the tensions inherent in a priori beliefs about society but should also be willing to serve society through their 'expert' knowledge (Popkewitz, 1984). Knowledge, thought of in this way, is a channel through which students and society can be served, rather than a means to financial reward or asset gain. We are all familiar with the academics or experts who appear occasionally on our televisions to give broad and balanced critique or insight into some abstract concept. But perhaps students and the public at large are less aware of the ways in which lecturers serve society through the development of knowledge and ideas, as well as through advances in science, technology and medicine. Presenting education and the journey through education this way could, I believe, be a witness to the Light that is there to illuminate all. Shedding light on society and our place in it is surely a sacred act by which society is served and individuals are developed.

One of the key sacramental tasks I have as a lecturer is to move students away from what Paolo Freire describes as a 'banking' model of education and towards a model of education which seeks to challenge not only assumptions about the world but also about specific disciplines which contribute to a student's university career (Freire, 1993). Freire's ideas about the 'banking' of knowledge is a dangerous assumption that students, and indeed members of the public, take for granted. This is a preconception of the role of education and educators that does not challenge the status quo of society for a number of reasons. Primarily it tacitly endorses the role of the lecturer as 'expert' and reinforces hierarchical structures within society as it places the student in the position of a consumer, storing up nuggets of information which can be called upon when needed and which are only available through the medium of the 'expert'. As a Quaker involved in education this is something which I must always address if I am to live out my Quaker testimony of equality. For students to be passive consumers, beholden to figures of authority and experts within society for the supply of information, demeans their personhood and dignity and denies them the awareness of their capacity for growth and renewal. At the core of my lecturing is the aspiration to develop in students their own critical capacity which would otherwise be drowned out by the competing voices from 'facts' appropriated from a consumerist and subservient concept of education and relationships.

Conclusion

Living up to the educational and spiritual ideals set out above challenges not only the students' thinking but also my own practices and professionalism. My practice is rooted in relationships. I strive constantly to make all participants feel comfortable to contribute to sessions and also to make them aware that they too are 'experts' in that they have a perspective unique to them, which should be used to help others. From a strictly educational perspective, my planning and lecturing style could be described as 'constructivist' in that I plan and foster activities and discussions which are largely collaborative in nature so that students learn together and from one another. For me this is the essence of my Quaker faith as lived out in my profession. Lecturing allows me to make students aware of their own unique gifts and talents and how they can use those talents to develop themselves as learners but also as active and discerning members of society, aware of the hierarchical nature of the society we live in and very often take for granted. From my perspective, this hidden curriculum (Giroux and Penna, 1983) within my lecturing makes it distinctively Quaker as it fosters the character growth and development that is a key feature of Quaker education in general (Meidl and Meidl, 2013).

Discussion Questions

1. Within your own teaching or learning context, what are the main obstacles or tensions between being an educational professional or similar and that of your faith or world-view?
2. The Quaker faith is one of uncertainty. Does your faith tradition and the position you take complement or challenge your view of education?
3. Is the role of education to lead to ongoing questioning of individual disciplines or to questioning of authority and the status quo?
4. What value does the study of philosophy and faith have in relation to life beyond university?
5. Is this a view of education from within an ivory tower or is it one that can be realized within your own teaching context?

References

Anchor, J. R., Fiserova, J., Marsikova, K. and Urbanek, V, 2011, 'Student Expectations of the Financial Returns to Higher Education in the Czech Republic and England: Evidence from Business Schools', in *Economics of Education Review*, 2011, 30.4, p. 673–681

Fox, G., 1656, cited in *Quaker Faith and Practice*, 2011 (4th edn) London: The Yearly Meeting of the Religious Society of Friends (Quakers) in Britain

Freire, P., 1993, *The Pedagogy of the Oppressed*, London: Penguin Books

Giroux, H. and Penna, A., 1983, 'Social Education in the Classroom: The Dynamics of the Hidden Curriculum', in *The Hidden Curriculum and Moral Education*, Giroux, H. and Purpel, D. (eds), 1983, Berkeley: McCutchan Publishing Corporation

Johnston, R., 2013, 'England's New Scheme for Funding Higher Education through Student Fees: "Fair and Progressive"?', in *The Political Quarterly*, 2013, 84.2, pp. 200–210

Meidl, C. and Meidl, L., 2013, 'Character Education in three schools: Catholic, Quaker and public', in *Education 3–13: International Journal of Primary, Elementary and Early Years Education*, 41.2, pp. 178–187

Pelikar, J., 1992, *The Idea of the University: A re-examination*, London: Yale University Press

Popkewitz, T. S., 1984, *Paradigm and Ideology in Educational Research: the social functions of the intellectual*, Lewes: Falmer Press

Quaker Faith and Practice, 2011 (4th edn) London: The Yearly Meeting of the Religious Society of Friends (Quakers) in Britain

Ritzer, G., 2004, *The McDonaldization of Society*, London: Sage

Shipway, B., 2011, *A Critical Realist Perspective of Education*, London: Routledge

Weil, S., 2009, *Waiting For God*, London: Harper Perennial

Wilson, V. and Kendall-Seatter, S., 2010, *Developing Professional Practice 7–14*, Harlow: Pearson Education

5

The sustaining of a Christian teacher's career in a secularizing context

Phillip J. O'Connor

Abstract

In this chapter, a Christian teacher's perspective is addressed by a consideration of what sustains a career in teaching in the face of marketization, secularization, and the politicization of the educational system. Teachers operate within a milieu of political, economic and professional ambiguities. This is a reflection on how a Christian faith (which operates with values of love, compassion, care, authenticity, empathy and respect for others) has contributed to a resilient approach that has informed and influenced a teaching career.

Keywords

Career sustainability; secularization; policy landscape; professional frameworks; marginalization; marketization; Christian-believing; values; theological approach; vocational and ministry

Context to the issues

My experience of teaching personal social health and citizenship education (PSHCE) is a thought-provoking journey. It embodies my conviction of its relevance to the lives of students and, perhaps controversially, affords me opportunities to inspire them, to inculcate values, beliefs, attitudes and skills that can contribute to their understanding and appreciation of educational achievement while becoming well-rounded, worthwhile citizens. From this, it might be obvious that my world-view rejects the preponderance of targets, outcomes and mere results, although these are all important for the overall attainment of pupils.

However, PSHCE also presents opportunities for tensions and complexities. For example, should the topics covered be addressed at home or by the school and to what extent should controversial issues be handled from a faith perspective? Also, what epistemology should be employed in ethical discourse? A theological approach to truth is considered necessary from a Christian perspective as this informs the basis of how truth claims are understood, interpreted and handled in relation to opposing debates. It is therefore necessary to contextualize my position regarding personal principles, morals, standards and biblical beliefs in the subject delivery given its sensitive, controversial, value-laden content. My position, together with the policy and legal frameworks within which I operate, will have some impact on the subject delivery regarding content, strategies and desired outcomes.

Clarifying a pedagogical approach to engage with this has been vital in informing and guiding my understanding, interpretation and practice of truth claims: be they transmissionist, constructivist or apologetic (Cooling, 2013). Furthermore, the strategies used and the outcomes desired for students have been illuminated, be they 'conservative, fundamental or evangelical.'

Identifying some areas of tension and of opportunity

When I relocated to England as a returning citizen in 2001, my first teaching responsibility was PSHCE. I was appointed department head at a West London Church of England school the following year with additional responsibilities for citizenship, careers and work experience. Despite my prior unfamiliarity with PSHCE as a subject, I embraced the experience as welcome yet challenging. It was welcome in that this was an area of interest comprising topics and subject aims I deem very relevant and applicable to students' lives. I envisaged this subject as an extension of the pastoral role I had had as youth minister while living and working in the Cayman Islands in an Evangelical church and teaching in its affiliated faith school. It was also welcome in relating some aspects of my religious upbringing to my biblical beliefs.

It was challenging because PSHCE was delivered through many, different and often under-prepared and reluctant form teachers. I found the coordination of this unfamiliar subject testing at times. This was mainly due to my then lack of specific subject knowledge and delivery strategies (my training, certification and subject-specialist status came later). Furthermore, the education system with its 'impersonally regulated professional stance' (Carr, 2000), with its very precise separation of 'professional from private concerns' (p. 11) highlighted a new challenge for me because it was not aligned to my world-view of teaching. Also noticeable was a general marginalization of a biblical perspective and faith position in favour of a more liberal and secular agenda in the curriculum, assemblies and policy documents. This could potentially be problematic from a Christian point of view.

Additionally, I was challenged by the low profile of the subject as well as the apathy and indifference of a large number of the students. Admittedly, the fragmented provision delivered through form-time by teachers who felt ill-equipped to do so did not particularly inspire the students.

In 2013, Ofsted stated that 'the PSHE curriculum was usually more coherent and comprehensive in schools that offered discrete PSHE lessons taught by specialists' (p. 30). A perception existed that the subject was not very useful; perhaps because of its non-academic status. Earlier research by Ofsted (2005) suggested that only 40 per cent of students saw it as relevant to their lives. I maintained that topics covered in PSHE and their inherent values were worth inculcating as they satisfied the aims of the subject.

But how should it be taught? My stance has always been that it is impossible to teach in a value-neutral way, void of the influence of our ideologies and personal beliefs, be they secular or religious. Straughan and Wrigley (1989), argue that 'even in the most neutral curriculum context, the job of teaching is intrinsically bound up with values' (p. 90).

Likewise, the tension when considering the relevance of a biblical view to citizenship and PSHE is well documented (Willmer, 1992; Hirst, 1965). It is argued that 'the corner stone of western liberal education is essentially secular' (Bryan 2012, p. 1). Revell and Walters (2010) recommend that 'a secular, atheist or agnostic belief position in the classroom should be recognized by all students as an identifiable belief position rather than a neutral stance' (p. 4). While Cook (1996) cautions against holding strong views and presenting them as authoritative, Cooling (2002) argues that biblical beliefs should be appreciated as a resource to be developed educationally instead of being deemed a dilemma to be 'privatized' or 'managed' (p. 4).

A specific example occurred years ago when I noticed that whenever some health professionals delivered sex and relationships education (SRE), their emphasis was primarily on issues of contraception, especially condom acquisition and use, as well as sexually transmitted infections. These are important issues to cover at the appropriate age and stage as pupils are prepared for the experiences, opportunities and responsibilities of later life. I felt, however, that this approach failed to address a wider discourse and understanding of the issues. The need, therefore, existed to follow up these lessons emphasizing issues of healthy relationships including love, trust, respect, empathy, care, support, fidelity and 'attitudes, values and virtues' (Arthur et al., 2010). My approach and strategy would also raise awareness of the position of those students with religious beliefs and their perspectives on complex and tension-riddled issues, for example of sexuality, abstinence and contraception. This could assist students to reflect on their learning 'in the light of their faith' (Hull, 1977, p. 19) and this reflection from a Christian standpoint enabled a critical or rational response to learning.

Introduction

Perceptions of teaching are based on economic, political, ideological, professional and religious construction. Therefore, the interpretations of its definition are contextual and open to dissimilar paradigms. These seek to achieve particular goals and outcomes to realize dissimilar agendas; be they faith-based, political or ideological, pupil-centred, scientific, rational, vocational or economic. For example, should education prepare the workforce to become worthwhile citizens who are socially and morally responsible and who participate in the democratic process? Should it inspire students to fulfil their God-given potential and embrace some aspects of spirituality? Or should it be a combination of these?

Teachers practice within a complex landscape riddled with ambiguities, fluctuations in policy and assessment frameworks, low morale, bureaucracy and an increasing workload. While these can present tremendous opportunities for personal advancement, inspiring and influencing the lives of students, they can also contribute to teacher 'stress and exhaustion' leading to the high rate of attrition, reported by Richard Garner (2015) in the *Independent* newspaper, to be 40 per cent of teachers quitting after having served only a year in the profession. Hutchings (2010) notes that 'in England, the number of teachers leaving the profession before they reach retirement age is higher than it is elsewhere in Europe' (p. 8). Similarly, Erricker and Erricker (2000) claim that education is distorted and altered by the stipulations and pressures of modernism and a capitalistic culture.

Yet, within this milieu, various pathways to teaching have been established to recruit and retain suitably qualified individuals into the profession. Alexander (2008) claims that teaching involves the broader issue of motives. The issue of initial examination of motivation for Christian educationalists is addressed by Worsley (2013) in *What Motivates Christian Educational Practitioners?* A close scrutiny, therefore, of our motives, symptomatic of our values, beliefs and ideology, might inform our true purpose for teaching. My view is that preliminary motive-clarification might guide and sustain during the inevitable challenges and vicissitudes of teaching, thus directing a greater sense of passion and purpose. However, research suggests that there is not necessarily a connection between future job satisfaction, sustainability and the circumstances under which a teacher's career is selected (Talts et al., 2011).

The educational landscape can be blurred by the relationship between motivation for entering the profession and sustainability. It is possible to enter the profession with clear and noble motives and be disillusioned later for many reasons, leading to low morale, apathy, indifference and/or attrition. The converse is also true. Nonetheless, this correlation is made more complex by perceptions of the marginalization of a faith position and religious beliefs, with debate as to the extent to which faith should be integrated into professional practice, or whether it is appropriate to do so (Smith and Shortt, 2003). Research by Bryan and Revell (2011) on religious education (RE) teacher-trainees suggests that, although issues of identity and faith are considered personally important, they fail to contribute to a perception of what constitutes the 'good teacher'. This perception embraces a *new* professional world-view of teaching which celebrates *rationality* and *objectivity* as benchmarks. However, Hill (2004) argues that 'good teachers are able . . . to develop the empathy needed to understand the motivational strength of the values held by others' (p. 58) whereas Hirst (1965) claims that objective reasoning, not Christian beliefs, should be the hallmark of educational reflection.

To further illuminate, contextualize and examine these issues, I have asked five questions to structure this chapter and provide a personal account from a Christian perspective within a macro-political milieu:

1. What are some of the challenges that might affect sustaining a teaching career in today's educational and economic climate?
2. How could the inherent issues and tensions that are implicit in bringing Christian faith into this educational context be identified and handled?
3. To what extent do educational approaches and metanarrative influence the pedagogy of a Christian teacher?
4. How does a biblical understanding relate to the teaching context and does it influence a sustained teaching career?
5. What additional challenges are presented by the current educational system and what helps sustain a life in teaching?

1. Educational and economic considerations

Perceptions of how a teaching career might be sustained or prolonged in today's harsh economic climate are well-documented (Barnes, 2012; Hutchings, 2010; Day et al., 2005). Few teachers are exempt from the extended pay freeze and constantly changing expectations and frameworks. Worsley (2013) identifies the Academies Act, competition, the 'standards agenda' and assessment culture as some of the challenges in education at the moment. These can potentially affect a teacher's decision whether or not to remain in the teaching profession. For example, it might be argued that the commercialization and marketization of education have contributed to a culture that promotes low morale, added work pressure and less teacher autonomy (through parentocracy, competition and political interference). Additionally, the more 'nurturing' aspect of teaching has been tremendously reduced or removed as targets, outcomes, assessment, competition, performance management, rigid and, arguably, uncaring, teaching and learning regimes are implemented.

Perceptions of these issues or the approaches teachers adopt to cope with them might be informed by one's teaching context, personal beliefs, values, ideology and motivation for teaching. These may embolden or discourage us to take up a position of resilience as we are shaped by the stories of our life experiences and our attitudes towards them. Our interpretations of them contribute to the metanarrative of our identity which forms a 'central commitment in our lives' (Cooling, 2002, p. 2).

While teaching and educational standards must be established and upheld, Ofsted's ambiguity and perceived legalistic character does little to contribute to a positive school ethos or to the personal health and well-being of teachers, as Worsley argues in his article, *The Standards Agenda and the Culture of Grace (A Conflict between Ofsted and the Church)* (2011). This perception is deemed 'unforgiving', due to its emphasis on 'standards'. A gap therefore exists for 'emotional intelligence and spiritual relativity'.

Other considerations relate to students' low aspirations, achievements and challenging behaviour and to a changing policy landscape, assessment criteria, 'target-driven narratives' (Barnes, 2012), long work-hours, excessive marking and the unrealistic demands and expectations placed on teachers. These can lead to teacher stress and disillusionment. While every effort must be made to inspire, encourage and implement different intervention strategies to ensure high pupil attainment, it must also be acknowledged that pupils attend school with their own unique challenges, and personal and family issues.

2. Christian faith and professional identity: issues and tensions

Besides economic and educational challenges, the second question explores the inherent issues and tensions implicit in bringing Christian faith into this educational context and its impact on career sustainability. The tension between private beliefs and professional identity is well-documented (Willmer, 1992; Hirst, 1965; Bryan, 2012). Bryan and Revell (2011) discuss the secular language of the Teachers' Standards and the potential challenges this poses for teachers of faith.

This is mainly due to the fact that except in faith schools, the policies and ideologies of education arguably are underpinned by a secular world-view. This suggests a 'disassociation between teachers' work, values and religion' (Bryan, 2012). While faith may be incorporated in teaching; Shortt et al. (2000) in their article, 'Metaphor, Scripture and Education', recognize a conflict in doing so explicitly. Their suggestion instead advocates a metaphorical model comprising principles and stories, given the problematic nature of adopting an authoritative biblical view to controversial topics encountered. This is particularly applicable in the teaching context of PSHCE, where a teacher of faith might present issues and topics of a sensitive and controversial nature in which the scope for tensions abound. Notably, major conflicts do relate to what constitutes controversial issues, how they are defined, what understanding of truth is adopted and to what extent personal Christian beliefs should influence professional practice in a secular context.

Remaining resolute, Pring (2000) argues that 'the teacher is not paid to transmit his or her personal views and certainties' claiming instead that authority exists in the command of the body of knowledge needed to develop and 'form the judgement of the learner' (p. 80). Yet Shortt (2012) argues that the stories of our faith positions can inform our teaching and learning and provide meaning and purpose. Such a metaphorical approach could arguably be non-adversarial compared with incorporating 'Christianity as a form of authoritarian meta-narrative' (Wright, 2004, p. 116). Tensions inherent in religious believing within a secular context therefore concern the legitimacy of being a PSHE teacher and the potential conflict this brings with a personal Christian faith and whether the two can be interwoven in a way which satisfies both.

Performativity is a concept that refers to externally set criteria and standards, articulated in a secular language and potentially in conflict with personal beliefs systems (Bryan, 2012). This emerging concept of teacher professionalism within a secular positioning portrays objectivity and neutrality as benchmarks, fiercely advocating a separation between the private and public spheres. However, there should be respectful appreciation of others' life-shaping biblical beliefs as a resource to be utilized in education rather than a problem to be 'privatized' or 'managed'

(Cooling, 2011, p. 4). In fact, Hart (1995) presents theology as an explicit activity of faith to be embraced unashamedly.

An additional related issue arising is that of conscience versus commitment. Cooling (2002) in *Commitment and Indoctrination: A Dilemma for Religious Education?* articulates this complexity. Like religious education (RE), PSHCE is a subject where it could be argued that the teacher's religious faith commitment might facilitate the propagation of personal views rather than the fulfilment of educational aims when dealing with sensitive and controversial issues. That is to say, religious dogma will dominate, resulting in indoctrination. This is unsubstantiated. The appropriateness of the classroom as a context in which to handle controversial issues is advocated by Arthur and Wright (2001), albeit within an approach that avoids indoctrination or the exploitation of pupils (Downie, 1990).

While an agenda arguably exists to 'secularize teachers' beliefs by banishing them to the private domain of an individual's life', respect for the rights of others is required in a plural society to ensure the preparation of students to formulate judgements on diverse and opposing commitments and beliefs (Cooling, 2002, p. 5). Liberal, radical or secular approaches should not be presented as rational, neutral or 'educationally superior' (p. 8). It is also important that shared goals are not in conflict with one's own metanarrative to avoid being 'personally compromised': there has to be 'courageous restraint' (p. 7). Adopting such an approach to teaching as a 'ministry' can guide, motivate and give meaning, fulfilment, satisfaction and purpose to life, thereby contributing to career sustainability, as an indelible impact is made on the lives of students and colleagues.

3. Educational approaches: influences on teaching

Within this context of complexity, my third question examines the extent to which some features of my educational approaches and metanarrative influence the pedagogy of a Christian teacher.

Arguments for teaching experiences void of our personal stories, beliefs, values and approaches are flawed. My evangelical Christian experiences form part of that metanarrative as well as my ministry/vocational positioning on practice, teacher-professionalism and hence on career sustainability. A new professional approach of the kind advocated in recent policy documents in the UK fails to celebrate the diversity of teaching approaches drawn from different cultures and belief positions and tends to mould teachers into 'inflexible clones of a rigid top down imperative' (Barnes, 2012, p. 10).

My initial Caribbean teacher-training experience tended heavily towards a didactic, teacher-led and centred approach which was also religiously influenced and inspired. It also focused heavily on teacher professionalism, dress code, being well-rounded, positive role-models, social graces and modern etiquette. However, my last 14 years teaching in England (since 2001), have been further enriched by a significant adoption of a wider diversity of educational approaches as advocated by Salandanan (2008) who believes that teachers should be equipped with knowledge of various strategies together with the proficiency to employ them. These have included employing a pedagogy that promotes active learning and that requires the teacher to act as a facilitator of learning. This pedagogical approach also requires the teacher to be reflexive.

As a teacher, my educational and theological approaches are intertwined. Bringing my initial motivation, values, beliefs and metanarratives to teaching reflects a desire to model my faith implicitly; yet the question remains as to the extent to which personal beliefs, secular or Christian, should be articulated in the classroom. Furthermore, the extent to which these inform and influence teaching and the criteria for judging success or measuring outcomes will also remain subjective.

I share the aim and desire of Barnes (2012) to encourage a 'fulfilling, affirming, liberating and sustaining' experience for children created through the 'curriculum and pedagogy' (p. 9). It is commendable, therefore, that Ofsted stipulates that the definition of achievement in PSHE should be broadened to account for values and attitudes as well as the acquisition of factual knowledge by students (Ofsted 2005).

4. An understanding of a faith position and approaches within a professional context

My faith position shapes my world-view and my teaching. My fourth question therefore addresses how such theological understanding and interpretation relates to the teaching context and how it influences and contributes to a sustained teaching career. Theology may be defined as a 'reflective religious discourse' (Astley, 1996, p. 68) or according to Hart (1995) as an 'activity of the mind' merged with the workings of human rationality: that is, 'thinking about faith and God in a "responsible way while seeking to comprehend and express that understanding"' (p. 73). The contribution of private beliefs to professional contexts has been recognized by Hirst (1965). However, he questions the appropriateness of the application of such truth in the public domain. Worsley (2013), on the other hand, argues that 'traditionally, the church has contributed to education in Mission, nurture and service' (p. 1).

Arthur et al. (2010) also take this viewpoint, recognizing the opportunities for a positive contribution of religion to civic education, through the democratic and effective moulding of individuals. Additionally, Hull (1976) identifies approaches for inculcating a Christian philosophy of education in civic education by employing broad moral principles from which educational conclusions are deduced, and by identifying appropriate scriptural references about education and then embedding them in educational contexts.

Adopting and applying theological approaches and professional identity to the context need not be disconnected, despite the inherent tensions. Besides seeing these professional challenges as opportunities to experience and share God's love, adopting a faith position could also help in contributing to a more holistic approach. In fact, 'Christian educators should also engage with secular social theory in order to counter the marginalization of religion' (Green, 2012, p. 10). Thus theological concepts are applied to 'areas beyond the community of faith' (Hull, 1977, p. 11).

Applying a Christian lens to my teaching and professional life can only be achieved through humility, integrity, respecting authority, authenticity and by cooperating with external top-down policy initiatives. This demonstrates Christian love and grace rather than a compromise of faith or a confrontation. Thus the Bible might 'inform and guide educational activity' and 'make a difference to the work of a teacher' (Smith and Shortt, 2003, p. 10). This might help to negotiate the legal and policy shifts in education, creating opportunities leading to a greater understanding and application of our interpretations of truth.

5. Sustaining a teaching career – some additional challenges and opportunities

In the fifth and final question I consider the sustainability of my career in relation to additional challenges and opportunities presented by the current educational climate in a macro-political sense. Arguably, education has become a commodity used to fuel the economy, simultaneously positioning children in such a system as 'products', according to Worsley (2013, p. 1).

Recent central pressures have greatly undermined teachers' powers, reducing the profession to mere mechanical execution of other people's education design (Carr 2000, p. 43). The marketization of education, parentocracy, choice and competition between schools mean that 'teachers have become publicly accountable to pupils and parents' (Bryan et al., 2011, p. 16; Day et al., 2005). Furthermore, the introduction of academies, free schools and other pathways add to this diversity, choice and opportunities for raised standards. Perhaps others would argue that this leads to fragmentation of the education system.

Despite these challenges, what is it that sustains a life in teaching? From a Christian perspective, it is the place of my personal values which include aspiration, perseverance, empathy, care, respect and love, plus the support of colleagues. In addition to my faith these have contributed to a resilient approach and, by extension, to greater sustainability. Also by adopting a vocational teaching world-view, I have been guided with a perspective of passion and purpose through my professional career challenges, ambiguities and vicissitudes.

The PSHE Association notes that, 'PSHE makes a major contribution to schools' statutory responsibilities to provide a curriculum that is broadly based, balanced and meets the needs of all pupils.' Under Section 78 of the Education Act 2002 and the Academies Act 2010, such a curriculum must, 'promote the spiritual, moral, cultural, mental and physical development of pupils at the school and of society, and prepare pupils at the school for the opportunities, responsibilities and experiences of later life'. Being thus influential in the lives of thousands of students is a responsibility, a great honour and a tremendous opportunity to live out faith in a life of Christian service and ministry.

These PSHE aims therefore, do illuminate and inform my approach, perceptions and priorities. Teaching cannot be merely technical, mechanical and outcome-driven: we are inspiring people, human beings whose processes, development and metanarratives do matter. Therefore by examining these five questions as well as my professional journey, teaching approaches, metanarrative and theological understanding within the context of career sustainability, I have been influenced to the extent that there is:

- Greater awareness of the tremendous opportunities and responsibilities afforded me to make an impact and a difference to the thousands of lives entrusted into my care as a part of my Christian ministry, duty and service;
- Greater flexibility, openness, raised awareness of, and empathy for, students' personal circumstances;
- Wider understanding of my world-view within a much broader context of pluralism, secularism and a macro-political landscape;
- Greater respect for others' values and beliefs while embracing my core commitments, non-negotiable positions and a pedagogical approach influenced by Christian values;

- Opportunity to reflect on and adopt an approach to truth and biblical interpretation of controversial or settled issues and further explore their impact on professional identity, being respectful of opposing views;
- Greater voice given to students and stakeholders for their own perspectives and contributions to better appreciate and 'understand (their) existing beliefs, knowledge and experience';
- Opportunity to revisit, reflect on and clarify my motives for teaching within this difficult recessionary climate and the associated economic, political and educational issues (Taber, 2007, p. 27).

Conclusion

Although the political, economic and professional context within which teachers operate contains ambiguities and challenges that can affect the length of time teachers choose to remain in the teaching profession, a Christian faith is resourceful. As I have discussed, the ongoing transformation in my educational approaches and metanarrative mean that I have aspired 'to create an experience for children that is fulfilling, affirming, liberating and sustaining' (Barnes 2012, p. 9). Despite the political, economic and professional context of education, my personal values (principles, standards and morals), my Christian beliefs and the support of family, friends and colleagues do all contribute to a resilient approach and by extension, teaching longevity.

Discussion Questions

1. Is sustaining a teaching career in today's educational, economic and political climate a goal worth pursuing?
2. Should gaining academic qualifications play a significant role in career advancement and provide a financial incentive?

3. To what extent are biblical beliefs and personal values compatible with teaching in the public domain?

4. In what ways can theological knowledge and approaches contribute to thinking in your teaching or professional context as a Christian?

5. How might the teaching profession, through senior leadership, government policies and inspection regimes, reflect more care, thoughtfulness and concern for the well-being of teachers?

References

Alexander, R., 2008, *Essays on Pedagogy*, Abingdon: Routledge

Arthur, J. and Wright, D., 2001, *Teaching Citizenship in the Secondary School*, London: David Fulton

Arthur, J., Gearon, L. and Sears, A., 2010, *Education, Politics and Religion: Reconciling the Civil and the Sacred in Education*, London: Routledge

Astley, J., 1996, 'Theology for the Untheological? Theology, philosophy and the classroom', in Astley, J. and Francis, L. (eds), *Christian Theology and Religious Education*, London: SPCK, pp. 60–77

Barnes, J., 2012, PhD thesis: *What Sustains A Life in Education*, Canterbury Christ Church University

Bryan, H. and Revell, L., 2011, 'Performativity, Faith and Professional Identity: Student Religious Education Teachers and The Ambiguities of Objectivity', in *British Journal of Educational Studies*, 59.4, pp. 403–419

Bryan, H., 2012, 'Reconstructing the teacher as a post-secular pedagogue: A consideration of the new teachers' standards', in *Journal of Beliefs and Values: Studies in Religion and Education*, 33.2, pp. 217–228

Carr, D., 2000, *Professionalism and Ethics in Teaching*, London: Routledge

Cook, D., 1996, 'Moral Relativism Schools and Societies', from *Sacred text to educational context*, Whitefield Institute Briefing Papers, 1.1

Cooling, T., 2011, *Is God redundant in the Classroom*, Inaugural lecture, Canterbury Christ Church University

Cooling, T., 2002, *Commitment and Indoctrination: A Dilemma for Religious Education?* Nottingham: Stapleford Centre

Cooling, T., 2013, 'The Formation of the Christian Teacher: The role of faithfulness to the Bible in conceptualising learning', in Morris, A. (ed.), *Re-Imagining Christian Education in the 21st Century*, Chelmsford: Matthew James Publishing

Day, C., Elliott, B. and Kingston, A., 2005, 'Reform, Standards and Teacher Identity: Challenges of Sustaining Commitment', in *Teaching and Teacher Education 21*, pp. 563–577, Australia: Elsevier Ltd

DfES, 2004, 'PSHE', in *Practice – Resource pack for Teachers in Secondary Schools*, Nottingham: DfES Publications

Downie, R., 1990, 'Professions and Professionalism', in *Journal of Philosophy of Education*, 24.2, pp. 147–159

Erricker, C. and Erricker, J., 2000, *Reconstructing Religious, Spiritual and Moral Education*, London: Routledge Falmer

Garner, R., 2015, 'Four in 10 teachers quit in their first year as stress and exhaustion take toll' in *'I' The Essential Daily Briefing* from the *Independent*, 1 April 2015, p. 4

Green, E., 2012, 'The contribution of Secular Social Theory to Research in Christian Education', in Smith, I. and Cooling, T. (eds), 2012, *Journal of Education and Christian Belief*, 16.1 [Spring 2012], Kuyers Institute for Christian Teaching and Learning, pp. 9–21

Hart, T., 1995, *Faith Thinking The Dynamics of Christian Theology*, London: Gospel and Culture

Hill, B., 2004, *Exploring Religion in School: A national priority*, Australia: Openbook Publishers

Hirst, P., 1965, 'Morals, Religion and the Maintained School', in *British Journal of Educational Studies*, 14.1, pp. 5–18

Hull, J., 1976, 'Christian Theology and Educational Theory: Can There Be Connections?', in *British Journal of Educational Studies*, 24.2, pp. 127–143

Hull, J., 1977, 'What is Theology of Education?', in *Scottish Journal of Theology*, 30.1, pp. 3–29

Hutchings, M., 2010, *What impact does the wider economic situation have on teachers' career decisions? A literature review* [Report DFE-RR136], Institute for Policy Studies in Education, London: Metropolitan University Research

Ofsted, 2005, *Personal, Social and Health Education in Secondary Schools*

Ofsted, 2013, 'Not yet good enough: Personal, social, health and economic education in schools', in *Personal, social and health education in English schools in 2012*

Pring, R., 2000, *Philosophy of Educational Research*, 2nd edn, London: Continuum

Revell, L. and Walters, R., 2010, *Christian Student RE teachers, Objectivity and Professionalism: A research project based on interviews with students from three universities investigating the way student RE teachers understand the relationship between their faith and professionalism*, Canterbury: CLIENT Faculty of Education

Salandanan, G., 2008, *Teaching Approaches and Strategies*, revd edn, Philippines: Katha Publishing Co., Inc

Shortt, J., Smith, D. and Cooling, T., 2000, 'Metaphor, Scripture and Education', in *Journal of Christian Education*, 43.1, pp. 21–28

Shortt, J., 2012, *Faith and Education Lecture*, Canterbury Christ Church University

Smith, D. and Shortt, J., 2003, *The Bible and the Task of Teaching*, Uckfield: The Stapleford Centre

Straughan, R. and Wrigley, J. (eds), 1989, *Values and Evaluation in Education*, London: Harper and Row

Taber, K., 2007, *Classroom-based Research and Evidence-based Practice – A Guide for Teachers*, London: SAGE

Talts, L., Kubb, A. and Muldma, M., 2011, *Factors Affecting the Sustainability of a Teaching Career*, International Conference on Education and Educational Psychology, Estonia: University of Tallinn

Willmer, H. (ed.), 1992, *2020: Futures of Christianity in Britain*, London: SPCK

Worsley, H., 2011, 'The Standards Agenda and the Culture of Grace (A conflict between Ofsted and Church)', in *Journal of Anglican Secondary School Head teachers*, September edn

Worsley, H., 2013, *What motivates Christian Educational Practitioners? (Theology as Resource in the school)*, Grove Booklets, Grove Education Series

Wright, A., 2004, *Religion, Education and Post-modernity*, London: Routledge Falmer

6

Are British values Christian values?
A reflection on the tensions between
British values and Christianity

ANDREA HAITH

Abstract

While successive UK governments have been preoccupied with the notion of 'Britishness', the 2010–2015 Coalition government took the concept to new heights. Under the new Teachers' Standards a teacher's performance is to be judged on their ability to be seen to not undermine 'fundamental British values' (DfE, May 2012). Just what exactly are 'fundamental British values'? On the back of the Britishness concept the government, in seemingly stark contrast to its predecessor, openly acknowledged the link between church and state. David Cameron claimed that Britain is a Christian country, which wholly embraces Christian values. This chapter explores the tensions inherent in the notion of 'British values' which the government upholds, predominantly around the notion of democracy. It also examines the Christian values which David Cameron suggests are indicators of the way in which this government is 'doing God' in politics. The conclusion is that there seems to be a chasm between what the government is saying and what the government is doing.

Keywords

'British' values; democracy; inequality; poverty; the Golden Rule; authenticity

Prologue

There is something rather un-British about seeking to define Britishness. Rather like leadership, it's a quality which is best demonstrated through action rather than described in the abstract.

As a Scot who has made his career in London and whose family is now rooted in England, I feel immensely fortunate to be a citizen of a cosmopolitan state where nationality is defined not by ethnicity but sustained by the subtle interweaving of *traditions* and given life by a spirit of liberty.

Britishness is best understood as an identity shaped by an understanding of the common law, refined by the struggle between the peoples' representatives and arbitrary power, rooted in a presumption in favour of individual freedom, enriched by a love of the quirky, local and unique, buttressed by anger at injustice, constantly open to the world and engaged with the suffering of others, sustained through adversity by subversive humour and better understood through literature than any other art.

But if you really want to understand Britishness you need to ask why the British find Tracy Emin lovable, regard Ealing comedies as sacred, look on the world of Wodehouse as a lost Eden, always vote for the underdog in Big Brother, make the landscape the central character in their Sunday evening dramas, respect doctors more than lawyers and venerate their army but have never had a soldier as a leader since the Duke of Wellington.

(Michael Gove, shadow education secretary, October 2007)

Introduction

The spark for this reflection is born out of a combination of personal experience and my own personal values. These include my role as a teacher and the litany of education policies imposed by governments which do not relate to my practice, my personal commitment to justice and my world-view of Christianity.

The new Teachers' Standards (Department for Education, 2012) foreground the upholding of fundamental British values as a central tenet of a teacher's work (Bryan, 2011). My performance as a teacher will be measured on my ability to be seen not to undermine fundamental British values. The Teachers' Standards represent a significant shift in emphasis in terms of the articulation of values and any reference to faith or religion in teaching; they also give rise to the notion of the teacher as cultural custodian, moral compass and upholder of the virtues (Bryan, 2011).

Discussions I have had with colleagues at all levels in education have shown that there is confusion and a lack of clear understanding of what British values are; more importantly, there is a lack of clarity as to what Mr Gove was, and what Nicky Morgan, the current secretary of state for education, is expecting of teachers. Indeed, recent comments by Ofsted's schools director Sean Harford, have intimated that inspecting British values has made life 'difficult' for Ofsted (Burns, 2015).

Further, since the inception of the Coalition government Prime Minister Cameron and his (then) minister for faith, Baroness Warsi, seem to set themselves apart from their predecessors by the fact that they 'do God'. Cameron's references to Britain's Christian heritage highlight the complex nature of education in Britain today. The cornerstone of Western liberal education – that education is essentially secular – is curiously situated with a country that has a Christian lineage and a prime minister who stresses the influence of Christianity on contemporary British society (Bryan, 2011).

In this chapter I want to examine the tensions inherent in the concept of British values. I also want to scrutinize Prime Minister Cameron's world-view that we are a Christian country by analysing what he says and what his policies do in practice.

The chapter is written with humility and out of a quest for social justice.

British values

Successive governments have been preoccupied with the question of Britishness especially post 9/11 and the London bombings on 7 July 2005. Soon after coming into power the Coalition government reviewed the previous government's *Prevent Strategy* (Secretary of State for the Home Department, June 2011). In a speech in Munich, David Cameron set out the government's approach to dealing with terrorism. Cameron stated that the doctrine of state multiculturalism has failed:

> we have encouraged different cultures to live separate lives, apart from each other and apart from the mainstream. We've failed to provide a vision of society to which they feel they want to belong. We've even tolerated these segregated communities behaving in ways that run completely counter to our values. (Cameron, 2011a)

Referring to what he termed as the *passive tolerance of recent years* the prime minister called for a 'more active, muscular liberalism'. For him, this is a society which believes in, and actively promotes, values such as 'freedom of speech, freedom of worship, democracy, the rule of law, and equal rights regardless of race, sex or sexuality' (Cameron, 2011a).

Subsequently, the new Teachers' Standards (DfE, 2012) were published. These 'define the behaviour and attitudes which set the required standard for conduct throughout a teacher's career' (DfE, 2012, p. 9). Teachers are expected 'to uphold public trust in the profession and maintain high standards of ethics and behaviour, within and outside school, by:

- not undermining fundamental British values, including *democracy, the rule of law, individual liberty* and *mutual respect*, and *tolerance* of those with different faiths and beliefs
- ensuring that personal beliefs are not expressed in ways which exploit pupils' vulnerability or might lead them to break the law' (DfE, 2012).

There are tensions here. The first question is whether these are 'British' values or rather a universal set of values common to democratic countries. Prentice has suggested one would expect that for something to be called a 'national value' it would be enshrined in the life of, and championed by, that nation to an extent where the rest of the world would recognize it as quintessentially so (Prentice, 2014). He goes on to suggest that if we assume 'values' are moral principles or, more vaguely, a shared moral understanding, then other countries do explicitly state these; for example, the French revolutionary 'Liberté, Egalité, Fraternité', the South African post-apartheid 'Rainbow Nation' ideal, and the USA's 'life, liberty and the pursuit of property' – adopted from Locke and reworded to equate property with happiness (Prentice, 2014). These are universally recognized and constitutionally enshrined to make it plain to their own citizens, and outsiders, what their identity is (Prentice, 2014, p. 2). A further tension arises in the Teachers' Standards, namely, how does the requirement to promote fundamental British values impact upon teachers who are not British?

Other tensions emerge regarding the multicultural status of our society: what distinguishes British citizens from long-term residents who have settled here from other EU countries, Commonwealth countries or the Republic of Ireland? (Beetham, 2008).

In order to highlight how problematic the notion of 'Britishness' is I want to use Beetham's ideas. He provides a detailed interpretation of the historian Linda Colley's historical narrative of Britain – *Britons: Forging the Nation 1707–1837* (Beetham, 2008). Colley claims that while England and Scotland can be described as 'old countries', Great Britain and, still more, the United Kingdom, are comparatively recent constructs patched together at different stages and in different ways (Colley, 2009, p. 21). She goes on to say that although successive Anglo-Norman monarchs strove to leave an imprint on Wales and Scotland and, after 1170, on Ireland, Parliamentary union between England and Wales only took place in the 1530s and 40s. Dynastic union was effected by James VI of Scotland when he inherited the English and Irish thrones in 1603 (Colley, 2009; Beetham, 2008). Colley points out that the making of England, Wales and Scotland into 'one united kingdom' by the name of Great Britain with a single Parliament at Westminster (until recently, that is, with devolution of government to Scotland and Wales) was only achieved through the Treaty of the Union of 1707 (Colley, 2009, p. 21).

Colley maintains that the British nation was subsequently 'forged' out of a number of constituents, namely, the Empire and the trading opportunities that went with it; from a common commitment to Protestantism; and by a monarchy at the apex of an increasingly interconnected landing ruling class (Colley, 1992; Beetham, 2008). Further, she maintains that all these elements were reinforced by wars against continental Europe and especially Catholic France, which served as the 'Other' against which British distinctiveness came to be most clearly defined (Colley, 1992, 2009; Beetham, 2008).

Beetham makes the following significant observations regarding Colley's account. First, British nationhood came to be 'added on' to other identities, Scots, Welsh, English or more purely local ones, and therefore being 'British' has always allowed for multiple identities (Beetham, 2008). He argues, however, that because the English have been larger in numbers and politically dominant, they have regarded 'English' and 'British' as interchangeable (Beetham, 2008).

Second, Beetham points out that Colley is suggesting that British nationhood has always been more civic than ethnic. What is meant by this is a commitment to, and identification with, certain common institutions, including the Westminster Parliament, rather than depending on 'blood and soil' (Colley, 1992, 2009; Beetham, 2008). Colley maintains that it was the common institutions of political and civic life that defined what was distinctively 'British'. (Beetham, 2008). For Colley, commitment to these institutions was out of self-interest rather than through emotionally based allegiance or ideology (Colley, 1992, 2009; Beetham 2008).

Colley claims that while a number of events in the early twentieth century led people towards an identity of Britishness (she cites such events as military service in successful wars, popular mobilizations at royal events and anniversaries), essentially, the

British nation was an elite project (Beetham, 2008; Colley, 2009). Colley maintains that all these defining elements of Britishness came to an end, or were eroded, during the second half of the twentieth century, and as such, she maintains, can no longer form the basis of a distinctively British identity or nationhood (Colley, 1992; Beetham, 2008). Beetham quotes Colley:

> As an invented nation heavily dependent for its 'raison d'être' on a broadly Protestant culture, on the threat and tonic of recurrent war, particularly war with France, and on the triumphs, profits and Otherness represented by a massive overseas empire, Britain is bound now to be under immense pressure . . . we can understand the nature of the present debates and controversies only if we recognize that the factors that provided for the forging of a British nation in the past have largely ceased to operate. (Beetham, 2008).

From this historical narrative it is evident that looking for a definition of Britishness today is problematic. However, Beetham argues that there are a number of legacies from the Empire which remain today and which are influential in reinforcing the notion of Britishness. These are, *inter alia*, our multicultural society, the way our economic system is run, the monarchy and the conflicts with Europe (Beetham, 2008). With this in mind I want to look at these components to show how the British values which Prime Minister Cameron puts forward, such as democracy and equality, are seriously flawed.

The multiracial and multi-ethnic composition of Britain is a product of the Empire (Beetham, 2008). Beetham argues that as a result of the number of inequalities and disadvantages, for example, in language and education, integration continues to be problematic (Beetham, 2008). When Prime Minister Cameron talks about 'liberty' and 'mutual respect' then clearly there is a tension. The concept of 'tolerance' of those with different faiths and beliefs, which Cameron emphasizes, also provides a tension. It implies an attitude of superiority coupled with paternalism. This tension is also evident by the way in which immigrants (legal and illegal) and asylum seekers are treated. It was only in July 2013 that Theresa May sent her 'Go Home' vans around the UK (Home Office Campaign, 'Go Home' Vans Scheme, 2013: quoted in the *Guardian*, October 2013).

Harries poses the question, 'is our much prized tolerance in the West really tolerance?' (Harries, 2010, p. 76). Harries goes on to suggest that one major factor bringing about tolerance has been the decline in intensity of belief (p. 76). One is reminded of G. K. Chesterton's widely quoted assertion that 'tolerance is the virtue of those who do not believe anything' (Harries, 2010).

The two-tier education system in Britain is exclusive (Williams, 2011). Beetham maintains that private schools reproduce social and economic privilege across generations through the preferential access of their pupils to the most prestigious universities and into the leading professions (Beetham, 2008). A true democracy would provide a common system of public education which is shared by all and through which individuals recognize and accept diversity (Beetham, 2008). Raising tuition fees has also excluded many young people from attending university.

Democracy is also unequal in terms of the model of capitalism in place and the fact that London is the finance capital of the UK (Beetham, 2008). The banking system is an open deregulated economy. As such, it is unfair, allowing bankers to earn high bonuses when austerity cuts are being implemented and decimating the welfare state. Ironically, it is the bankers who plunged Britain into disaster (Jones, 2014). The financial model also allows tax avoidances and evasions which enable wealthy corporations and individuals to escape their obligations (Beetham, 2008). What does democracy mean in this context?

At the same time, Beetham argues, this form of capitalism has caused successive British governments to opt out of European Union treaties which would secure workers in Britain the same employment rights enjoyed by all member states (Beetham, 2008). What does democracy mean in this context? Does this not show a lack of integrity, an abuse of power and greed?

Beetham highlights a further tension arising from the fact that Britain remains a monarchy, in that we have been left with 'the remnants of an aristocratic social order, complete with titles and ceremonial and within this people are viewed as subjects rather than citizens' (Beetham, 2008). The fact that in citizenship ceremonies those acquiring British citizenship through naturalization have to swear 'true allegiance to Her Majesty Queen Elizabeth the Second, her Heirs and Successors' shows how ingrained the monarchy is in our society. It is perhaps ironic that today in practice it is, of course, the government through Parliament which exercises this sovereignty (Beetham, 2008).

There are tensions with the constitutional and electoral basis of the UK. Several commentators have suggested that a single written constitution might help to cement the UK in contemporary society (Colley, 2009) However, despite the fact that there have been a number of influential constitutional documents over the centuries relating to the whole of Great Britain and the UK there has been no attempt at a single written constitution, directly as a result of the monarchy and the fact that it was the centre of a worldwide empire (Colley, 2009, p. 27). Colley argues that monarchical empires do not favour written constitutions: rather, those in charge of empires are concerned to exercise often widely different levels of authority over peoples in geographically dispersed territories (Colley, 2009, p. 28).

Colley argues that the current 'first past the post' system of elections to Westminster rewards parties whose support is geographically concentrated (Colley, 2009). Under the current system both Labour and Conservatives have a close connection with particular parts of the UK. Colley asserts that had we used the fairer system of proportional representation in 1997 it is unlikely that the Conservatives would have been wiped out in Wales and Scotland and thus made to appear an *English* party (Colley, 2009, p. 27).

Arguably, the modern honours system remains open to abuse (Plain Language Commission, January 2015). In 2006 police were called to investigate allegations that fundraisers for both Labour and Conservative parties had offered supporters a life peerage in return for their financial support.

There are other tensions within the constitution. The House of Lords, as the second chamber in Parliament, remains wholly unelected. Wilks-Heeg et al. (2012) argue that this is unique to the UK among established democracies. A significant minority of government ministers are drawn from the House of Lords and are therefore not only unelected but also unaccountable to MPs. The principle behind the second chamber is that it should act as a check for legislative proposals. In practice, however, it is restricted by the principle of House of Commons primacy, which stems from the Parliament Acts 1911 and 1949. The justification usually offered for this is its unelected nature.

There have been tensions in relation to the rule of law and democracy. Post 9/11, New Labour sought derogation from the Human Rights Act 1998 to detain 'suspected terrorists' (Section 23, Anti-Terrorism, Crime and Security Act, 2001). Grube (2011) demonstrates contradictions in relation to the Anti-Terrorism, Crime and Security Act 2001 and the Terrorism Act 2006.

Before concluding this discussion on British values I want to return to the concepts of mutual respect and tolerance. In Colley's historical narrative she suggested that wars against continental Europe were powerful in forging the British nation (Beetham, 2008). There remained bitter and opposing opinions within the 2011–2015 Coalition government over Europe. One area of dispute is that of the European Court of Human Rights and the rights it affords the citizens of its member states; namely, the right to reside and work in another member state, the right to vote in another member state, the right to enjoy a range of social benefits there linked to work, incapacity or retirement. Britain has already opted out of the treaties that provide citizens with employment rights. Smith provides a detailed account of how the Coalition government was committed to preserving and restoring the rights and civil liberties which they viewed as fundamental to British society (Smith, 2013). She describes how they were keen to bring in a British Bill of Rights to ensure that the European rights law is implemented in a way that preserves the security and sovereignty of the UK. Smith outlines how the Conservatives believe that the Human Rights Act has been exploited by lawyers who have used it in such a way that it subverts the original intention of the legislation; their contention is that the balance has tipped too far in favour of protecting the rights of those suspected, or guilty of crimes rather than the rights of the honest citizen (Smith, 2013). The Conservatives also believe that an unelected (and arguably unaccountable) judiciary should not have the power to veto human rights initiatives put forward by an elected government (Smith, 2013). Is this not ironic, given the Coalition government's proposals for reformation of health and education which are radical, long-term policies for which no one voted (Williams, 2011)?

The first half of this chapter has sought to show that the concept of Britishness is value-laden and that the values, which the government define as 'fundamentally British,' are replete with tensions.

Prime Minister Cameron's concern was to foster cultural integration and social cohesion by reinforcing British values and suppressing English-national identity (Cambridge, 2011). In fact, as we have seen, what he described as British values are traditional English values. There was no mention of the English context in the Coalition government's language. Scruton (2006) maintains that British values are Enlightenment values with no intrinsic connection to the history, loyalty and shared experience that define our country. For him, values are matters of practice, not of theory. You learn them by immersion. I think the concept of British values is essentially a political concept and much of what Cameron says is political rhetoric. The values he describes are vague and a mask for the government's actual principles. Prentice argues that democracy is more of a process than a value, which is something bigger (Prentice, 2014).

Christian country?

Linked to his adherence to the concept of 'British values', David Cameron claims we are a Christian country. In December 2011, in a keynote speech marking the 400th anniversary of the King James Bible, David Cameron attacked a 'slow-motion moral collapse' in Britain and called for a revival of traditional Christian values.

Arguing for an approach which moves away from what he called 'the moral neutrality and passive tolerance' of previous years, Cameron defended the role of religion in politics:

> We are a Christian country. And we should not be afraid to say so. Let me be clear: I am not in any way saying that to have another faith, or no faith, is somehow wrong . . . I am also incredibly proud that Britain is home to many different faith communities, who do so much to make our country stronger. But what I am saying is that the Bible has helped to give Britain a set of values and morals which make Britain what it is today. (Cameron, 2011b)

Cameron has listed Christian values in society as 'responsibility, hard work, charity, compassion, humility, self-sacrifice, love, pride in working for the common good and honouring the social obligations we have to one another, to our families and to our communities' (Cameron, 2011b).

The first point I want to make about the values he lists is that the Bible has something to say about each of the values he cites but they are not distinctly Christian. Other holy books make reference to these values and indeed they can be found in moral codes of non-believers.

Second, it is what Mr Cameron hasn't included which makes me suspicious of his agenda. The Golden Rule is fundamental to Christianity, 'So in everything, do to others what you would have them do to you, for this sums up the Law and the Prophets' (Matthew 7.12 NIV).

Closely linked to the Golden Rule is the parable of the Good Samaritan. This implies that we are to show compassion and love for those we encounter in our everyday activities. We are to love others (v. 27) regardless of their race or religion; the criterion is need. If they have a need and we have the supply, then we are to give generously and freely, without expectation of return (Luke 10. 25–37).

Distinctly Christian values are rooted in the narrative and life of Jesus of Nazareth. Pritchard maintains that 'Christianity is a spiritual and an embodied faith, so it insists on the inconvenient truth of a particular historical life and asks us to make that life a lightning rod by which to judge the Christian nature of the enterprise' (Pritchard, 2012). This is echoed by Cooling when he says the claim to be distinctively Christian is not the claim to be exclusively different or superior, rather it is highlighting the distinctive outcome of seeking to be faithful to Christian beliefs in the way one acts (Cooling, 2010).

The Coalition government introduced a number of policies that had a significant impact on the fabric of our society and which highlight the relationship between capitalism and poverty. Some of these consequences are:

- there were 3.5 million children living in poverty in the UK in 2013. This is 27 per cent of children, or one in four (Child Poverty Action Group);
- approximately 40 per cent of adults in the most deprived areas of the UK lack the literacy skills of an average 11-year old (National Literacy Trust, 2015);
- there is unequal access to schools graded by Ofsted as 'Good' or 'Outstanding';
- people on benefits have been demonized (Jones, 2014). There has been a resurgence of the seductive language of 'deserving' and 'undeserving' poor (Williams, 2011);
- punitive measures have been put into place for so-called 'abuses' of the benefit system;
- disabled people are being discriminated against by having their benefit reduced if they have a spare bedroom;
- the NHS is at breaking point due to sustained cuts, increasing privatization and unfair and incoherent financial penalties;
- a radical educational policy is in place which is not evidence-based;
- our treatment of minority groups is selective and discriminatory – 86 Gypsy families on Dale Farm were evicted in 2011 from their homes of ten years.

If Cameron's values were distinctly Christian why do we have such inequalities? There is no compassion, self-sacrifice or love for those individuals who are suffering under the government's policies. Application of the Golden Rule might lead politicians to consider alternative approaches.

In the Munich speech Cameron argued that religious faith can inspire people to make more ethical decisions. Rowan Williams argues that ethics is essentially about how we negotiate our own and other people's vulnerabilities (Williams, 2012). Furthermore, he suggests that our ethical seriousness is tested by how we behave towards those whose goodwill or influence is of no 'use' to us. Therefore the moral depth of a society can be assessed by how it treats its children, disabled, elderly or terminally ill. Williams emphasizes the importance of the Christian ethic, the duty of care for the neighbour.

If we are a Christian country shouldn't we be negotiating conditions in which the most vulnerable are not abandoned?

The final point I want to make about Cameron's 'Christian' values is this. He talks about 'pride in working for the common good' and 'honouring the social obligations we have to one another, to our families and to our communities' (Cameron, 2011b). Ironically, pride in Christianity is considered to be the root of all human error and failure (Williams, 2012). What does Cameron mean by the common good? What does he mean by our social obligations?

Devolving power from Whitehall to local communities has been one of the government's priorities in its drive towards the Big Society. Davies maintains that this localism has led to inequalities in, and between, communities because of cuts to local authorities, cuts to charities and civil society organizations, which are expected to pick up the responsibilities shed by government (Davies, 2011). In the youth-work sector the Coalition government's reworking of institutional and funding arrangements that have been in place for 70 years has left many young people vulnerable (Davies, 2011).

What does Prime Minister Cameron see in our communities? Does he see child poverty, does he see poor literacy and does he see estates of unemployed people?

In Christianity 'koinonia' is an important concept. Koinonia is a Greek word meaning 'that which is common' and is often translated as 'fellowship' or 'community'. Other translations might include 'union' 'partnership' or 'being yoked together'. A yoke is a shaped piece of wood which goes across the shoulders often linking two animals; by combining strength it helps the work to be done and burdens to be carried. Koinonia expresses the quality of the relationship within the Christian community. It is based on fellowship with Jesus. Through Jesus, Christians are all members of the same family. A central element of being in a family is interdependence: all are needed and valued and each person is important to the whole. The same message is found in Paul's image of the Christian community as the body of Christ. Each member of the body shares the joys and sufferings of the others and each depends upon everyone else.

Michael Sandel (2009) has written, 'to achieve a just society we have to reason together about the meaning of a good life, and to create a public culture hospitable to the disagreements that will inevitably arise' (in Harries, 2010, p. 128).

Harries describes how Amartya Sen maintains that a case can be made for each of the dominant political philosophies of our time (Harries, 2010). Sen argues that no one can totally exclude the validity of the other perspectives. He says that as a result of this in any situation we have to make a judgement. For Sen, a good society is one in which we take all voices and the needs they represent into account; these include voices from outside our borders (see Harries, 2010, p. 128). Sen looks to the parable of the Good Samaritan as a model for taking the outsider into consideration and not drawing the definition of our neighbour in narrow terms (Harries, 2010, p. 128). So, for both Sandel and Sen, the essence of democracy is reasoning together, taking into account the key values of liberty and equality, but doing so in relation to the actual practical outcomes of different societies, not imposing an abstract philosophical blueprint (Harries, 2010, p. 128).

In light of this, much of what Cameron says could be seen to be paternalistic. Prime Minister Cameron's 'Christian' values are not distinctly Christian. A distinctively Christian approach is inspired by reflection on the teachings of the Christian traditions about what it means to flourish as a human being

(Cooling, 2010). The government's emphasis on individualism seems counter to the Golden Rule. Their policies value consumerism and profit.

Maybe Prime Minister Cameron needs to re-evaluate his concept of Christian values or at least practise some of what he preaches. We need a greater emphasis on the values, which offer 'a vision of a good person and a good society'. For Cooling, values towards this end are integrity, openness, authenticity, empathy, honesty and trustworthiness (Cooling, 2010). Maybe Prime Minister Cameron could take into account the concept of 'courageous restraint'. Cooling describes this as,

> a person's willingness to stand back from what is naturally their first priority in order to respect the integrity of other people. It means being willing to let fairness temper one's advocacy of the truth as you understand it. It means holding the golden rule that one should treat other people as you hope they would treat you in similar circumstances. It means being willing to accept the truth that you personally hold dear is contestable in a wider society. Welcoming the expression of points of view that you think are flawed – willingness to look at a diversity of views allowing developments that personally may be seen as retrograde. (Cooling, 2010)

Now, that's a distinctively Christian approach.

Discussion Questions

1. What are fundamental British values?
2. What is democracy?
3. What is inclusivity?
4. Can poverty ever be eradicated in a system of unregulated capitalism?
5. Can distinctively Christian values provide a basis for a 'just' and 'good' society?

References

Beetham, D., 2008 'What is Britishness? Citizenship, values and identity', *Red Pepper*, www.redpepper.org.uk/what-is-britishness-citizenship/ [accessed 2 February 2014]

Bryan, H., 2011, 'Reconstructing the teacher as a Post-Secular Pedagogue: A Consideration of the New Teachers' Standards', in *Journal of Beliefs and Values: Studies in Religion and Education*, 33.2, pp. 217–228

Burns, Judith, 2015, 'British values "a tough call" for inspectors-Ofsted' from *Education, BBC News*, 20 March 2015, www.bbc.co.uk/news/education-31991767 [accessed 23 March 2015]

Cambridge, D., 2011, 'Deconstructing British Values', http://britologywatch.wordpress.com/2011/02/ [accessed 2 February 2014]

Cameron, D., 2011a, Speech delivered on 5 February 2011 at the Munich Security Conference, www.gov.uk/government/speeches/pms-speech-at-munich-security-conference [accessed 2 February 2014]

Cameron, D., 2011b, King James Bible speech, Oxford, 2011, www.britishpoliticalspeech.org/speech-archive.htm?speech=326 [accessed 6 July 2015]

Child Poverty Action Group, www.cpag.org.uk/child-poverty-facts-and-figures

Colley, L., 1992, 'Britishness and Otherness: an argument', in *The Journal of British Studies*, 31.4, pp. 309–329

Colley, L., 2009, *Britons: Forging the Nation 1707–1837*, New Haven and London: Yale University Press

Cooling, T., 2010, *Doing God in Education*, London: Theos

Davies, N., 2011, 'Does religion have a place in politics?' www.in-debate.com/2011/10/religion-in-politics/ [accessed 6 July 2015]

Department for Education, 2012, *Teachers' Standards*, London: HMSO

Grube, D., 2011, 'How can "Britishness" be Re-Made?', in *The Political Quarterly*, 82.4, pp. 628–635

Harries, R., 2010, *Faith in Politics*, London: Darton, Longman and Todd

HM Government, 2011, *Prevent Strategy*, Secretary of State for the Home Department, London: HMSO

Human Rights Act 1998, www.legislation.gov.uk/ukpga/1998/42/contents

Jones, Owen, 2014, 'It's socialism for the rich and capitalism for the rest of us in Britain', *Guardian*, 29 August 2014

Jones, Owen, 2014, *The Establishment And How They Get Away With It*, Harmondsworth: Penguin

National Literacy Trust, www.literacytrust.org.uk/policy/forum [accessed 6 July 2015]

National Society, 2009, 'Christian Values for Schools', www.christianvalues4schools.co.uk [accessed 26 February 2014]

Plain Language Commission: Clear English Standards, *Invidious Honours System open to Abuse*, http://clearest.co.uk/news/2015/1/18/Invidious_honours_system_open_to_abuse#

Prentice, G., 2014, 'Replacing British Values', http://nationalcollective.com/2014/01/05/gav-prentice-replacing-british-values/ [accessed 2 February 2014]

Pritchard, J., 2012, *The Gospel and Educational Values – The Church of England's Contribution*, Cambridge: Grove Books

Sandel, M., 2009, in R. Harries (2010), *Faith in Politics*, London: Darton, Longman and Todd

Scruton, R., 2006, 'Values are not learnt through teaching', *Daily Telegraph*, 16 May 2006, p. 20

Smith, L., 2013, 'Repealing the Human Rights Act', www.abouthumanrights.co.uk [accessed 9 March 2013]

Warsi, S., 2013, 'Speech at the University of Cambridge: Churchill's archives "Faith in Politics" Conference', http://sayeedawarsi.com/2013/11/12/speech-at-the-university-of-cambridge-churchill-archives-faith-in-politics [accessed 2 February 2014]

Wilks-Heeg, S., Blick, A. and Crone, S., 2012, 'British Politics and Policy: 2012 Democratic Audit Report', London School of Economics, http://democracy-uk-2012.democraticauditarchive.com/assets/documents/how_democratic_is_uk.pdf [accessed 10 March 2014]

Williams, R., 2011, 'Leader: The Government needs to know how afraid people are: We are being committed to radical, long-term policies for which no one voted', *New Statesman*, www.newstatesman.com/uk-politics/2011/06/long-term-government-democracy [accessed 27 February 2014]

Williams, R., 2012, *Faith in the Public Square*, London: Bloomsbury

Part Two

'Living with Faith: making sense of faith in professional contexts'

7

Looking backstage: insights on professional dilemmas in a faith-based development

Martin B. Jamieson

What is needed is a more comprehensive approach involving a new development strategy which will focus primarily on meeting the basic needs of the total population . . . Such a strategy should also aim at a fuller utilization of locally available resources in all production efforts . . . in short, a strategy for a more self-reliant approach to development. (Bacchus 1983 p. 196).

Abstract

Development work is arguably awash with professional, political and ethical tensions. This chapter presents development work from a personal faith-based perspective, navigating through a range of critical issues that create four tensions. The first involves the location of the various 'actors' in the development. Writers including Pieterse (2010), Vogel (2012), Faik, Thompson and Walsham (2013), frequently describe participants in development as 'actors' and this chapter expands this metaphor to discuss the 'stage' as the location of their act. The second occurs when expectations for development clash with the intentions of those bringing intervention. This includes looking at the changing perceptions of participants whose expectations are challenged (Crossley and Vulliamy, 1996). The faith positions of all stakeholders are brought into tension as cross-cultural, and cross-faith, work is accomplished through a range of strategic roles. The final tension examined is sometimes exacerbated by 'inappropriate international transfer' and poor communication during cross-cultural exchanges (Crossley and Vulliamy, 1997).

Keywords

Development; self-reliance; inclusion; partnership; participation; empowerment; tension

Introduction: Looking backstage

Some years ago I visited the Thames-side site where Shakespeare's Globe Theatre was being built. Taking photographs and walking around the replica of the playhouse with my daughter, I longed to return to watch a play by Shakespeare as I believed that it would be so much enhanced by this replica of the original setting. When, at last, I was able to get a ticket I stood with the other 'groundlings' in the crowd at the front of the stage. These were conditions similar to those experienced by early Elizabethans and I believed myself to be experiencing Shakespeare as authentically as it could be. As groundlings we even participated in crowd scenes as the actors leapt from the stage and used the audience as living scenery. Of course there were many differences, comforts of modern times, but the illusion was powerful and the experience enjoyable. As a history teacher, becoming authentic in the historical setting was always a significant factor in my enthusiasm for the past, so when my attention turned to educational development I approached the task with a penchant for authenticity.

This chapter employs the metaphor of the 'stage' to explain the project undertaken by the charity I set up in Malawi, and the 'actor' as anyone whose interaction with it leads them to tread the boards of that stage. This is because the stage is neutral to the content of the play, and the participating actors, depending upon each other, only require the stage to be a platform for their presentation. What is presented is not the stage, but the play performed by the actors. In this metaphor for development the 'actors' included are: the headteachers and school staff members, parent teacher association members, school management committee members, primary school advisors and the district education manager. The 'stage' being constructed in rural Malawi is a 'teacher's centre'. From an early start in 2012, a group of Malawian friends and I set out to register legally a non-governmental organization (NGO) called Livingway Education. This local NGO would work with teachers in the Salima District of the central region of Malawi, where many of my friends live. More specifically, the NGO works with two of the 12 zones in the district. The friends now form the trustees of the NGO while two, including myself, retain the status of 'director.'

Aside from the construction of the teacher's centre our project included the addition of a guest house as an integral and essential element of the project. It is through the income generated by the guest house that educational activities will be funded, making the aim to become self-sufficient ever more of a possibility.

It was hoped that this centre would help to serve 18 local primary schools by hosting workshops, seminars and meetings and contributing to the production of basic materials for use in the classroom. It was hoped also that the centre would host visiting speakers from other parts of Malawi and that volunteers from abroad would add to the input with the approval of the district council. At every level, from the district commissioner down, it was expected that there would be collaboration and dialogue with other 'players' over education, and indeed, even by early 2015, this is what has been happening – but not without some initially unexpected tensions. These tensions form the subject of this chapter.

While I and my friends have built the stage, the pulling together of the script would be a collaborative affair between all local actors with minimal input from the friends or myself. The development work I had been involved in previously had revolved around the almost permanent presence of an external agency, and had been limited by other assumptions about the value of both the intervention and the host's own programmes. I wanted to avoid what I saw as an ethnocentric and colonialist position, and instead create a space for a response to challenges that would lead increasingly towards self-reliance, rather than one that could only be sustained through external agency. By privileging the indigenous voice within the concerns, the consequences would be entirely owned by those who would have to live with them. As a part of my doctoral research it is my intention to examine the processes and attitudes of 'players' surrounding the construction of this 'play' but this chapter focuses upon the challenges surrounding the positioning of the players and the tensions inherent to the project rather than the methodological struggles I contend with as a researcher. Here, I only want to explain the background to the development, the play, itself.

So, now that you know what the play (the project) is about, where the play will take place (the project location) and the metaphor used to frame intervention, you may be expecting to hear what is to be done. In short, you want the play to begin – but wait, I have yet to arrange the scenery on the stage. This scenery is the sociological 'context' within which the play is to be performed. Knowledge of this scenery is of paramount importance, whether the intention is to enact sustainable educational development consistent with the aims of the UN declaration in 2002 that 2005–2014 would be the 'Decade of Education for Sustainable development' (UNESCO 2005) emphasizing that education is an 'indispensable element for achieving sustainable development' (UNESCO, 2005), and the Bonn Declaration (2009), or, indeed, to conduct culturally sensitive research (Stephens, 2005, 2007).

The 'context' revealed

There are three aims of the project. First, it is to provide a stage upon which Malawian education professionals may apply *any* perspective consistent with Christian thought to their pedagogy.

Second, the 'stage' should provide space for reflection, deliberation and debate over educational issues. This space exists within an organization that is both self-sufficient *and sustainable from its own resources*. Above all, as Crossley and Vulliamy (1996) would approve, it is rooted in the local context and seeks to be sensitive to 'local needs and conditions'. Third, the project is an 'ethical play' within a Christian-led educational NGO intent on supporting and encouraging pedagogic development from a Malawian perspective and epistemology. As a development worker (and researcher), I need to be positioned where the change in attitude from dependency to self-sufficiency can be observed through the 'delicate interdependence of constructed narratives' with participants (Gergen and Gergen, 1983), using an 'appropriate' development strategy that will meet people's needs (Bacchus, 1983) and sensitively highlight where innovation and new processes might be applied and evaluated (Vulliamy, 1990).

As explained above, the underlying intention is to create a space where no single view is prescribed, but *many may be explored*. This exploration might find resonance with the claims made by David Margolies that Shakespeare's plays were tightly controlled experiments to disguise the obvious and 'disturb the audience', indicating that there should be more ambiguity about educational answers to intriguing questions. Recent attempts to improvise Shakespeare by the Improvised Shakespeare Company (ISC, 2015), in a style the author may have used, and original plays reinterpreted freely for a modern audiences, point to a postmodern approach to older metanarratives. Livingway Education's developmental 'stage' is prepared to allow fresh Malawian interpretations to questions posed elsewhere. When the main actors, and the supporting cast in this development, have examined, adopted and reviewed the variety of stakeholder views on an issue, educational practise may evolve naturally. It may not be a polished play whose ending is predetermined, but rather will become one that is authentically created to fit social, economic and political markers understood by the current players on the stage. If I may put down the stage metaphor for a moment, then our project may be described in this way: 'We provide workshop opportunities so that solutions to current educational difficulties may be discovered, through collaborative dialogue, by those to whom the responsibility has been given. Real answers, to local problems in education, will be found by teachers working in local schools, rather than applying dictated answers given by outsiders.'

The challenge is to use the space provided cooperatively, through dialogue, to find the most suitable pedagogic responses (McClintock et al., 2003). For example, teachers can gather to discuss the demands of the 2013 Education Act. In Malawi the Act reversed a previous position and declared that henceforward all teaching, from standard one, aside from the teaching of Chichewa, was to be in English. Ensuing dialogue may lead to what Denzin and Lincoln (1994) labelled messy, multi-voiced texts but, as the project progresses, it is hoped that a more authentic text may emerge from the actors, engagement (Rogers, 2012).

Tensions pull at, and shape, the potential for self-development, which is one intention of the project. If the tensions can be managed, Christian players backstage might provide a developmental paradigm capable of rejecting the need for the neo-colonial oversight hinted at earlier. Arguably, this oversight has a tendency towards corruption and the erosion of social capital, as it is claimed that aid 'engenders laziness' (Moyo, 2009). Heralding an end to the traditional dependency on donor support, and pointing the way towards self-sufficiency, this anti-colonialist development paradigm (Young, 2001) may provide some opportunity to develop the good governance that will 'trump all' (Moyo, 2009), and ensure that solutions to problems are found, not by Western interventionists, but by their African partners. According to Freire, this requires a dialogic mindset with faith, not only in God, but also in people who are determined to see the world unveiled (Freire, 1970).

Tensions 'backstage'

Working against this are four observable tensions within the project:

Location: in the first place tensions may exist because I am a foreigner, an outsider. I do not even live in the area being developed (although residing seven months out of 12 in 2014–2015 makes it feel as though I do!). While I can greet my friends in the vernacular I do not speak the language fluently. Tension is also created when I switch between the roles representing my various responsibilities (researcher, founder, donor, director and educational consultant) on the project.

As one of the NGO's directors I am hoping to be able to demonstrate that a model of development need not descend into another form of 'north-south' oversight, a disguised neo-colonialism. Passionate Marxist and anti-imperialist Kwame Nkrumah (1965) looked to African unity to end neo-colonialism, Parenti (1995) believes that Schiller's 'cultural imperialism' (Schiller, 1976) still oppresses developing countries and believes, like Moyo (2009), that the continuing supervision of southern actors by ones from the north causes problems for the long-term development of African countries. More circumspectly, Young suggests that when development comes by empowering non-governmental civil actors, fundamental human needs can be addressed (Young, 2001). This emphasis on the local actors shows local empowerment, and the setting of a self-reliant agenda, to be the key to resisting neo-colonial pressure (Saïd, 1993).

The key to empowerment is a secure relationship between the parties facilitating vision transference through 'participatory competence' (Kieffer, 1984; Anderson et al., 1994; Young, 2001) encompassing personal, social, educational, economic and political dimensions consistent with Frerian *'conscientização'* that requires participants desiring emancipation and empowerment to become fully conscious of what has oppressed them. This project departs from any neo-colonialist accusation by implementing an exit strategy that prescribes time limitations for the northern partner, and provides details of power transference through local ownership.

Any donor might be considered colonial if their object is to enhance their own reputation or further their own interests. This is obvious, but when the donor appears altruistic by providing advice linked to the funding of projects, it is less so. There may even be a rhetoric which states that 'aid' or 'skills transfer' is not the result of superiority on the part of the donor, but if compliance is still expected for funding to be released, then this remains a form of oppression. This reality is not always understood by the recipient, as 'Pedagogy of the Oppressed' demonstrated (Freire, 1970). However, by providing a forum for debate where local theory might develop, and giving support for autonomous innovative action, I may be a catalyst in the production of a better script. Once completed, with a 'proper use of context' the project's 'script' will have achieved a measure of legitimacy (Stephens, 2005).

Expectation: The second tension concerns the dominant expectation of the people in the area that NGOs bring material benefits, seek to import Western ideas, are run by non-indigenous personnel and want to 'help' Malawi 'catch-up' to the Western 'ideal.' Challenging this perception often provokes tensions between stakeholders.

As explained earlier, my position is that of a 'donor' from a developed-world country contributing funds for the construction of a guest house and teacher centre. Even though the teacher centre's activities will be funded by the profits created by the guest house, stakeholders may expect donations to continue pretty much indefinitely. These stakeholders may have assumed that continuing support, and control, of the project would come from the funding partner. If that had been the case I would be following a pattern described elsewhere as neo-colonialist.

The initial problem, then, is how to resist such expectation. In the first place, expectation cannot be rejected only verbally as local stakeholders still expect to see both the material benefits, and the domination of developmental process, coming from the northern partner. Merely stating an opposite position is insufficient and all actors need to be involved in ongoing dialogue. My identification as 'donor' and the NGO's as 'recipients' must be constantly re-examined so that it becomes clear that once the construction phase is complete, transference of ownership will take place.

Another difficulty to overcome is the effect my continuing presence has on the site. So long as I remain present it may be expected that my wishes are to be considered of greater worth than those of local managers. Deference to my donor role will reinforce this view and so I guard against it by reiterating the equal partnership principles and resisting calls to intervene.

Some visits to the site have been made specifically with the purpose of transferring vision ownership through workshop and seminar opportunities. An initial workshop empowered trustees, through discussion and collaborative learning, to assimilate the purpose and aims established by myself and counterpart director. After this, the trustees demonstrated their understanding by taking leading roles in further training.

Other donors in the area reinforce the expectation of the local community by either shipping in quantities of material goods that enable a few individuals to profit, despite the goods being of little relevance to the donor's stated purpose or activities, or by providing cash handouts that encourage further passivity, bolstering a dependency mindset. These actions are not seen by the donor as a bribe to effect compliance, nor is it understood to be a means by which the donor's views might be favourably heard, but it does reinforce the view that development is a process that provides goods in return for compliance with donor objectives. Often the measures being implemented fail to take into account the current restrictions prevalent in the recipient's situation.

The answer to this is not easy. It is only by becoming as invisible as possible that effective development will occur without altering the natural development of the schools in the project area. Emma Crewe (1997) tries to 'uncloak' the silent assumptions of developers who take for granted that their position as Western players gives them the right to interfere in countries deemed to be undeveloped. She presents a case study where cooking stoves are wrongly heralded as a superior alternative to traditional methods and reports on the similar marginalization of indigenous knowledge found by Brokensha, Warren and Werner, 1980; Chambers, 1983 and Hobart, 1993. She then points out that 'technical knowledge is not measured and valued according to its utility' and that in many ways an innate superiority is assumed by the donor partner (Crewe, 1997). Elsewhere it is claimed that making use of indigenous knowledge may be vital to all development projects if sustainability is to ensue (Senanayake, 2006).

To reduce expectations, and limit the expectations my presence creates, I must step down and slip backstage, promoting the roles of indigenous actors rather than my own. While it may have been expected that I would lead workshops and meetings I often bow out after introductions have been made. My Malawian co-workers lead seminars and workshops, reducing language difficulties and helping participants to become fully engaged. The ensuing discussions may then reflect a reality that embodies the culture of the participants and, rather than privileging a voice from a distance, reduces tension by emphasizing a local view.

Faith position: Despite being 'sent out' by my home church, which is Methodist, I have an eclectic church background. This leaves me with few certainties and a desire to practise inclusivity in all things. Those I work with are from Pentecostal, Baptist and Seventh Day Adventist backgrounds, but the wider group of actors are from other faith backgrounds. While differences initially challenge those I am working with, they have faced the tensions with me, and most now benefit from diversity.

Co-creating an NGO with an educational focus working from a faith position made me both insider and outsider. With regards to faith and education I am an insider because I am a Christian teacher, but remain an outsider, in Africa, with regards to culture and ethnicity. However, my 'insider' status is compromised in that while I have been a teacher I am one no longer, and therefore may be viewed a relative outsider. My status with regards to faith may also be questioned while I continue to maintain a more or less inclusive stance with regards to belief. While my ethnicity places me outside the group studied, my 12-year association with some of the NGO members and community members may invoke honorary insider status.

Although many in the local community are not Christian it is expected that the project activities will reflect not only different faith perspectives but the views of others who are either sympathetic to the concept of championing inclusive practice in education, enhancing a spiritual dimension to pedagogic practice, or both. From the outset, efforts were made to engage others from different faith per-spectives and to explain the purpose and aims of our NGO. As a result, local Muslim leaders gave approval to the organization and assisted us when we bought land for the project. While a Christian-led organization, the philosophy is to be as open as possible and to provoke inclusion as a philosophical goal. This aim was applauded during meetings with local leaders of both faiths.

It may be that the transparently Christian brand of the NGO may mitigate against its philosophically inclusive rhetoric and this may need to be reviewed if the NGO is to gain widespread acceptance for its actions. It is necessary to consider the views of all stakeholders, before, during and after any activity, in order to retain credibility and build on initial support.

If there is to be an underlying theological motivation behind the activity of the NGO it must surely lie in the perception that inclusivity is the fundamental key to understanding the declared 'gospel' being brought to bear. When God 'so loved the world' (John 3.16) he made no exceptions, and called all to join him. There should be no hint of any judgement of another, merely the articulation of a 'call' to participate and collaborate, from each of our unique selves with the one God who is 'other' to us all. While following the tenets of Brazilian liberation theology, as espoused by Paulo Freire may be seen as virtuous and praiseworthy for championing personal and social liberation, and education for all, proselytizing for a particular faith position would be an antithesis of that liberation and therefore rejected.

Communication: Finally, there is a tension between the need for accurate accounts as well as the reporting of progress, and the allowances that need to be made for cross-cultural differences in representation. One instance that may be used to exemplify this tension is the way in which my Malawian friends rarely give a neg-ative response to a request, and nothing is said that might cause damage or hurt. During our NGO's management meeting I would ask what was said when the spoken voice was in Chichewa, and a simple translation was given. Suspecting a deeper reality, I probed further in order to reveal a more accurate story.

The tensions that exist between groups of individuals when collaborating on a project may be exacerbated when factoring in cross-cultural differences in understanding. Whether this is in the carrying out of a task, accepting responsibility or determining the value of a statement passed on down the chain of command, interpretations and response are often misunderstood. At the heart of this tension is the need for someone to have overall authority for the project. In the first instance, despite my intentions, it became clear that I was that person. At an early meeting of workers the question was asked about who owned the project. The workers answered unanimously 'Jamieson' despite the fact that ownership was vested in the NGO, Livingway Education. At the very least they may have assumed that the trustees owned the project, but communication on this issue was not clear.

On describing the tensions arising from research, Dwyer and Buckle (2009) make points that equally apply to development activity initiated by an outsider. They point out that while benefits of access, acceptance, trust, openness and shared distinctiveness can be of assistance, assumptions of similarity can result in 'inadequate descriptions', 'clouded perceptions' and other conflicts of interest. For example, early in the project, my views were sought and every suggestion followed without reference to other voices. This was at a time when it was only the two directors – one Malawian, the other English – who were providing direction for the building work. Later, when the debate over ownership had been settled and a Malawian management team was introduced, my suggestions were considered, but not necessarily followed. The Malawian director expressed the view that this was 'much better' (supposedly because there were more voices able to support an alternative to my suggestion) as it allowed for a more collegiate response.

The tensions described, particularly the tension between the insider-outsider participant, and the cross-cultural setting in which the project is set, need not be seen as 'constructed dichotomies' and 'entrenched perspectives' (Dwyer and Buckle, 2009) but the boundaries between which we may explore the alternate perspectives of the actors positioned within the event. Admitting that there is a 'richness in the space between' Dwyer and Buckle ask us to 'embrace and explore' complexities thrown up by the tensions. It is through such exploration of the 'boundaries between', that measures to contain the tensions have been developed.

Measures to induce self-reliance: Measures taken before and during the construction phase of the project are taken to defuse tension and build internal strength and ownership. In some ways what follows is positive and encouraging – at other times the reverse. It is necessary to be honest about the achievements and give reasons for both success and failure. These measures include:

- making a Malawian the co-director of the NGO;
- ensuring that all trustees of the NGO are Malawian;
- allowing decisions to be made by the trustees without reference to my wishes;
- openness of lines of communication;
- openness as regards finance;
- openness with regards to the exit strategy;
- vesting power in a management committee.

Another step, although not taken as a result of this thinking, was to make all the signatories for the bank accounts of the NGO Malawian. As the UK director I am not a signatory on the account as I am not a resident of Malawi.

All the above measures have been taken with the intention of reducing the tensions described and to affect a transfer of developmental ownership and organizational power. Pieterse challenges the westernization of developing nations and suggests that 'local culture and cultural diversity' should be valued, presumably above that of external interest (2010, pp. 76–78). When this is the case and local communities take greater responsibility for development it is hoped that the result will be beneficial to civil society and converge with governmental objectives. At the same time it is still necessary to involve all actors in the dialogue leading to changes in community capacity. When faith-based organizations are grounded in local values and culture they have the potential for generating goodwill and accountability between the various actors (Ashman, 2001; Olarinmoye, 2011 and 2012).

Conclusion

These measures have been taken to reduce the perceived tensions associated with this development project and to promote self-reliance. They are also an attempt to prevent any critique of the development as neo-colonial and present instead a move to empower and legitimize development from the perspective of the developed rather than that of the developer. Development that does not empower local enterprise towards self-reliance is likely only to produce time-locked 'improvement' which, however called for, or appreciated, cannot really be termed a 'development'. When responsibility is assumed by the beneficiaries, and the work sustained independently of outside agency, sustainable educational development worthy of the term has occurred. Empowering communities towards self-reliance may be the best way to see that the educational goals of the local community will be met.

Discussion Questions

1. How can an educational development programme facilitate transformative action?
2. Will holding a specific faith position increase tensions and reduce whole community inclusivity?
3. How can those initiating development position themselves so that reflective practice can lead indigenous knowledge to precipitate local ownership?
4. What roles can all participants take in order to increase the likelihood that self-reliance will occur?

References

Anderson, S. C., Wilson, M. K., Mwanasa L. K. and Osei-Hwedie K., 1994, 'Empowerment and social work education and practice in Africa', in *Journal of Social Development in Africa*, 9.2, pp. 71–86

Ashman, D., 2001, 'Strengthening north-south partnerships for sustainable development', in *Non-profit and Voluntary Sector Quarterly*, 30.1, pp. 74–98

Bacchus, M. K., 1983, 'Towards a development strategy for education and educational research in third world countries', in *International Journal of Educational Development*, 3.2, pp. 193–201

Brokensha, D., Warren, D. and Werner, O. (eds), 1980, *Indigenous Knowledge Systems and Development*, Lanham: University Press of America, pp. 7–8

Chambers R., 1983, *Rural Development: Putting the Last First*, London: Longman, p. 6

Dwyer, S. C. and Buckle, J. L., 2009, 'The space between: on being an insider-outsider in qualitative research', in *International Journal of Qualitative Methods*, 8.1, pp. 54–63

Crewe, E., 1997, 'The Silent Traditions of Developing Cooks', in Grillo, R. D. and Stirrat, R. S. (eds), *Discourses of Development: Anthropological Perspectives*, London: Berg, pp. 59–80

Crossley, M. and Vulliamy, G., 1996, 'Issues and trends in qualitative research: Potential for developing countries international', in *Journal of Educational Development*, 16. 4, pp. 439–448

Crossley, M. and Vulliamy, G., 1997, 'Qualitative research in developing countries: issues and experience', in Crossley, M. and Vulliamy, G. (eds) *Qualitative Educational Research in Developing Countries: Current Perspectives*, New York and London: Routledge, p. 23

Denzin, N. K. and Lincoln, Y. S., 1994, 'Introduction: Entering the field of qualitative research', in Denzin, N. K. and Lincoln, Y. S. (eds), *Handbook of Qualitative Research*, London: Sage, p. 15

Faik, I., Thompson, M. and Walsham, G., 2013, '*Facing the dilemmas of development: understanding development action through actornetwork theory*', Centre for Development Informatics, www.cdi.manchester.ac.uk/resources/ant4d-working-papers/ [accessed 6 July 2015]

Freire, P., 1970, *Pedagogy of the Oppressed*, New York: Continuum

Gergen, M. M. and Gergen, K. J., 1983, *Studies in Social Identity*, New York: Praeger

Hobart, M. (ed.), 1993, *An Anthropological Critique of Development: The Growth of Ignorance*, London: Routledge

Kieffer, C. H., 1984, 'Citizen empowerment: a developmental perspective', in *Prevention in Human Services*, 3.2–3, pp 9–36

McClintock, D., Ison, R. and Armson, R., 2003, 'Metaphors for reflecting on research practice: researching with people', in *Journal of Environmental Planning and Management*, 46.5, pp. 715–731

Moyo, D., 2009, *Dead Aid: Why aid is not working and how there is a better way for Africa*, New York: Farrar, Strauss, and Giroux

Nkrumah, Kwame, 1965, *Neo-Colonialism: The Last Stage of Imperialism*, London: Thomas Nelson and Sons

Olarinmoye, O. O., 2011, 'Accountability in faith-based development organizations in Nigeria: preliminary explorations', in *Global Economic Governance Working Paper*, 67, p. 3–5

Olarinmoye, O. O., 2012, 'Faith-based organizations and development: prospects and constraints', in *Transformations, An International Journal of Holistic Mission Studies*, Oxford: Sage, 29, pp. 1–14

Parenti, M., 1995, 'Imperialism 101: An introduction to the process by which political and economic domination is achieved', in *Against Empire*, www.michaelparenti.org/Imperialism101.htm [accessed 06 July 2015]

Pieterse J. N., 2010, *Development Theory*, 2nd edn, London: Sage, pp. 76–78; 190–191

Rogers, M., 2012, 'Contextualizing theories and practices of bricolage research', in *The Qualitative Report*, 17.48, pp. 1–17

Saïd, E. W., 1993, *Culture and Imperialism*, New York: Alfred A. Knopf, pp. 220–238

Schiller, H. I., 1976, *Communication and Cultural Domination*, New York: International Arts and Sciences Press, pp. 9–10

Senanayake, S. G. J. N., 2006, 'Indigenous knowledge as a key to sustainable development', in *The Journal of Agricultural Sciences*, 2.1, pp. 87–94

Stephens, D., 2005, 'Culture in Educational Research in Africa: From the Methodological to the Practical', in Daniel Hammett and Ruth Wedgwood (eds) *The Methodological Challenges of Researching Education and Skills Development in Africa*, Edinburgh: Centre for African Studies, pp. 26–46

Stephens, D., 2007, *Culture in Education and Development; Principles, Practice and Policy*, Oxford: Symposium, pp. 25–52

The Improvised Shakespeare Company, 2015, *Show description*, www.improvisedshakespeare.com/about/ [accessed 19 January 2015]

UNESCO, 2005, *United Nations Decade of Education for Sustainable Development (2005–2014): Framework for the UNDESD International Implementation Scheme*, Paris: UNESCO

UNESCO, 2006, *United Nations Decade of Education for Sustainable Development (2005–2014): International Implementation Scheme*, Paris: UNESCO, p. 10

UNESCO, 2009, *Bonn Declaration UNESCO World Conference on Education for Sustainable Development, 31 March – 2 April 2009*, Bonn: UNESCO, http://unesdoc.unesco.org/ images/0018/001887/188799e.pdf

Vogel, I., 2012, *Review of the use of 'Theory of Change' in international development*, Department for International Development (DFID), pp. 3–4

Vulliamy, G., 1990, 'How can qualitative research contribute to educational policy making in developing countries', in *Journal of Educational Development*, 1.10 (2/3) pp. 151–156

Young, R., 2001, *Post colonialism: An Historical Introduction*, Oxford: Blackwell pp. 383–426

8

Re-visioning the teaching methodology in African Pentecostal Church Education (APCE)

Nana Kyei-Baffour

Abstract

This chapter reflects on the prominent didactic teaching methodology employed in African Pentecostal Church education and presents an alternative approach to practice. Due to the pneumatocentric nature of ministry which African Pentecostals engage in, there is a tacit tendency to neglect some of the other relevant structural ingredients required for effective ministry as well as healthy and holistic growth of the congregation. In this chapter I have reflected on the character of African Pentecostal faith, our practice of adult education and the ongoing teaching methodology in our churches, as well as personal reflections on my application of constructive-didactic methodology as an effectual alternative to didactic methodology for adult education in our churches.

Keywords

Pentecostalism, Church education, teaching methodology, learning process, African Pentecostal Church (APC)

Introduction

The African Pentecostal faith is said to be a protégé of the modern Pentecostal movement of the West which began at the beginning of the twentieth century (Davis, 1993, pp. 11–31). According to Anderson (2004, p. 104), this faith movement was brought to the continent by Western missionaries around 1907. Despite being a foreign type of Christianity, Anderson (p. 103) has observed that it has become the fastest growing and largest Christian movement on the continent since the beginning of the twenty-first century with a staggering record of thousands of churches being planted. The spirit of this sweeping growth seems to have accompanied the high influx of migrants from Africa into the United Kingdom.

The nature of this faith tradition is notably identified as one rooted in a theology which is spiritually oriented. In general, the APCs actually prefer that their doctrinal position be identified as *beliefs* and *practices* as opposed to theology because of their strong orientation to praxis rather than theory. They are more experientially inclined rather than being cognitive in their faith practice: they place emphasis on practical theology in their day-to-day lives rather than philosophical or speculative theology. They emphasize knowing and experiencing God by being filled with and baptized by the Holy Spirit to empower and invade all aspects of the worshipper's life, including the worshipper's world-view and daily activities. This type of spirituality is what Anderson (p. 210) refers to as 'pneumato-centric spirituality' and Lovelace (1985) describes as 'Pentecostal spirituality'.

In general, the term 'spirituality' seems to have been identified as an ambiguous word due to its several interpretations. Swinton (2001, p. 21) asserts that it was primarily understood as a religious concept but has now been used by researchers and scholars from various disciplines who have ascribed different meanings to it. In the same line of thought, McCarthy (2000, p. 193) has observed that the religious prism is no longer the only construct used to understand the term because different professional bodies in both 'religious and scientific' disciplines have worked on spirituality;

likewise many magazines and professional journals carry articles explaining the term. Lartey (2003, p. 140) refers to it as an 'omnibus term', and according to Koenig, 'spirituality is sufficiently broad, vague and undefined to include almost everyone' (2007, p. 38). It therefore seems difficult to give one touchstone definition but, when put in context, a working definition could be identified and described.

From an anthropological view, Swinton suggests that, 'Spirituality . . . is a way of being and experiencing that comes through awareness of a transcendental dimension and that is characterized by certain identifiable values in regard to self, others, nature, life' (2001, p. 20).

In this definition one could identify spirituality at three different levels of human experience: *intra*, *inter* and *transpersonal* experience. It does reflect the academic perspective of spirituality, which sees the phenomenon as a dimension of human experience with no specific reference to whether the individual is religious or non-religious, as noted by Sheldrake (1999). Again, the definition does not seem to refer to a defined *authority* or a *deity*. These interpretations, however, may not suit the way in which the term is used in African Pentecostalism.

African Pentecostal spirituality recognizes total submission to the intuitive guidance and leadership of the Holy Spirit, his control over the lives and activities of the congregation, their total reliance on the Holy Spirit for understanding and interpretation of the world, ascribing authority to God through the Holy Spirit and acceptance of the infallibility of their sacred text (the Holy Bible). It maintains a view that there is an absolute truth that rests with God and the key to this knowledge is through the Holy Spirit. These are the key elements of African Pentecostal spirituality, which provides a belief system for guidance to determine the lifestyles and practical decisions of church members. So what the African Pentecostals (hereafter APs) practise is as a result of their beliefs and values. The APs' worship is characterized by charismatic phenomena that emphasize the manifestations of the power and gifts of the Holy

Spirit through their lives and in their service to God. Among these spiritual gifts are miracles, faith healings, exorcism, prophecy, spiritual revelations and *glossolalia* (a term in Greek meaning speaking in an unknown tongue, see Holdcroft, 1979, p. 121). In a typical African Pentecostal church (hereafter APC) the common ecstatic phenomena include miming, shouting, the raising up of hands, jumping, clapping of hands, falling, prophetic utterances, sessions for faith-healing prayers, exorcisms and prayers for miracles. Though this kind of faith position has stimulated a lot of debate and divisive opinions among contemporary evangelical scholars, it does not seem to have diminished the passion of its proponents. The African Pentecostals (like Pentecostal worshippers in other parts of the world) ardently promote, pursue and practise these charismatic activities in their lives and churches.

The APs' insatiable quest for spiritual experiences and the leading of the Holy Spirit during their gatherings takes away the recognition of a written liturgy as seen in the Church of England and Roman Catholic Church. The APs believe in free worship, meaning that they are not bound by following words written down for prayers or preaching. In addition to their charismatic-oriented services, the APs' worship is also characterized by the use of musical instruments played loudly and songs sung loudly while the congregants dance energetically to worship God. The common ecclesiological structure within the APCs has two dimensions. It is usually either a two-tiered system where the minister leads the congregation with a body of deacons or a three-tiered system where the minister leads with a body of elders and then a squad of deacons. The minister, who is usually called Pastor, is recognized as one with divine calling so is a special representative of God among the congregation. The pastor is therefore charged with total responsibility and given authority to provide spiritual oversight of the congregants. In this regard, the minister becomes a powerful figure among the group. The minister is seen as the most highly respected custodian of divine knowledge and information from whom the instructions regarding all aspects of life flow to the rest of the congregation. The pastor therefore is the architect behind the educational programmes in the church as well as the main figure to deliver knowledge and information in the learning process of the adult congregants.

The practice of adult education within APCs

The significance of education has not eluded religious communities. This could be because for a community to secure its continued existence, develop and prosper there should be a process of sharing and transmitting their accumulated traditions, knowledge, ideologies, experiences and skills to the next generation. There are explicit scriptural references in the Bible where God commanded the Israelites to engage in the process of education to ensure their prolonged existence. Moses was charged to deliver a message about their religious education:

> These are the commands, decrees and laws the LORD your God directed me to teach you to observe in the land that you are crossing the Jordan to possess, so that you, your children and their children after them may fear the LORD your God as long as you live by keeping all his decrees and commands that I give you, and so that you may enjoy long life. Hear, Israel, and be careful to obey so that it may go well with you and that you may increase greatly in a land flowing with milk and honey, just as the LORD, the God of your ancestors, promised you. (Deuteronomy 6.1–3, NIV)

God gave the above command to the Israelites through Moses for the Jewish community to continue its existence, preservation of their culture, growth and success. So in order to achieve these objectives, God charged them to engage in teaching his commands and ordinances to the whole community including their children. This model of imparting divine knowledge and information to the community of God's people was not limited only to Old Testament times but rather it transcended to the New Testament era as well, and continues to the present day. According to the Gospel of Matthew (the Great Commission, Matthew 28.19, 20) Jesus commanded his disciples to teach the new believers to observe his commands and ordinances in these words: 'teaching them to obey everything I have commanded you'. Later in the Pauline epistles, he charges Timothy and Titus to educate the Christian communities in the cities and islands such as Ephesus and Crete with sound doctrine, how to live honourably and preserve the traditions of the Christian faith community (1 Timothy 1.3–10; 4.11–16; Titus 2.1–5).

The contemporary Pentecostal movement, of which the APCs are part, also seems to have embraced and ardently continues this tradition of teaching their church members biblical knowledge. In fact the APCs adhere closely to this tradition since they accept the Bible as an indisputable revelation of God's mind to humankind. To them, the Bible is the unparalleled and infallible authority that provides the context for their beliefs, decisions and praxes. It provides a lens through which they view and interpret the various aspects of society and the world at large, from politics to economics, health care to education, science and technology to art and entertainment. Hence it is an important manual for their Church education.

Reflections on the ongoing teaching methodology within APCE

Didactic methodology

Both the Great Commission and Paul's charge to Timothy, the young pastor (refer to 2 Timothy 3.16–17), serve as impetus and model for practising education among the APCs. They engage enthusiastically in the teaching process as part of their worship in perpetuating their faith tradition. There is no officially recognized and institutionalized teaching methodology in the APCs but there is a predominant practice. In this pedagogical practice, the Bible is the main textbook. Mostly on Sunday mornings and mid-week meetings in the evenings, the Bible is taught from the pulpit to the pew. While the Bible as the main teaching manual within the APCs may not be questioned, the methodology being used to engage in the teaching–learning process appears to require a critical attention. During the teaching–learning sessions, the pastor, who is recognized as the most credible person with divine vocation and authority vested in him or her to lead the congregation, carries the responsibility of church education, hence is the qualified teacher to deliver the lessons while the congregation sit and listen. The methodology is a teacher-centred approach or what I will call a didactic methodology. From the pulpit, the minister systematically and authoritatively delivers direct instruction on whatever topic may be of interest at the time. The congregation sit down quietly and become receptors of knowledge and information while the minister teaches.

Being an AP minister, I have been employing this methodology over the years and through my experience I have made the following observations. First, the approach makes the teacher (the pastor) a powerful figure among the congregation, exerting authority and control in the church auditorium. Second, the minister is described as an expert on whatever topic is being taught because he or she has a divine vocation. Third, the minister becomes a respectable role model to the congregation since he or she is the sole actor or actress in the theatre, to whom the audience look up. These observations consequently confer on the minister the monopoly of the management and ownership of the teaching–learning environment, hence impacting on the learning process of the congregants. They are not able to approach their learning with a significant measure of control and the level of participation required in an andragogical model of education; neither are they able to engage in their learning with an interdisciplinary approach expected in adult education. This could be because as custodians of the divine commission given us we, the AP ministers, are very protective of the divine instruction to the extent that we guard the content of our instruction in order to avoid any presumed form of adulteration of the divine doctrine, against which the apostle Paul warned Timothy and Titus in his pastoral letters to them. So we become somewhat unconsciously selfish in the course of our teaching methodology, giving priority to instruction. AP ministers place much more importance on the content than the process in adult education and this contradicts the views of Paraskevas and Wickens (2003) who posit that in adult education, the process needs more focus than the content.

Why this methodology is prominent within APCE

I have observed through experience and with conviction that there are some persuading factors which have contributed to the prominent usage of didactic methodology in our church education process and these are explored below.

Cultural element

The African culture is noted for its practice of oral tradition as a model in teaching methodology. In this context, history, anecdotes, information, traditional knowledge and religious beliefs are narrated orally or imparted from a speaker to a group of recipients. The people in African society are therefore culturally used to sitting down quietly and listening to lectures being delivered by elders or people with authority. Mbiti (1975, p. 4) remarks that this has been the practice from generation to generation where the African people depended on oral tradition to engage their communities in the teaching and learning process. This pedagogical model has been an old tradition in both the faith and secular education systems in African society where the pupils or students are often passive recipients of information, rather than actively involved in gathering information.

Moreover, another feature which favours this form of teaching–learning format is the uncompromising respect which African society has for gerontocracy. One of our traditional values is an acknowledgement that elders, by virtue of their experience, knowledge and skills, occupy top positions in society because they are custodians of customary laws, wisdom and traditional knowledge, and they have the responsibility of transferring or interpreting this to others. So in the process of transferring this treasure of knowledge and wisdom to others by way of oral tradition, the sole responsibility of the audience is to sit quietly and listen while the teacher (narrator/elder) alone directs all the teaching–learning activities. In terms of teaching methodology, the oral tradition format becomes a teacher-centred approach.

This pedagogical culture has transferred into the APCs. The congregants see ministers as being elders and custodians of divine knowledge and wisdom to whom the congregation should look for interpretation: inadvertently the methodology is practised among the APCs as a result of its strong integration within the fibre of African culture.

Our philosophy for Church education

I have learned that the philosophy which underpins our Church education process has influenced our choice of methodology employed in our teaching. Erkiliç (2008) comments that philosophy is central to the process of education. The philosophy of education in the APCs is one that springs out of a concept which is divinely oriented, imparting divine knowledge and information as the Holy Spirit inspires and directs. Within the scope of this philosophy, we hold the view that we have been divinely mandated to teach God's people with divine knowledge and doctrines to preserve the Christian faith and traditions. Therefore we are custodians of divine knowledge and we have got to carry out this duty with the due diligence it deserves, without adding nor removing from the scriptures or bending it in any way but forcefully delivering our message. So the appropriate method for discharging this task should be able to captivate the audience to abide by the commands and information we teach, just as it was in the Mosaic era (see Deuteronomy 4.9; 11.19). There should be no room for disobedience or adulteration. Our educational philosophy therefore allows us to engage in enculturation, using didactic methodology as the appropriate approach. A representation of this type of education was practised in ancient Greece where philosophers were engaged in a process called 'Paideia', a process of culturing the soul (Kelsey, 1993, p. 6) to educate their youth in Greek traditions. This process shaped their youth to emerge as good citizens with self-discipline and absolute devotion to their traditions.

Within the APCs, the congregation also acknowledges the minister's divine mandate so the authority and authenticity of the minister's teaching activity and the didactic method employed are rarely questioned. Hirst (1974, p. 80) would tag this as a primitive type of education – passing on of customs and beliefs uncritically because it does not give opportunity for reasoning and critical reflections. However, for the purpose of preserving traditions the AP ministers would see this methodology as the only way to deliver biblical teachings authoritatively, given their educational philosophy.

Why there should be a paradigm shift in this methodology

My experience as an Ed. D student

Having been on the Ed. D programme, I have been challenged to appraise the teaching practice within the APCs, hence my own teaching methodology. I now understand the pedagogical importance of starting with my congregants learning processes and attending to the learning environment. In this way my practice will be relevant to the contemporary believer.

The above challenge came about as a result of my forensic analysis of the didactic teaching practice within the APCs which suggested that such approach could hardly produce an audience who have an objective critical approach to issues. I am conscious that though the nature of professional knowledge (that is divine knowledge) we the AP ministers teach our congregation is different from secular knowledge, we cannot shy away from accepting the fact that we need to have adequate understanding of its proper dissemination to make it relevant to the twenty-first century believer. I have realized that our teaching should stimulate critical thinking of the audience rather than just limiting ourselves to giving them knowledge while they become passive recipients. We currently hold a didactic theory of knowledge because undoubtedly, we affirm that our professional knowledge is God-given while we are only instruments to pass the knowledge on to the audience. So we are quite cautious not to add or remove as explicitly written in scripture that: 'See that you do all I command you; do not add to it or take away from it' (Deuteronomy 12.32, NIV). So we are careful not to cause any form of adulteration to this divine command. But this does not however deter us from understanding the learning process of the congregation and so employing a methodology which can stimulate our audience to reflect from their own life experiences. Jesus, our indisputable model, from whom we draw our inspiration, applied a question-and-answer method to get his audience thinking and engaging.

My Pentecostal epistemology had closed my mind against any knowledge outside Pentecostal philosophy. I was reluctant to welcome another form of methodology to acquire knowledge. This is because my pentecostal spirituality refutes epistemological plurality which postmodernism philosophy promotes. An integration of reason, science, faith and authority as the possible multiple ways to build knowledge was anathema to me. But this paradigm has become very powerful in our contemporary world affecting the way we think and know. So I needed to reassess my own views as well as my teaching strategy in order to educate my church members and make them relevant for society.

My experience as health care chaplain

My experience of working in the National Health Service as health care chaplain has informed my teaching praxis in the Church. As a chaplain I have learned that there has been a shift in the religious landscape of Britain since 1948 when the chaplaincy ministry was integrated into the health service. The lone ranger dispensation and dominance which Christianity had enjoyed as the only prominently known faith in British society has faded away since the 1970s. This is due to the increasing growth of multiculturalism within British society. As the influx of migrants from other cultures into the UK increases, so do the diverse faith groups. This has undoubtedly resulted in multiplicity of faith groups in Britain and the religious complexion of the nation has therefore changed. I meet patients and people from non-Christian faith groups. My interactions with them and the support I give them come from an objective approach without any trace of prejudice. The new volunteers and trainee chaplains whom I train come from different religious communities. There is a diversity and equality element to respect as well as the challenge of living in a tolerant society in the face of conflicting religious views. In this sort of situation, the minds and attitudes of our church members must be enlightened to engage with the community objectively without any prejudice. Therefore my usual teaching trajectory as a Pentecostal lecturer has been challenged to shift. My formation as a Pentecostal minister had impacted on my thinking and hermeneutical processes which unconsciously made me bias towards positions and interpretations which are different from mine. I was indoctrinated with Pentecostal beliefs alone with no opportunity to consider other world-views objectively.

So my experience in the health-care environment informs me that the didactic teaching methodology is losing its sustainability in modern society.

Constructive–didactic methodology – an alternative approach

On reflection, a new pedagogy is required to engage our congregation. The acceptance and practice of this consideration will create a paradigm shift in our adult education in the Church to develop congregants who are independent, critical and reflective thinkers with good analytical skills but still work and walk within the limits and standards of biblical teachings. I hold the view that this could be achieved through our (the ministers) renewed understanding of the nature of our professional knowledge and learning, a careful reconsideration of our Pentecostal epistemology, a good study of practical andragogical systems and the various barriers that may hamper adult learning within the Church education environment as well as a good reflective process on the purpose of our education. Having appraised my teaching methodology through these lenses, I have brought some changes into my teaching by employing a constructivist approach to learning while I still take leadership in the learning environment. So the approach I have been applying is what I call a constructive–didactic methodology. In this method, there is a recognized partnership between the members and myself in the teaching–learning sessions so it is no longer a teacher-centred approach but a combination of teacher-and-student-centred approach. In this andragogical practice, I use a cooperative learning approach on some topics to encourage learning through shared experiences. This style promotes community and social growth. As the members learn in groups, they are able to interact, reflect critically and healthily as well as appreciate one another's competence. Second, I utilize enquiry-based learning to stimulate critical reflective thinking through their own experiences and life challenges. They do this in groups or on an individual basis. Moreover, I employ an interactive approach by asking the congregation questions directly from the pulpit. In all these styles, diverse topics from politics to sociology, technology to medicine, the economy to education are treated against the backdrop of the Bible. I am conscious of the nature of my professional knowledge, being divine command, so I set boundaries in order to avoid diverting into compromising areas. I therefore provide guidance in the learning process since this type of education has a spiritual connotation but my practice would counter Rogers' (1983) theory that adults learn well when they have control and direction over the learning process. The guidance I provide aims to empower them to take ownership of their learning outside the church. I also supply notebooks and pens for them to capture the lessons being learned. I have witnessed progressive participation from church members both during teaching sessions and in carrying out other tasks in the church. Due to the presence of collaborative control which I have established within the teaching environment their learning process has been enhanced. They show active involvement, readiness to contribute, evidence of growth and taking ownership of their faith which is the aim of our teaching ministry as stated in Ephesians 4.12–14 that we the ministers are to equip God's people for works of service, so that the body of Christ may be built up. 'Then we will no longer be infants, tossed back and forth by the waves, and blown here and there by every wind of teaching.'

The progress I have witnessed is because the learners have realized that their involvement in the learning process is a testament to their self-worth because the process recognizes and draws out from their rich experiences, confirming their competence. Self-worth theorist, Covington (1992) sees self-worth as an impetus for achievement in the classroom and this works well for us. The apostle Paul also put value on his ministry (Romans 11.13) and on his own competence (2 Corinthians 3.6) to underscore his successful ministry when he said: 'I have fought the good fight, I have finished the race, I have kept the faith' (2 Timothy 4.7, NIV).

Though Knowles (1990) suggests that adult learners get motivated to learn if they participate in planning and evaluating the learning process, I would differ on this point. His assumption might easily work within secular adult education but the spiritual element of our teaching task does not easily permit such an inclusive planning in Church education. There is an acknowledged understanding among the congregation that planning for the teaching–learning process comes within the jurisdiction of the minister's divine commission so I see it as a significant aspect of my teaching task and I would not relinquish it to anyone. Even evaluation is done with extreme care since we are cautious not to compromise the direction of the Holy Spirit. I am not against evaluation in any form because the Bible encourages self-evaluation (2 Corinthians 13.5).

Conclusion

A didactic approach to teaching could possibly make learners bias to other views with closed minds since there is no opportunity to interact and participate in the learning from their own experiences. Mezirow (1991) has noted that one of the goals of adult education is to recognize the rich body of experience of the adult learner so failure to recognize this important element could hamper transformative learning. A reflective learning process which involves active participation of the members from their experiences will encourage active learning with change in perspectives. I have realized that by drawing from their own experiences to engage in the teaching–learning process, they are effectively able to jettison some old views and concepts while forming new and relevant ones to help them adapt to modern life in the twenty-first century. The learning environment becomes a collaborative setting to enhance adult learning. The strategy to achieve this is involving them. So we the AP ministers must adopt a teaching approach that can equip our congregants to meet the changing faces of society. I would propose that our education praxis be organized around the experiences of the congregation and actively but cautiously involve them in the learning process so as to equip them well to interact with diversity competently. In Jesus' teaching ministry, he often employed the method of starting with his audience and their own life experiences which he would use to demonstrate or illustrate teaching points. His use of parables in the Gospels confirms this fact. He involved his audience by getting them to think from their own world of experience and knowledge. Therefore I am confident that my adapted constructive–didactic methodology is not out of place but rather a real paradigm shift in our Church educational process.

Discussion Questions

1. In what ways could church ministers be better equipped to engage in church adult education?
2. In what ways can Church education be beneficial to society?
3. What would be the relevant model for Church education among the African Pentecostal Churches?
4. Should the spirituality be replaced by teaching methodology in Pentecostal adult education?
5. Do church ministers need special training for their adult education in the church?

References

Anderson, A., 2004, *An Introduction to Pentecostalism: Global Charismatic Christianity*, Cambridge: Cambridge University Press, p. 104

BBC.co.uk, 2006, 'Pentecostal Church Sees Growth', BBC News, Tuesday 19 December http://news.bbc.co.uk/1/hi/uk/6192785.stm [accessed 2 March 2015]

Covington, M. V., 1992, *Making the Grade*, Cambridge: Cambridge University Press

Davis, C., 1993, *Azusa Street Revival*, Springdale: Whitaker House

Erkiliç, T. A., 2008, 'Importance of Educational Philosophy in Teacher Training for Educational Sustainable Development', in Middle-East *Journal of Scientific Research*, 3.1, www.idosi.org/mejsr/mejsr3(1)/1.pdf [accessed 20 March 2015]

Hirst, P., 1974, *Moral Education in a Secular Society*, London: University of London Press

Holdcroft, L. T., 1979, *The Holy Spirit: A Pentecostal Interpretation*, Springfield: Gospel Publishing House

Kelsey, D. H., 1993, *Between Athens and Berlin: The Theological Education Debate*, Eugene: Wipf and Stock

Knowles, M., 1990, *The Adult Learner: A Neglected Species*, Houston: Gulf Publishing

Koenig, H. G., 2007, *Spirituality in Patient Care: Why, How, When, and What*, 2nd edn, West Conshohocken: Templeton Press

Lartey, E. Y., 2003, *In Living Color: An Intercultural Approach to Pastoral Care and Counselling*, 2nd edn, New York: Jessica Kingsley Publishers

Lovelace, R., 1985, 'Baptism in the Holy Spirit and the Evangelical Tradition', in *Pneuma*, 7.2, pp. 101–123

Mbiti, J. S., 1975, *Introduction to African Religion*, Oxford: Heinemann Educational Publishers

McCarthy, M., 2000, 'Spirituality in a Postmodern Era', in Pattison, S. and Woodward, J. (eds), *The Blackwell reader in Pastoral and Practical Theology*, reprint, Oxford: Blackwell Publishing, p. 193

Mezirow, J., 1991, *Transformative Dimensions of Adult Learning*, San Francisco: Jossey-Bass

Paraskevas, A. and Wickens, E., 2003, 'Andragogy and the Socratic Method: The Adult Learner Perspective', in *Journal of Hospitality, Leisure, Sport and Tourism Education* 2, www.hlst.ltsn.ac.uk/johlste [accessed 11 March 2015]

Rogers, C. R., 1983, *Freedom to Learn for the 80s*, Chicago: C.E. Merrill Publishing Company

Sheldrake, P., 1999, 'The Study of Spirituality', in *Theological Trends*, www.theway.org.uk/Back/39Sheldrake1.pdf [accessed 2 March 2015]

Swinton, J., 2001, *Spirituality and Mental Health: Rediscovering a Forgotten Dimension*, London: Jessica Kingsley Publishers

Warfield, B. B., 1995, *Counterfeit Miracles*, Edinburgh: The Banner of Truth Trust

9

The academic tail wagging the curacy dog: a theology of learning and formation

Trevor Gerhardt

Abstract

Curacy, the second stage of training and education of Anglican priests for ordained ministry has changed significantly from its historical precedent. Training and educational design of curacy vary in their effectiveness in preparing priests for Christian ministry. This complexity will be explored in order to suggest a 'theology of learning and formation' for curacy. Such a proposed model, aiming towards a theology of learning and formation must have a balance of vocational, mastery and developmental curricula. This is enhanced by incorporating self-directed, experiential and transformative learning, applying sound principles of pedagogy and andragogy. The emphasis in curacy will focus initially on an apprenticeship training model.

Keywords

Theological education; curriculum; formation; models; learning

Introduction

I am the programme director of curacy training for the Diocese of Rochester. I am passionate about preparing people for ministry, having been a Baptist pastor, missionary and university chaplain in the past. I am committed to adult education and discipleship. I am fervent about the Church's role in society. Due to my tradition being that of an ordained Baptist minister, I had to learn quickly how ministers are trained in the Church of England when I first started in this post as curacy programme director.

Trainee Church of England ministers undertake a period of study at a prescribed higher educational institution (HEI) prior to ordination. This is compulsory, with the expectation of at least a Diploma in Theology as an academic award (Ministry Division, 2006, p. 80). This period is called Initial Ministerial Education, years 1 to 3 (IME 1–3), and is followed, post-ordination, by what is called a curacy post (IME 4–7) as an 'assistant curate' in a local parish under the supervision of a trained and experienced training incumbent. Those who are full time and who receive a stipend are called stipendiary curates. Those who are part time and who are financially self-sufficient – many are in some form or other of employment – are called self-supporting ministers (SSM).

Curacy is very complex. It involves training and educating adults; many who train as ministers as a second or third career bring with them various transferable skills. Some curacies involve further academic training, requiring informed practice regarding curriculum design and andragogy appropriate for the audience and the role in which they are being trained. Most curacies involve a model of training that is either that of an apprentice or that of an assistant, or both. In this chapter I define and explore these key terms. Engaging with the complexity found in curacy, I will attempt to formulate a 'theology of learning and formation for curacy' by using three archetypal stories created from my experiences, combined with the actual experience of five curates from other dioceses across England as case studies. Such a theology can become a model for good practice.

Archetypes

The three archetypes presented below, created from common experiences I have had as a programme director, represent some of the main intricacies on which this chapter will focus. These archetypes emphasize the complexities of professionalism, academia and pedagogics and the models of training used in supervision.

Since the Middle Ages clergy have been seen as professionals, joined later by physicians and lawyers (Crook, 2008, pp. 11, 15). Not all curates are academic and not all curricula and course programmes for curacy are academic. Higton (2012, p. 181) suggests that 'formation in virtue is bound to take the form of apprenticeship', however, Longden (2012, p. 124) in his doctoral research of curacies found that there are conflicting models of assistantship and apprenticeship. The fact that curates are called *'assistant* curate' does not help, yet it is very clear (at least now) that curacy is a designated training post (Formation and Ministry Team, 2013, p. 5).

Story 1 – Professionalism

An IME 4–7 director called Ray had a curate named Mary who was a qualified and practising barrister training to become a priest. Mary was a self-supporting minister (SSM), choosing to become ordained while still working as a barrister. Her previous educational training and professional working context influenced her understanding and engagement with her IME 1–3 and curacy process. Ray was struggling to get her 'on board', as she did not understand the learning and formational process of curacy. Mary was happy to do the parish skill-based 'bits' but the learning 'bits', described by her as academia, she perceived as an unhelpful distraction. Mary was an extremely motivated learner but displaced this motivation in resistance to the curacy process as she could not see the relevance of further learning and formation.

Story 2 – Academia and pedagogics

Tom, another IME 4–7 director, had a curate named Joe who was also an SSM curate working in the care industry. Completing his IME 1–3 training, Joe clearly struggled with the academic part-time college course and with critical think-ing and producing essays. Tom was not struggling to 'get Joe on board' but rather Tom was struggling to 'keep Joe on board'. Tom recognized that the taught components of the curacy are not just about satisfying academic assessment and that if Joe were to be withdrawn from the university-validated course, the taught components would still continue. It would just be the assessment that would be different. How could the curacy process of learning and formation be shaped to help Joe flourish?

Story 3 – Models of training

Jill, another IME 4–7 director, describes Jack as a married sti-pendiary curate in his mid-twenties who completed his IME 1–3 with a Masters award. Jack audits the university-validated curacy programme producing 'learning evidence' as a form of assessment. Jack is very academically capable, motivated and treated by his training incumbent more as an assistant than an apprentice. Jack is given a lot of freedom, with very little direc-tive input regarding further learning and formation. How can further learning and formation be identified and applied that is appropriate for Jack?

Mary, Joe and Jack are all very different curates. These three archetypes demonstrate the mixed economy of the complexities of curacy and the difficult task of formulating a coherent, consistent and applicable 'theology of learning and formation' that will be suitable and fair for all.

Theology, learning and formation: university-validated curacies

Curates often ask, 'Why do we have to learn this stuff?' and there is a range of possible answers. Newman considered sound intellec-tual formation, such as an academic curriculum, an end in itself. He saw such intellectual formation as 'needing no other utility to make it a good worth pursuing. Intellectual formation only becomes itself – only becomes formation rather than deformation, and only becomes truly intellectual – to the extent that it leads towards that end' (Newman, 1976, p. 97). According to Thompson (2004), academic learning:

> Involves the individual's structured absorption of knowledge, through research, reading, lectures, seminars and tutorials; and the processing and correlating of that knowledge and the production of assessed material e.g. essays, exam papers, seminars, verbal dialogue, etc. It is not immediately obvious how academic learning so defined can assist ministerial training or formation. [As in the example of Joe] (p. 269)

The emphasis of a vocational/professional curriculum is on using the material in order to do something else. The emphasis is on using the knowledge to do something (Atherton, 2013). Finally, a developmental/constructive curriculum is concerned with advanced skills and is centred on the development of the student as found in material related to reflection and reflective practice. In order to analyse the complexity of curacy, these definitions are helpful as a point of departure to help create a theology of learning and formation.

Although there are many biblical passages that can be used in relation to this discussion on curacy, the following passage from the New Revised Standard Version (NRSV) is of theological interest: 'But solid food is for the mature (τελείων), for those whose faculties [their senses (αἰσθητήρια)] have been trained (γεγυμνασμένα) by practice [constant use (ἕξιν)] to distinguish good from evil' (Hebrews 5.14). 'Babes' or 'infants' (NIV/NRSV) (v. 13) represent those new to learning, especially in moral philosophy, in contrast to the 'mature', who are those 'trained' or 'practised' (Attridge, 1989, p. 160). The versions of the Bible referred to above each articulate distinctive characteristics. Farley (1996, p. 37) asks how educated people with highly professional roles in secular society, for example Mary in the first story above, exhibit a 'literalist, elementary school level in their religious understanding'. There is an expectation of clergy in training of a progression in theological education and that this progression, as it relates to curates specifically, includes knowledge as well as character formation so as to attain 'full age' or maturity (KJV/NRSV) and not be 'dull' (NRSV). Furthermore, the writer of Hebrews 6.12 uses the phrase 'ought to be teachers' (NRSV) to indicate those who have a 'mature grasp of a subject' in contrast to those unable to teach because they 'refuse to grow up in knowledge' and 'never grow up in behaviour' (Barclay, 1976, pp. 50–51). Curacy resonates with Barclay's interpretation of this passage in the sense that there is not just an expected progression in knowledge and in character but also in the mastery of a subject, in this case practical theology and its application to and implications for ministry in changing contexts. This is what is understood by theological reflection. According to the passage, this is achieved through 'exercise' or 'practice' (*dia ten hexin*, KJV/NRSV) which is used only here in the entire New Testament and can be understood as the 'building up of experience through continued process in the past'; a 'steady application' developed as a 'skill' (Guthrie, 1983, p. 136). The result of this process is mature judgement (v. 14).

Curacy resonates with a curriculum which is vocationally and developmentally oriented, resonating with the passage from Hebrews. This dispels the assumption that the academic tail wags the curacy dog. The shift in Protestant schools in the seventeenth century resulted in theology becoming the referent for doctrines, beliefs or systems of belief and once this was located in the schools which educated clergy, 'theology became the umbrella term for the cluster of sciences or disciplines which organized that education' (Farley, 1996, p. 39). This arguably restricted theology to a teacher–scholar model and created the assumption that any university education therefore followed an academic curriculum. However, as Higton (2012) states, 'Christian learning is that of a saint (*formation*) rather than that of a master (*competence*). The excellence of the saint . . . is more thoroughly kenotic in form ("self-emptying" of one's own will and becoming entirely receptive to God's divine will)' (2012, p. 181). Curacy and learning is complex. Banks (1999, p. 3) concurs that seminary education (such as IME 1–3) is too focused on cognitive learning at the expense of personal development and practical experience.

Learning is described by Higton (2012, p. 194) as continuous. This highlights the importance of the process of learning and the

priority of lifelong learning that simply starts in IME and continues throughout life as an ordained minister (Archbishops'
Council, 2001, p. 26). Wickett (2005, pp. 155–157) in this context describes three kinds of appropriate learning, namely self-
directed, experiential and transformative. What kind of learning,
shaped into an effective and affective programme and curriculum,
will meet the expectation of faith communities, bishops and the
Church of England?

Pedagogy and andragogy

Considering the context of curacy, Knowles (1980, p. 13) argues
that an adult learning experience should be a process of self-
directed enquiry enabling adults to be active participants. This
kind of learning will be unique and different from the more 'scientific'
educational context of law as illustrated by the example of Mary
(story 1). Knowles, (p. 40) defines a purely knowledge-driven curriculum as pedagogy, and defines pedagogy literally as the art and
science of teaching children, that is the transmission of knowledge and skills from an adult to a child (teacher–scholar) which
involves fact-laden lectures, rote memorization and examinations.
This view by Knowles is not definitive. Andragogy, the art and
science of teaching adults, is goal-oriented, activity-oriented and
learning-oriented, resonating with the three forms of learning suggested earlier which together with pedagogy can work towards
achieving competent reflective practitioners.

Competent people are people who are able to apply their knowledge (the base knowledge acquired at IME 1–3) under changing
conditions (Knowles, p. 19), which in this case is provided by the
parish setting in which they are placed for at least three years during
curacy. 'To produce such competent people', continues Knowles
(p. 19) 'is to have them acquire their knowledge [and skills, understanding, attitudes, values and interest] in the context of its application', which in this case is theology applied in local parish and/
or working contexts. Banks (1999, pp. 19–20) notes the importance of the development of one's *habitus* or disposition in this

process using *theologia* (that is, the human capacity for intuitive knowledge of divine things which is called theological wisdom) which takes place through formal, structured learning as well as through the institutional culture and structure in which this learning is set (mastery/induction). Curacy can provide such a rich, diverse pluriform context. Such learning is inclusive for those who, like Joe in story 2 above, do not excel in academic study: 57 per cent of clergy do not have a degree (Furlong, 2000, p. 264).

The programme and curriculum of a university-validated curacy must be about skills and values as well as specialized knowledge (competence, mastery and development). This enables us to avoid a dualism between academia and vocation. Criticism of curacy (IME 4–7) identified by Burgess (1999, pp. 94–95) in the past include: the duplication of IME 1–3; poorly presented or inadequately prepared curriculum; little flexibility in what people did in curacy training and a failure to recognize experience and skills gained prior to ordination. Subjects covered often reflected more the presuppositions and hobby-horses of the organizers than the realities of the ministries in which people were engaged.

These can be avoided by incorporating and shaping the curacy around a university-validated course (or policy) with well-defined learning outcomes (LOs). Well-expressed statements of intended LOs help students to identify their own targets, and work systematically towards demonstrating their achievement of these targets; in the context of benchmarking, LOs can provide one of the most direct indicators of the intended level and depth of any programme of learning (Race, 1999, p. 10). More broadly, validation also adds incentive and value, affirming its quality and aiding confidence in the wider society (Ministry Division, 2006, p. 80).

Curacy with university validation is, however, not held up as the perfect solution and comes with a caveat, as stated quite vigorously by Piper (2013, p. x), when he says:

Ministry is professional in those areas of competency where the life of faith and the life of unbelief overlap . . . that overlapping can never be central . . . professionalism should always be marginal, not central; optional, not crucial . . . the pursuit of professionalism will push the supernatural center more and more into the corner while ministry becomes a set of secular competencies with a religious veneer.

Furthermore, Ramsden (2003, p. 220) adds that we need to question the validity of external quality assurance processes not because we do not want to be accountable, but because they generally display a flawed understanding of the essentials of teaching and learning. One of the struggles of theological curricula in recent years has been that of trying to bridge the gap between the academy and the demands of ministry and life in the Church and in the wider world (Fuller and Fleming, 2005, p. 163). Higton (2012, p. 180) offers a solution in that 'academics and research take place within communities of character and therefore make the university, in pursuit of these, schools of virtue . . . the picture of learning as a spiritual discipline, deeply forming the knower's character'.

Assistantship and apprenticeship

Vocation is understood as 'such a direction of life activities as renders them perceptibly significant to a person because of the consequences they accomplish, and also useful to his associates' (Dewey [1916] 1966, p. 307). Such an instrumental emphasis, if taken too far, will change education so that technical capability is privileged over deep understanding (Atherton, 2013). The shift between education and training actually supports the ethos of curacy. The competence-based curricula are based on this model, another aspect that is part of the curacy process. Recent changes in Church of England legislation, including *The Clergy Terms of Service Measure* and *The Clergy Discipline Measure* have brought the need for enhanced attention to assessment at the end of the curacy. The vocational and mastery curriculum as described in this context of curacy therefore by default, particularly due to the empathies of formation, will naturally also incorporate a curriculum of a developmental nature, particularly if there is an emphasis on reflection. The question therefore, allowing for the three modes of learning and the appropriate three forms of curricula, is whether an apprenticeship or assistantship model maximizes this intent.

An apprenticeship is a period of preparation for the mastery of a craft (Berry, 2004, p. 23). It is the format most commonly used for learning a skilled trade, allowing for a learning-on-the-job experience (Knowles, 1980, p. 132). Using this description by Knowles, there are a number of similarities to the way a curacy is shaped, justifying the apprenticeship model:

- the curate and training incumbent enter into a *curacy agreement* stipulating among other things the number of hours for work and study, expenses, etc.;
- the training incumbent in that capacity agrees to the regular supervision of the curate in the tasks and skills they are to learn and master;
- the diocese issues each curate with a *statement of particulars* in which the time frame of the training post is defined (in our diocese, 3–4 years for stipendiary curates and 3–6 years for SSM curates).

Contributing to this discussion, Higton (2012, p. 181) adds that formation in virtue is bound to take the form of apprenticeship and that such virtue is acquired by means of involvement in a practice sustained by a particular community (*such as the IME 4–7 programme and the local parish placement*). 'It is a skill in pursuit of the good that orientates that practice and gives the person the capacity and disposition reliably to advance towards that good. A person formed in that virtue has internalized the good of the practice, until that good has become his own good' (Higton, 2012, pp. 175–176).

Assistantship or pupillage is the preparation for a profession (Berry, 2004, p. 23). Pupillage, according to Russell (1980, p. 24) was the dominant preparation for clergy historically and is what we would understand by assistantship. The assistantship model therefore resonates with the definitions and descriptions of professionalism. These include autonomy of role, altruistic service, professional association with self-regulation, specialized skills and training, a long period of education and socialization and control over recruitment, training, certification and standards of practice (Russell, 1980, p. 13).

Longden (2012, p. 118) found that there is a 'reframing of curacy away from assistantship towards apprenticeship'. Regardless of the model used, its failure or success is largely dependent upon the dynamics of the training incumbent–curate relationship as well as the other factors already mentioned.

To what degree does the training incumbent–curate relationship, distinctive to curacy, equate to learning that is largely vocational, constructed to ensure the application of sound principles of pedagogy and andragogy using the three learning styles described? And do the assistantship and/or apprenticeship models support such a task? A group of five curates from across England were interviewed on this matter. Reflecting on their curacy thus far, they were asked to discuss: 'why do we have to learn all this stuff?' and whether their experience of curacy thus far emulated the model of assistantship and/or apprenticeship?

Actual experience

These five curates from other dioceses in England met with me as a focus group in order to share their experiences of curacy. Their names have been changed to ensure anonymity. Each experience adds to and accentuates the rationale already discussed.

Mark is a stipendiary curate from East Anglia and describes his curacy training as being 'more about practical advice rather than the theological justification for it'. Mark explained that due to the large theological differences between curates, training incumbents and parishes, the training provided, in order to avoid conflict, focused on practical aspects which most can agree on, such as how to conduct a funeral. This no-frills focus embraces the curriculum of vocation and seems to divert into the area of training quite substantially. Mark, however, added that you are still required to master the skills and it is this mastery which forms part of the assessment of the curate. This was further illustrated in the context of leadership where you learn to 'test things in practice'. This will indicate the relevance of the skill (taught material) and also your mastery of the skill (application in context). Mastery therefore implies learning the 'reality of the context and how the "theory" applies'. Mark said that IME 1–3 gave him 'less immediate experience of parish' than IME 4–7. What was missing in the conversation with Mark in relation to his curacy was any indication of an academic and/or constructive curriculum. What was emphasized was vocational and mastery curriculum with self-directed, experiential learning. According to Mark, his training incumbent voiced the opinion that the curate was 'there to learn'. Mark reported feeling like an apprentice sometimes (learning with less autonomy) and an assistant at other times (contributing with more autonomy).

In contrast Harry, a stipendiary curate from central England, described his curacy as a combination of skills training and theological reflection. Harry is part of a curacy that has a validated academic award as part of the curacy process. Harry describes his curacy as 'not looking at specifics but the overarching theology behind our thinking'. In seeking to describe his curacy within the curriculum being discussed in this chapter, Harry said his curacy was, 'partly to maximize potential, also partly mastering . . . and therefore you can use it'. This approach enabled curacy to cover 'blind spots in a general sense' (beyond the local parish context) which included 'unrehearsed debate'. From the discussion, the curriculum dominant in Harry's curacy reflects mastery and development using learning that is more transformative and self-directed. Harry did not feel his curacy was academic, but had 'quite a clear sense of being an apprentice and an assistant' and was 'very grateful for it being both'. This worked because there were very clear boundaries and roles defined by the training incumbent and these were communicated to the parish.

Tom, a stipendiary curate from south-east England, also had a curacy that was part of a validated academic award but described his curacy as 'a bit of everything' describing it as theory and reflection upon actual experience. The intention was to construct a reflective practitioner. Tom felt the curacy programme had been well shaped with much thought. He mentioned an example of past generations training as curates simply meeting in a pub and being asked, 'So how is it going?' In comparison, therefore, he felt much more supported by the process which was about 'broad practice and perspectives'. Tom too felt that IME 1–3 was 'removed' and that IME 4–7 'made sense'. Curacy was described as 'unpacking the trunk' of things placed in it by IME 1–3. This statement points to the utility of curacy and the more formal academic nature of IME 1–3. The discussion described a vocational, developmental curriculum with certain aspects of mastery, all shaped around self-directed, experiential and transformative learning. Tom agreed that there was constant change between the model of apprentice and that of assistant because the context and training was changing resulting in different and appropriate models been applied accordingly particularly in creating greater autonomy of action.

A stipendiary curate from the west Midlands named Edward was the only curate who had a curacy shaped around a highly driven portfolio model to enable self-directed learning. This was illustrated by the example of sessions about schools and a session entitled, 'being it', a session reflecting on what it was like three months into your curacy as an ordained deacon. Edward understood this as 'being able to master certain subjects, but also being able to use other bits' by which he meant that it is often the context that defines the value of 'stuff' taught or applied. With the use of reflection, this curacy too resembles what was described by Tom above. Edward felt greater autonomy was linked to status (the longevity of the position held) creating trust which would cause transition between the models of apprentice and assistant. He felt, though, that he inhabited an assistant-colleague model.

The only SSM curate, named Jay, from the south-west of England described his curacy as skills-based, 'practical as much as anything else'. These 'things we can use' he described as being 'well inter-related'. Jay, however, may be the exception to the rule due to his context and vast experience, being treated differently by his training incumbent and IME 4–7 director. It was difficult to establish whether his experience of curacy was general to all or very specific to his unique situation. However, what was described had a very dominant curriculum of vocation (to training) context with little discussion about mastery and development (although implied). By implication the learning was more self-directed and experiential and less about transformation, although this again may be implied. Jay felt he was treated only as an assistant and expressed aspects of power and insecurity by his training incumbent when treated like an apprentice.

These five actual experiences resonate with what is being suggested by this chapter in order to formulate 'a theology of learning and formation'.

Conclusion

The five curates illustrate the diversity of contexts, approaches and shapes involved in curacy curriculum and learning. Their stories resonate with the archetypes. The five curates described healthy pedagogy and andragogy. Most described a vocational curriculum which was self-directed and experiential particularly because of the parish context, that is the unique context of curacy. There was an implied mastery and developmental curriculum with transformative learning due to an emphasis on the use of reflection. None referred to their curacy being academic even though two of the five interviewed were part of an academically validated curacy. This is encouraging as often, in my role as programme director, I have to address this misconception by those seeking to do their curacy in the Diocese of Rochester and by a few curates initially when they start their curacy. The focus group revealed that most operated in both the models of an assistant and an apprentice. The only area that was lacking was a clearer identification and emphasis of developing character (virtue) through a developmental curriculum and transformative learning. A greater emphasis on the apprentice model, as argued by Higton (2012) and Longden (2012) initially may help in this regard.

A 'theology of learning and formation' for curacy must have a balanced curriculum of vocation (competence in skill), mastery (induction) and development (virtue) using a balance of self-directed, experiential and transformative learning applying sound principles of pedagogy and andragogy with a greater emphasis initially on an apprenticeship model. This implies that programme directors like myself need to have a greater awareness of the programmes we create as part of curacy, particularly if these programmes are shaped around a university-validated award; that programmes need to have a greater holistic understanding by all participating in them; and that training incumbents in particular need to be trained and educated in this regard especially in terms of the implications of which models they use in supervision.

Discussion Questions

1. What are the strengths and weaknesses of the model presented in this essay i.e. what are the gaps?
2. Can the ordained ministry be captured in the model presented in this essay i.e. is it distinctive in its Christian expression?
3. Should one form of curacy be dominant? If so, why?
4. Is the shift from models of pupillage (assistantship) towards apprenticeship a shift away from notions of clerical professionalism? And, if so, what are the implications as related to questions 2 and 3?
5. Does curacy underpinned by university-validated teaching enable a Christian presence in higher education that would not be there otherwise?

References

Archbishops' Council, 2001, *Mind the Gap*, London: Church House Publishing

Atherton, J. S., 2013, Curriculum, www.learningandteaching.info [accessed 6 September 2013]

Attridge, H. W., 1989, *The Epistle to the Hebrews: A Commentary on the Epistle to the Hebrews*, Philadelphia: Fortress

Banks, R., 1999, *Reenvisioning Theological Education*, Grand Rapids: Eerdmans

Barclay, W., 1976, *The Daily Study Bible: The Letter to the Hebrews*, Edinburgh: Saint Andrew Press

Berry, T., 2004, 'The social construction of the ministry student', in *Contact: The Interdisciplinary Journal of Pastoral Studies*, 114, pp. 23–30

Burgess, N., 1999, *Into Deep Water: The experience of curates in the Church of England*, Bury St Edmunds: Kevin Mayhew Ltd

Crook, D., 2008, 'Some historical perspectives on professionalism', in Cunningham, B. (ed.) *Exploring Professionalism*, London: Institute of Education, pp. 10–27

Dewey, J. [1916] 1966, *Democracy and Education*, New York: Macmillan/ The Free Press

Farley, E., 1996, 'Can church education be theological education?', in Astley, J., Francis, L. J. and Crowder, C. (eds) *Theological Perspectives on Christian Formation: A reader on theology and Christian education*, Grand Rapids: Eerdmans, pp. 31–44

Formation and Ministry Team, 2013, *Handbook for Training Incumbents and Assistant Curates (2013–2014)*, www.rochester.anglican.org [accessed 19 December 2013]

Fuller, M. and Fleming, K., 2005, 'Bridging a Gap: A Curriculum Uniting Competencies and Theological Disciplines', in *Journal of Adult Theological Education*, 2.2, pp. 163–178

Furlong, M., 2000, *CofE: The State It's In*, London: Hodder and Stoughton

Guthrie, D., 1983, *Tyndale New Testament Commentaries: Hebrews*, Leicester: IVP

Higton, M., 2012, *A Theology of Higher Education*. Oxford: Oxford University Press

Knowles, M. S., 1980, *The Modern Practice of Adult Education: From Pedagogy to Andragogy*, Chicago: Association Press

Longden, L. P., 2012, *Mission-Shaped Curacy? Reshaping Curacy for Effective Formation for Authentic Ministry in the Twenty-First Century Church of England*, Ph.D. thesis, University of Birmingham

Ministry Division, 2006, *Shaping the Future: New Patterns of Training for Lay and Ordained*, London: Church House Publishing

Newman, J. H., *The Idea of a University Defined and Illustrated*, Ker, I. (ed.) 1976, Oxford: Clarendon Press

Piper, J., 2013, *Brothers, We Are Not Professionals*, Nashville: B and H Publishing

Race, P. (ed.), 1999, *2000 Tips for Lecturers*, London: Kogan Page

Ramsden, P., 2003, *Learning to Teach in Higher Education*, 2nd edn, London: Routledge Falmer

Russell, A., 1980, *The Clerical Profession*, SPCK: London

Strong, J., 'A Concise Dictionary', in Zodhiates, S. (ed.), 1984, *The Hebrew-Greek Key Word Study Bible, Authorized Version*, London: Eyre and Spottiswoode

Thompson, R., 2004, 'Academic Theology and Ministerial Formation: Towards a contemplative approach', in *Theology*, July/Aug, 838 pp. 265–273

Wickett, R., 2005, 'Adult Learning Theories and Theological Education', in *Journal of Adult Theological Education*, 2.2, pp. 153–161

The diocesan education officer's tale: voices of church, culture and state in church school education

TATIANA WILSON

Abstract

This chapter explores the idea that schools need to be accomplished in speaking the dialects of the church, culture and state in order to develop accessible ways of expressing the school's Christian character and the opportunities that they provide to the students and families they serve. It suggests that by offering a clearly Christian world-view schools can be inclusive and support students to explore a vision of 'the good life' for themselves with depth and rigour. Finally the role of the diocesan education officer is explored within the context of Church of England schools, suggesting that Church of England schools are treasures within our education system.

Keywords

Church of England; Christian distinctiveness; leadership; language; Christian values; Christian worship; education

Introduction

I have always felt that my roles in education have been an expression of my faith. Jesus calls Christians to be 'salt and light'

(Matthew 5.13–14). In Jesus' lifetime salt was highly valued for its preservative and flavouring properties. Thus a Christian's expression of their faith is that of a preserving force working to prevent societal decay in the world and adding flavour in the communities we serve. As salt counteracts the power of sin, so the Christian's calling to be light is to make visible and illuminate. Jesus described himself as the 'light of the world' (John 18.12) and Christians are called to reflect the difference Christ's presence has in our lives. Personally, I have felt that this means that I should add something positive to all the people I work with and the students I serve as part of my role, especially those who are vulnerable and marginalized in some way.

For the majority of my working life I avoided working for church schools feeling that Jesus' teaching to be 'in the world but not of it' (John 17.11–16) meant that I should not be in a 'Christian ghetto' but rather within my local community. For the most part this has meant that I have chosen to live near enough to be able to walk to my workplace, as this has enabled me to gain a greater understanding of the community I serve. I started my career in deprived areas of London before moving to the West Country and have always seen education and schooling as having the potential to break cycles of poverty.

My first experience of working in a church school was as an acting headteacher of a Church of England school. My expectations did not match reality. For a start, very few families or teachers considered themselves to be Christian. In this particular school there did not seem to be a common understanding of what it meant to be a church school and of how what was being offered was different from neighbouring community schools. In my previous community school there was a group of parents who met regularly, and a staff prayer group who met at other times to pray for the school community. Periodically a local church would leave chocolate bars in our pigeon-holes thanking us for the work we were doing, and often supported community initiatives and projects from parenting support to gardening. Another local church, which I did not attend, on hearing that my husband was seriously ill with a form of leukaemia, prayed for him and us as a family until he was better. Many of these practices were either not present in the church school I was now leading or in embryonic form. The school's previous church inspection report reflected this. When I asked the diocese for support in identifying core Christian values that should underpin the school (an action point from the report) I was told this was for us to work out for ourselves.

During my interview for the post of acting headteacher I was asked how I would recognize worship rather than assembly in the context of the school. This is not an easy question to answer when serving a multicultural, multi-faith and belief community. Planning can shape worship but is not in itself worship. For me worship is an individual's personal response to God.

All these experiences provoked my thinking. I wondered:

- What makes church schools special and does it matter?
- What impact should church schools have serving a diverse community?
- What difference should this make for me as a leader? My staff? The children in our care? Their families?
- How should church schools fit within the church community? Within the community of other schools in the locality?
- What is the heritage of Church of England schools and how could this be reflected in them today?

Later that year, when my contract ended, I found myself at a crossroads trying to decide whether to continue to pursue a career as a university lecturer or to continue as a headteacher (before returning to teaching I had spent three years lecturing and research-ing in initial teacher education). I was qualified to do both but nei-ther felt the right shape for me. I found myself reluctant to pursue either. Then the possibility arose of applying for the position of education officer for a diocese. I knew little of diocesan Boards of Education when I applied for the position. However, reading the job description and person specification I realized that the role described my interest of linking faith and education in a way that made a difference in the communities we serve. I applied for the post and was fortunate enough to be appointed.

On taking up the role I imagined that working for the Church of England meant there would be a rich heritage of resources to draw on. Coming from an academic background I thought I would search out the relevant journals in church school education to find out what was current and topical. I also wanted to find out about Christian pedagogy and from where the Church of England drew its influence, for example the Jesuit tradition and beyond. I was surprised to find that no such canon was being advocated nationally, that there were no seminal texts to refer to and that when talking to schools the only shared language they had to describe 'Christian distinctiveness' nationally were the National Society's Statutory Inspection of Anglican Schools' (SIAS now SIAMS) grade descriptors.

The diocese I was working in had recently restructured and I was allocated just over 50 schools with which to build a working relationship and support their school improvement. It was decided that in the first few months we would visit each school and have a 'listening visit' from which we could then develop a strategic plan as a team. These proved to be very informative. What emerged was that school leaders and staff were very open to supporting and developing the Christian element of their school but needed support on how to do this. School leaders wanted to be offered some strategies for things they could develop in school as well as links to other schools working in similar ways. They also often wanted help with how to express the Christian aspects of their church school in an accessible way.

Rhea (2011, p. 3), in his analysis of Christian universities, discusses the two 'dialects' of student formation: 'the language of the church and the language of the culture'. He argues that in order for universities to be effective they need to be accomplished in both. In a similar way, it could be argued church school leaders need to develop accessible ways in which they express both the Christian character of their school and the opportunities that they provide to the students and families they serve. Rhea (2011, p. 4) proposes that 'those who will be the greatest change agents in the lives of students are those who can competently "speak" with two important registers or dialects . . . As (they) become fluent . . . they will speak with a wise and compelling voice.' This metaphor of speaking different dialects has a parallel in the New Testament story of Paul addressing Athenian philosophers in a meeting of the Areopagus (Acts 17). This portrays the scholar and evangelist Paul as so conversant with the Greek culture of the time that he was able draw on their understanding of 'God' before explaining his own. Similarly Rhea's concept of 'dialect' challenges church school leaders to immerse themselves in the cultures of the communities they serve without resorting to 'preaching' at them. Furthermore it could be argued that leaders need to be fluent in another dominant dialect in the current context: the language of accountability to the state, through the Department for Education (DfE) which funds schools and Ofsted (Office for Standards in Education) which inspects them.

The language of the Church

Before analysing the dialects of culture and state there follows a critique of Rhea's (2011) analysis of the Christian world-view. Rhea identifies three constructs which underpin the essence of the Christian world-view: an identity in Christ, wisdom and spiritual formation. Central to the identity in Christ is the 'Immanuel Principle' which is that 'God is with us'. All students who attend a church school should know that the Christian view of God is one of relationship and that God is with them. Jesus' incarnation as a human is the greatest testament to this. How each person responds to this is an individual choice. For Christians this truth offers the hope of knowing that 'nothing [they] will ever do or not do can separate them from the love God' (Rhea, 2011 p. 6; Romans 8.38–39). Foster and Helmers (2008) developed this concept further by looking at the grand narrative of the Bible as one in which God was with people. Biblical characters' responses to these encounters with God shaped them as people and caused them to develop practices and new ways of living. The same is true of Christians throughout history and today. In a church school these stories can be explored both through religious education and collective worship enabling students to consider the possibility that they are part of a bigger narrative.

Therefore, church schools need to consider what education is for. Implicit in Foster and Helmers' (2008) analysis is a vision of education that is not solely about factual knowledge but about enabling young people to flourish by growing in wisdom. Rhea calls this 'skill in living' and argues that any education that does not pursue wisdom is 'short-sighted and lacking' (Rhea, 2011, p. 6). Rhea expands this by drawing on Calvin's understanding of wisdom as comprising two parts: *'the knowledge of God and of ourselves'* (Calvin, trans. 2008, Rhea, 2011, p. 6). It could be argued that church schools face a significant challenge in finding sufficient time for this necessary private reflection in an already crowded, grade-focused curriculum.

Another challenge facing Church of England schools is that they often serve diverse communities. Therefore, when considering 'wisdom' it needs to be recognized that the Christian world-view is only one lens through which students view the world. Nevertheless there is merit in considering one world-view in depth for all students. This approach offers students the opportunity to explore issues of faith, belief, ethics and values with depth and rigour. It is hoped that students see the relevance of Christian faith in the way it is lived out either by the school as an institution or by an individual as a Christian. The challenge for the teacher or school leader is to enable a depth of learning that will help to shape the child as they mature into adulthood. As their own world-view is compared and contrasted it is to be expected that disagreement and debate will ensue. However this does not need to be positioned by the school as being about winning and losing. It is a question of perspective governed by the metaphors schools choose to hold on to. Shortt, Smith and Cooling (2000) explore this, drawing on the work of Lakoff and Johnson (1980), who suggest that argument and debate are often seen as warfare. They posit that the internal culture of schools would change by replacing warfare as the metaphor for argument or debate with dance.

The metaphor of dance presupposes collaboration, movement and partnership, while the metaphor of warfare presupposes the annihilation of 'the other'. Thus changing the metaphor of debate in schooling from warfare to dance is a step towards wisdom for those of all faiths and none. It could therefore be argued that church schools are at their most Christian when they invite students to 'dance with them'. The students' role within the dance is crucial; the perspectives and ideas they bring to it will shape it and each other in the process.

In a similar way, church schools should not avoid exploring the idea of spiritual formation with students, as without it students cannot fully grasp the essentials of the Christian faith, which is relational and transformative. For Christians, transformation comes through the power of the Holy Spirit. It is no accident that the fruits of the Holy Spirit are love, joy, peace, long-suffering, gentleness, goodness, faith (Galatians 5.22b). The Holy Spirit enables Christians to demonstrate these qualities when human effort is not sufficient. Spiritual formation is, at its centre, about the transformation of the heart. Smith (2009, p. 9) poses the question: 'What if education wasn't first and foremost about what we know, but about what we love?'

And then an alternative vision is offered by Smith, who suggests that: 'Education is not primarily a heady project concerned with providing information; rather education is most fundamentally a matter of formation' (2009, p. 26).

A church school's ethos helps students to make positive choices about the type of person they are and aspire to be. Church schools can offer an explicit framework to support this. Many church schools are developing this further, exploring how core Christian values can be taught through the curriculum as well as experienced in the daily life and rhythms of the school.

The language of culture

All students bring with them a 'cultural capital' which may or may not fit with that of the school they belong to. Raffo and Hall (2006) offer a case study of a student teacher working in different schools as a way of unpacking the 'way various experiences intersected and then impacted on her ability to learn and develop' (p. 64). They did this drawing on Bourdieu's 'thinking tools' of habitus, capital and field. They concluded that differing social relations and cultural contexts significantly influenced her experiences. This meant that she thrived in one context and struggled in another in which she found it hard to draw positives from her experience. The importance of a person's cultural capital is therefore significant. Olneck (2000, p. 319), drawing on Bourdieu (1977), describes this as a negotiation between different kinds of value: those of institutional expectations; ways of knowing and reasoning; and schemes of appreciation and understanding. The question remains of who decides these values, and how far individuals are encouraged to take agency in negotiating them by the institutions they work in.

The importance of these negotiations can also be seen in the work of Vincent and Braun (2011). In their analysis of working class students studying for Level 2 and 3 childcare qualifications they found a disconnection between their cultural capital at home and that at college. Braun (2012), drawing on Bourdieu (1977), explains that habitus is, therefore 'always constituted in practice' but can be transformed by the social fields negotiated through a person's life course. It is therefore vital that schools create bridges between students' own positioning and the school's ethos so that they can explore their emerging identities in a rigorous way and develop as rounded individuals. The power relationships at play here must be acknowledged, as all education is a political act (Freire, 1998, p. 41). Therefore church school education should be concerned with formation rather than squashing (forcing to conform).

Rhea (2011, p. 8) suggests that a goal of effective Christian education is to enable students to form a discerned critique of the 'words, symbols, and images of the cultural texts' that surround them. A part of this must involve recognizing the Experimental, Participatory, Image-driven and Connected (EPIC) culture of children and young people (Sweet, 2000). Students have a variety of competing world-views and values which they need to negotiate on a daily basis. Young people are more connected than ever and the influences on them stretch far beyond their homes. Exploring these through the lens of a Christian world-view is not about proselytizing. As Rhea (2011, p. 14) says, it is the duty of a Christian education to equip students with the intellectual tools and disposition to consider fundamental questions, including those of faith and identity.

By the same token one can argue that each school has a culture which also needs to be discerned and critiqued. The social constructivist theory of Vygotsky (1978, p. 88) suggests these dispositions are themselves in part formed by the 'intellectual life of those around them', including teachers and fellow students. This poses a challenge to church schools, namely how to renew and invigorate the intellectual life of adults who work in them. For both Vygotsky (p. 88) and Bruner (1986, p. 72) language is the key mediating tool in this process. It is therefore imperative that schools develop a shared vocabulary to support this process of negotiated discernment. If, as Smith (2009, p. 26) suggests, education is about enabling students to know 'what they envision as the "the good life" or the ideal picture of human flourishing', then it follows that schooling needs to support students to interrogate the cultures that they encounter and develop strategies for accepting or rejecting different visions of 'the good life' and in turn create their own personal scripts. Arriving at a co-constructed description of 'the good life' is, therefore, a fundamental question of education.

The language of the state

Recent education policy in England, of both Labour and Coalition governments, has shunned such language. Rather, consecutive secretaries of state for education have categorized state education as something that needs to be 'fixed' (Helm, 2014). As Ball (1990, p. 31) points out, this 'discourse of derision' is nothing new. It finds its roots in a distrust of teachers' professionalism and, citing the need for accountability of their performance, has devised ever more instrumental tools, including inspections, league tables and performance-related pay, to garner acquiescence. A recent example of this can be seen in the intervention of Tristram Hunt MP, the shadow secretary of state for education, in his proposal of a new licensing system for teachers in January 2014. His stated intention is to 'allow the best [teachers] to advance and the worst to be weeded out, while bringing teachers' status closer to that of professions such as lawyers and doctors' (Helm, 2014). Since the late 1980s governments of all persuasions have blamed a significant proportion of the profession whose performance is perceived to be poor.

Twenty-two days after the Coalition government came to power in 2010, the General Teaching Council, the organization responsible for teachers' self-regulation, was disbanded, its powers now the fiefdom of the secretary of state for education. Further, the 2010 White Paper, *The Importance of Teaching*, while describing teaching as a 'noble profession' (p. 7) identified numerous shortcomings it wanted to address. These included: the existing teacher standards being unclear (p. 25); teacher weakness, unprofessional conduct and incompetence (pp. 25–6); passive professional development (p. 19); restrictions on classroom observation and monitoring (p. 24); out-of-date literacy teaching (pp. 24, 43); prospective teachers fearing for their safety in school (p. 32); poor behaviour in schools (pp. 32–33); bureaucratic Initial Teacher Education; and low entry standards for new teachers resulting in a less talented workforce than other sectors (pp. 20–21). Thus, a pattern emerges, whereby government pronouncements which appear to bolster the status of the teaching profession simultaneously contain a subtext of control and criticism. In this sense the language of the state can at best be seen as bifurcated and at worst duplicitous.

In contrast to this, schools maintain a vocational habitus (Braun, 2012; Vincent and Braun, 2011). Stanfield and Cremin (2012) suggest this does not sit comfortably with Conservative ideological interest. This can be seen in the current emphasis upon recruiting elite graduates/high flyers/ex-soldiers to the teaching profession. This sustains the discourse of derision by insinuating that the extant workforce is intellectually suspect and/or weak and/or ill-disciplined. As Braun (2012) argues, this ignores the traditionally vocational culture of the profession. Such schemes as 'troops to teachers', whatever their efficacy in real terms, positions the state as taking 'bold' action, again with the subtext of maintaining authority within the 'field' of education. This use of language does not sit comfortably with the ethos of Church of England schools. Central to the Christian faith is a commitment to love one's neighbour as oneself. For schools this can be expressed as having an ambition to see others thrive.

How far the language of the state has moved from one envisioning 'the good life' and individual thriving can be seen in the way that schools are now required to report on pupil attainment. This is conveyed in league tables based on attainment and progress in reading, writing and maths at primary school and by EBacc subjects: English, mathematics, history or geography, the sciences and a language in secondary. While important these are narrow measures and cannot describe a child as a whole. The challenge for school leaders is to hold in tension the requirement of the state and the needs of the children they serve. Often there is no such tension but when there is, they need to find a wise way forward. A topical example of this is the decision some schools made about entering their students early for their GCSE English after changes meant that only the students' first attempt would count in the school's league tables.

The role of the diocesan education officer

In the light of this, what do I perceive my role to be as an officer supporting church schools? And what are the challenges I face within it? Bishop Stephen Cottrell exploring Christian leadership drew on the 'parable of Trees' found in Judges 9.8–15 (Lewis-Anthony, 2013, p. 22). The parable explains how the olive tree, the fig tree and the vine were approached to lead but turned the role down as they produced important things of benefit to others.

Eventually the bramble is approached and is appointed as king over the trees, enabling those it reigns over to flourish. In a similar way I do not consider myself to be particularly exceptional but hope that by working alongside colleagues I can enable them, and in turn their schools and communities, to flourish.

I see my role as that of awakening in others the possibility of what a church school could be. Within this is an inherent challenge; people need to understand the value of what is being asked of them. Part of this involves having a long-term perspective that sees the developing ethos of a church school as something that matures over time. Working with whole staff groups, and governors where possible, is helpful as one is able to develop a shared understanding of what is meant by Christian distinctiveness across the whole school community. In addition, as an officer I need to understand each school I work with and be flexible enough to modify my training and resources to meet their specific needs. I also need to be open to criticism and to see the colleagues I work with as co-constructors of the materials I develop and refine. On a personal level there is also the challenge to 'practice what I preach' and therefore to live a life that reflects authentically the Christian life lived out in the everyday, to continue to deepen my faith, and to grow and learn in the process.

Conclusion

There is a story that Michelangelo was once asked about sculpture. He explained that it was quite simple. Inside each block of marble is a beautiful statue. All you need is a hammer and a chisel to get rid of the stone that is in the way. Zander (2012) describes this as an alternative theory of education: 'It is eye-to-eye, working together, to get rid of the stone that is in the way of that beautiful statue.' It is important that whatever pressures face me I do not lose sight of this vision in the people I encounter or teach each day.

Smith (2009, p. 26) regards high educational standards as central to Christian education. Striving for excellence and maximizing students' potential beyond exam results needs to be taken seriously. It is not an 'either/or' model but a 'both/and' one. Church schools enable this through their Christian world-view ensuring that training, transformation and transition lie at the heart of the education they offer (Zigarelli, 2012). A Christian vision for education should therefore centre on all reaching their God-given potential and on individuals being as ambitious for 'the other' as for themselves. The role of the diocesan education officer is, therefore, countercultural, agentive and properly empowering. By replacing the binary language of war with that of the dance, by encouraging individuals to take agency as they negotiate the competing zones of influence in their lives, and by challenging the narrow measure of educational success with a vision of living 'a good life' I hope to enable church schools to see themselves as a distinctive force for good. Having started my educational journey sceptical of the value of Church of England schools I now believe them to be treasures within our educational landscape.

Discussion Questions

1. What is education for?
2. Who is it education for?
3. Should church schools exist?
4. What can church schools offer that is different from other schools?
5. How can church schools claim to be inclusive and distinctive at the same time?

References

Ball, S., 1990, *Politics and policy making in education: Explorations in sociology* 33, Abingdon: Routledge

Bourdieu, P., 1977, *Outline of a theory of practice*, Cambridge: Cambridge University Press

Braun, A., 2012, 'Trainee teachers, gender and becoming the "right" person for the job: care and authority in the vocational habitus of teaching', in *Oxford Review of Education* 38.2, pp. 231–246

Bruner, J., 1986, *Actual minds, possible worlds*, Cambridge, MA: Harvard University Press

Calvin, J., 2008, *Institutes of the Christian religion*, H. Beveridge, trans., Peabody, MA: Hendrickson Publishing, originally published in 1536

Deem, R. and Lucas, L., 2007, 'Research and teaching cultures in two contrasting UK policy contextx: Academic life in education departments in five English and Scottish universities', in *Higher Education* 54: 115–133

Foster, R. and Helmers, K. A., 2008, *Life with God: A life-transforming new approach to Bible reading*, London: Hodder and Stoughton

Freire, P., 1998, *Pedagogy of the heart*, New York: The Continuum Publishing Company

Gunter, H. M. and Forrester, G., 2009, 'School leadership and education policy-making in England', in *Policy Studies* 30.5, pp. 495–511

Helm, T., 2014, 'Labour says new licensing plan will improve status of teachers: Unions have doubts but are ready to discuss proposals that aim to raise standards in the classroom', in *Guardian* 12 January 2014, www.theguardian.com/education/2014/jan/12/labour-licensing-teachers-plan-improve-status [accessed 20 February 2014]

Lakoff, G. and Johnson, M., 1980, *Metaphors we live by*, Chicago: University of Chicago Press

Lewis-Anthony, J., 2013, *You are the Messiah and I should know*, London: Bloomsbury

National Society, www.churchofengland.org/education/church-schools-academies.aspx [accessed 20 February 2014]

Olneck, M., 2000, 'Can multi-cultural education change what counts as cultural capital', in *American Educational Research Association Journal* 37, pp. 317–348

Raffo, C. and Hall, D., 2006, 'Transitions to becoming a teacher in an initial teacher education and training programme', in *British Journal of Sociology of Education*, 27.1, pp. 53–66

Rhea, B., 2011, 'Exploring Spiritual Formation in the Christian Academy: The dialects of Church, culture and the larger Integrative Task', in *Journal of Psychology and Theology* 39.1, pp. 3–15

Shortt, J., Smith D. and Cooling, T., 2000, 'Metaphor, Scripture and Education', in *Journal of Christian Education* 43.1, 22–28, www.staplefordcentre.org/files/files/Metaphor_Scripture_and_Education.pdf [accessed 19 February 2014]

Smith, J. K. A., 2009, *Desiring the kingdom: Worship, worldview and cultural formation*, Grand Rapids, MI: Baker Academic

Stanfield, J. and Cremin, H., 2012, 'Importing control in Initial Teacher Training: theorizing the construction of specific habitus in recent proposals for induction into teaching', in *Journal of Education Policy*, 28.1, pp. 21–37

Sweet, L., 2000, *Post-modern pilgrims: First century passion for the 21st century church*, Nashville: Broadman and Holman Publishing

Vincent, C. and Braun, A., 2011, '"I think a lot of it is common sense . . . " Early years' students, professionalism and the development of a "vocational habitus" in *Journal of Education Policy* 26.6, pp. 771–785

Vygotsky, L. S., 1978, *Mind in society: The development of higher mental processes*, Cambridge, MA: Harvard University Press

Zander, B., 2012, *B Work – How to give an A*, www.youtube.com/watch?feature=player_detailpageandv=qTKEBygQico [accessed 19 February 2014]

Zigarelli, M., 2012, 'Training, Transformation, and Transitioning: A Blueprint for a Christian University', in *Journal of Research on Christian Education* 21, pp. 62–79

11

The church school as a pilgrim community

JANET NORTHING

Abstract

The landscape of education has changed dramatically since the start of the new millennium and the need for church schools to be clear about their identity and role is essential. This is made clear in *The Church School of the Future Review* (Archbishops' Council and the National Society, 2012) that calls for church schools to be explicit about their Christian distinctiveness and ethos. Drawing on my experience within Christian ministry and primary school headship, this chapter explores the use of metaphor to draw out the unique features of a church primary school. Focusing on the church school as a pilgrim community, it explores the difference between the notion of pilgrims and tourists to suggest that the role of Christian educators is to translate Christian practice into Christian pedagogy.

Keywords

Pilgrim; tourist; hospitality; community; journey

Introduction

The new millennium has seen unprecedented changes take place in the landscape of education. These include the reduction in

Local Education Authority control; the academies programme; the creation of free schools; teacher's pay and conditions being linked to test results, and pupil behaviour. At times the perception of these reforms for those working within education has been characterized by an increasing sense of fragmentation and lack of cohesion. Against this backdrop, the need for church schools to be clear about their identity and role in a new and evolving education system has become paramount. This point is made clear in the *Church School of the Future Review* which states that, 'At a time of educational change and challenge, the need to be unambiguous and explicit about the key characteristics of church schools becomes a priority' (2012, p. 15).

It was just over 200 years ago that the Church of England recognized the need to provide education for the poor in every parish in the country. At its outset the two key characteristics of this provision were first, that the education church schools provided should be distinctively Christian, and second that it must be inclusive. Today this inclusiveness can be interpreted by the manner in which church schools welcome those from different faith backgrounds or none, different ethnicities, children with special educational needs, those with a range of disabilities, gifted and talented pupils as well as those from a complete span of socio-economic backgrounds.

Believing in the church school ethos and the positive contribution it makes to education within an increasingly secular and relativist culture, I feel it appropriate to add my thoughts to the debate around the distinctiveness of provision that a church school offers. As a worshipping Christian traditionalist in the Anglican Church, my epistemological stance is shaped by a range of life experiences, including that of being headteacher of a Church of England primary school for over six years and an inspector of Anglican schools for the National Society. In this chapter I use a theological paradigm and a critical realist view of knowledge to explore the use of metaphor. My aim is to draw out a perception of the unique features of a church primary school that I believe correlate to a pilgrim community. I then go on to compare this briefly with other contemporary models of a church school.

The pilgrim metaphor is not necessarily the first image that comes to mind when considering education in general and Christian education in particular. However the concepts of pilgrim and pilgrimage do have significant biblical roots and these will be explored further in this chapter. In discussing the application of biblical metaphors to an educational context Smith and Shortt (2002, p. 120) make this point:

Metaphors encode the expectations we have of the educational process. They play an important role in shaping and expressing our basic vision. If metaphors are not water lilies on a pond, decorative and opaque, but can instead be windows through which the light of a particular vision of reality is refracted, then an exploration of how metaphors can refract a biblical vision is of considerable significance to Christian educators.

Although not applying the pilgrim metaphor to a school context, the Church of England in its publication *Children in the Way* (1988) explored the pilgrim model of the Church, with children as fellow travellers: 'Those involved on the journey are inextricably bound up one with the other. All are in some way responsible one for the other, all are learning, all are sharing in the communal life' (1988 p. 34).

A further example of the manner in which the pilgrimage metaphor gives recognition to the fact that the Christian nurture of children involves a partnership between the Church, family and school is found in the *Church of England Children's Strategy* presented to the General Synod in 2003, which stated that:

The Church's primary aim for children is their spiritual development that they should come to worship, know and love God in sacrament and through personal prayer in pilgrimage with other Christians in a way suitable to their age, culture and stage of faith. (Archbishops' Council, 2003, p. 7)

From a Christian perspective the notion of pilgrimage can be understood in various ways. The first as a literal physical journey to a holy place linked to the life of Christ or one of the saints; the second as an allegorical view of life that is ultimately completed at its journey's end in heaven; and third in a purely spiritual sense that places value on the part human experience plays in the development of spiritual maturity. While each is distinct they all have in common a sense of movement towards transformation and wholeness. This, I suggest, is also the aim of Christian education within the setting of a church school: 'The church school offers a spiritual and moral basis for the development of human wholeness . . . here we can begin to discover who we are, why we are, and perhaps most importantly – what we might be' (Archbishops' Council, 2001, p. 15). For me, a sense of pilgrimage lies at the heart of a church school, for it takes the community who belong to it on a journey that goes beyond the literal and physical dimensions of education. This distinctiveness of provision epitomized in the metaphor of a pilgrim community is an area I will now explore in more detail.

At the outset of our metaphorical journey we must acknowledge that the concept of pilgrimage is, of course, not exclusively Christian. All major world religions have their famous pilgrimage sites that, for a variety of reasons, hold special significance to believers. In all major religions the focus of a pilgrimage involves a journey or exploration of moral or spiritual magnitude. 'Pilgrims are persons in motion passing through territories not their own seeking something we might call completion, or perhaps clarity will do as well, a goal to which only the spirit's compass points the way' (Niebuhr, 1984, pp. 4, 7).

The starting point for a pilgrim's journey will be different for each individual. Some will start from a position of faith while others may hope to find faith or meaning along the way. This means that the objective behind pilgrimage involves a pilgrim in both physical and spiritual activity. Pilgrimage is not centred around rest and recreation, a fact that immediately sets the pilgrim apart from tourists or travellers whose motivation for moving from place to place may be due to other factors entirely. To set out on a pilgrimage is to throw down a challenge to everyday life. Its prime purpose is to find oneself and to return home changed and made more whole as a result of the experiences one has had along the way. Similarly, Christian education can be compared to a journey that itself offers the potential opportunity for the development of human wholeness: 'For the pilgrimage that is Christian education we . . . need to know where we are, and where we shall be going' (Astley and Day, 1992, p. 13).

A current and frequently used metaphor for the Christian spiritual journey used by Donnelly (1992) suggests that there are five marked distinctions to be made between pilgrims and another metaphor alluded to earlier, that of tourist. While in this chapter distinctions are made between these two metaphors, I am also aware that these can also be transitional themes throughout our lives. Sometimes in one context we may fulfil the role of pilgrim and in another that of tourist, neither are these necessarily fixed positions: 'anything that upsets the fixed programme of the tourist brings a threat of insecurity. And it is from the streets of insecurities that the pilgrims gather, in the marketplaces of the world, seeking fountains of "maybe" faith' (Fahey, 2002, p. 218).

This dichotomy between pilgrims and tourists is explored further by Woodiwiss (2011) in the context of first-year undergraduate students in an American institute of higher education. Using six of the nine characteristics of a tourist put forward by the British sociologist John Urry, Woodiwiss likens their college experience to that of a tourist. In response he set up a project at Erskine College designed to move students beyond what Urry refers to as the *tourist gaze* (2002) to an attitude more consistent with the search for a Christian identity. Similarly, while teaching secondary school students David Smith a teacher of modern languages, became aware that the pedagogy he delivered in the classroom was exclusively focused on preparing students to be tourists in a foreign land rather than on the Christian practice of hospitality. In the context of learning a modern language, the skills of language acquisition had become inextricably linked to a means of self-gratification rather than focusing on the Christian notion of serving others. Both Woodiwiss and Smith recognized the potential impact of language and context on the spiritual journey.

The problems faced by Woodiwiss around cultural context and age profile are, I believe, naturally overcome within the context of a primary school. In my experience as a headteacher, the culture of a church primary school naturally has a strong sense of family or community about it due largely to the fact that children, along with their families, spend seven of their formative years learning, eating, worshipping and playing together.

In using the metaphor of pilgrim community to represent the church school, I propose to use Donnelly's distinctions and apply the image of tourist in a similarly metaphorical way to support my belief that the distinctiveness of a church school education lies in the way it allows for the community to be transformed from tourists into pilgrims. The journey that is pilgrimage in this context relates specifically to the time a child spends in primary school, 'where faith is lived and which therefore offer opportunities to pupils and their families to explore the truths of the Christian faith' (Archbishops' Council, 2001, 3.12, p. 11).

So as we begin our journey the first distinction is to ascertain that a pilgrim is aware that there is an inward dimension to the journey. In this way a more allegorical interpretation of pilgrimage can be applied that recognizes there is more to the journey than that which is perceived by the senses. The tourist meanwhile settles for the more literal interpretation (Urry, 2002). For the tourist the journey is a leisure activity and they do not set out with the intention of being changed inwardly. In my experience, within the setting of a church school, daily acts of collective worship are pivotal moments in the life of the community providing opportunities for prayer and reflection. In the majority of church primary schools, collective worship focuses on Christian values made distinctive through biblical links and the life of Christ. The major Christian festivals are celebrated and the Church's liturgical seasons followed, so providing opportunities for the development of a personal spirituality, an understanding of the central place of Jesus Christ and a Christian understanding of God as Father, Son and Holy Spirit (Archbishops' Council, 2013). The church school community also has a daily prayer life with prayers being said at meal times and before going home and areas within classrooms are set aside for prayer and reflection. It is perhaps not surprising therefore that former Archbishop of Canterbury (2002–2012) Rowan Williams should describe the church school as a 'kind of church' (Astley, 2002), a viewpoint that I will return to later.

Second, pilgrims invest something of themselves on the journey. However, to set out on a pilgrimage involves putting aside time and energy for both planning and completing it. Pilgrimage has a different focus; it is not the same as holiday. For a pilgrim the reality lies in the re-creation made possible by the experience of the journey. A Christian pilgrim is concerned with ridding themselves of peripheral distractions in order to obtain a new identity with Jesus Christ taking centre stage. For the pilgrim the journey provides the space and time to put life into perspective. In biblical terms this is beautifully narrated in the Emmaus story found in Luke 24.13–33. Following the dreadful events of the crucifixion, two of Jesus' disciples head away from Jerusalem leaving everything behind them. As the disciples travel, a stranger joins them, walking beside them on the road. The journey allows time for different relationships to develop and new understandings to emerge. The disciples had set out on their journey with downcast faces, as men without hope and yet, motivated by love of a fellow pilgrim, they offer hospitality to the stranger. As they share a meal together they ultimately recognize Jesus in the breaking of bread. This episode is filled with Lucan theological motifs identified by Fitzmyer (1985, p. 1558) that are helpful in understanding the transformative potential of the journey that is often only fully realized at the journey's end, when the pilgrim becomes aware that they have a new perspective on that which perhaps had seemed insurmountable before. The geographical setting of the road to Emmaus, the revelation of the risen Christ to the journeying disciples whose recognition of him comes not from sight but with eyes of faith, and the fact that it is at the point of returning home that the disciples fully comprehend who Jesus is and are able to make sense of what has happened to them are all key features of the narrative.

In a similar way, a child who spends their formative years in a church school community will experience a distinctively Christian interpretation of what it means to be human as they travel through school. This will have a profound impact on their perception of themselves as a unique human being, precious and loved by God, and positively inform what they go on to become. As the *Church School of the Future Review* states: 'The enabling of every child to flourish in their potential as a child of God is a sign and expression of the kingdom and is at the heart of the church's distinctive mission' (2012, p. 3).

It also provides a spiritual and moral foundation for children to begin to formulate a values system that will help them to make informed decisions about what matters in life and what is secondary.

A third distinction is to be found in the way a pilgrim's intention is to be affected by the journey to such an extent that there is an element of transformation that occurs. Journeying is a recurring theme in the Bible and includes Abraham's call to leave his own home and set off for a place that God would reveal to him, the desert wanderings of the Israelites, the journey to Bethlehem by Mary and Joseph, along with their flight into Egypt. The supreme example, of course, is to be found in the life of Christ, the perfect pilgrim, exemplified in the events of his passion and resurrection. Within the Old Testament one account in particular features transformation as a result of hospitality. Genesis 18.1–15 recounts how, in the heat of the day, three strangers suddenly appear in front of Abraham at the door of his tent. He asks them to break their journey in order that he may wash their feet and give them food and water that they may refresh themselves before continuing on their way. Abraham welcomes them as special people even though they are complete strangers. His concern centres round his desire to ensure that when these men continue their journey, their experience of his hospitality will impact positively on their condition both physically and spiritually. When they are ready to leave, Abraham travels with them to see them on their way. Hospitality involves a desire to ensure that people leave in a better condition than when they arrive and while these changes may occur in the life of a tourist they are not necessarily planned or expected. Similarly, in the Gospel narratives we read how Jesus places special importance on the giving and receiving of hospitality, particularly when it is directed towards those considered the least important members of society. In biblical times children too were included in this category, and in Mark 9.33–37 we see demonstrated the inclusive nature of God's grace in Jesus' acceptance of the child as a model pilgrim when he says, 'Whoever receives one such child in my name receives me; and whoever receives me, receives not me but him who sent me' (Mark 9.37). In this context Jesus rebukes the ambitious nature of the disciples by pointing to children as examples of trust. The point is made that in the same way that children know they can never earn the gifts they are given, no more can the disciples earn their place in the kingdom of God (Mann, 1986, p. 377). While the aim of a church school is not to convert children to Christianity, there is little doubt that the love, nurture and hospitality that they receive as part of their journey through school will have an impact on their lives, enabling them in turn to make informed choices about the type of person they want to be and the values system that they wish to live by.

Our fourth distinction is acknowledging that for the pilgrim both the journey and the arrival are of equal importance. For those engaging in pilgrimage the internal dimension of the journey is very often not fully revealed until it is over and the pilgrim returns home. A biblical example to illustrate this can perhaps be found in the Gospel accounts of the transfiguration of Jesus (Matthew 17.1–8). Jesus takes three of his disciples up to a high mountain and there he is transfigured before them, appearing with Moses and Elijah. Peter speaks saying, 'Lord, it is well that we are here; if you wish I will make three booths here, one for you and one for Moses and Elijah.' Peter thinks that the glorious messianic kingdom has arrived and is therefore reluctant to move on and come back down the mountain. In these moments Peter is perhaps tempted to adopt the *tourist gaze* but Jesus uses this glimpse of glory to strengthen the disciples for the events of the passion soon to unfold. Times of spiritual transformation are given for a reason and it is in the returning home that their impact can be fully understood and appreciated. This is in contrast to the tourist whose major delight is in being away on location and sometimes the return home is not so well anticipated. In the context of a church school it is important that children be equipped with the skills and knowledge they need for the journey in order that they do not lose interest along the way. The essence of a church school pilgrim community lies in the promotion of a Christian pedagogy that views everyone as learners. In putting forward its 'Pilgrim Church Model' (Archbishops' Council, 1988, p. 34) it is suggested that:

> As in a pilgrim group, the young may find some situations easier to surmount than their elders. Sometimes they lead the way and are not always the followers-on. The pilgrim model suggests learning from shared experience and shared stories. It implies developing new skills, adapting and changing attitudes, and looking for new visions.

Within the context of a pedagogy that now focuses much more on drawing out children's ideas, helping them to extend their knowledge base and explore their experiences, I believe this pilgrim church model could equally be applied to a church primary school.

A fifth and final difference between pilgrims and tourists lies in the formation of community. While tourists may be content to experience things alone or in a chosen group, pilgrims consciously construct community and make connections with each other as they journey together: 'A spiritual community comes into being with ties of faith stronger than ties of one's own family of origin' (Donnelly, 1992, p. 7). Profoundly, the church school is ultimately a community where the Christian faith is made both visible and tangible. In discussing the characteristics of a church school, Purnell (1995, p. 131) comments on the kind of challenge which the community accepts when it becomes church in a school setting, and that the aim of the school is therefore directed 'at meeting pupils where they are on their faith journeys and, in the light and power of the gospel, at accompanying them on their way towards becoming fully human.'

Having applied the metaphor of pilgrim community to a church school I will now briefly turn my attention to other theological models that have been used to describe such a community, three of which are referred to by Worsley in his summative reflection (2013, p. 263 onwards). As mentioned earlier, when he was Archbishop of Canterbury, Rowan Williams described a church school as 'a kind of church' (Astley, 2002). While there are some obvious similarities to be drawn, equally there are many differences not least of all in the purpose of the buildings: a church being a place set aside for public worship and a school for education; a church being a fellowship of believers and a church school a place for followers of the Christian faith, other faiths or no faith whatsoever. Perhaps, though, there is one sense in which this description is an accurate one, for the metaphors of pilgrim and tourist both validly represent the extremes of Christian commitment and spirituality. There are pilgrims who are committed, involved, seeking transformation and community; and there are also those who are uncommitted, uninvolved and who form the tourist population of church congregations in our country (Donnelly, 1992, p. 9).

In describing the church school as a 'threshold community' Astley (2002, pp. 6–15) cites the French theologian Bouteiller who describes those at the edge of the church as 'threshold Christians'. This metaphor is further applied to a church school setting by Worsley (2013) who makes the point that the threshold position can mean different things depending on where people are in their understanding of the Christian narrative: 'The Church school is not merely about the Church's influence in finding a new generation of people to boost its own membership, but it offers a threshold of free entry and free exit. People can travel in either direction' (Worsley, 2013, p. 268).

In comparing the two metaphors of 'pilgrim community' and 'threshold community' there would appear to be considerable differences in understanding. Using the earlier comparisons of pilgrim and tourist it could be argued that in enabling members of the community to position themselves on the margins, a church school could perhaps be encouraging the *tourist gaze* to predominate in its Christian ethos. In suggesting that 'movement across thresholds is an on-going process for the learning person', Worsley (2013, p. 269) makes a valid pedagogical point. In my experience as a headteacher, individual members of the school community have the freedom to move both towards and away from faith within the pilgrim model but, by definition, the momentum of the community as a whole can only be forward as opposed to the more static image of a threshold community.

A further metaphor to describe a church school is that of family or covenant community. In its report *Going for Growth* (2010, p. 1) the Archbishops' Council of the Church of England states that: 'The task of Christian nurture must be seen not only in domestic terms, as something taking place within families and generations of the Church, but also within the larger context of the Church's universal mission to humanity.'

Not without limitations in terms of its potential to be exclusive and self-centred, the experience of family life for some may mean that this model does not carry entirely positive connotations. In contemporary British society children's experience of family is diverse and often fragmented due to marriage breakdown, conflict and sometimes violence within the family unit. In the image of the Church as a family of God there are some attractive ideals to be expressed around dependence and nurture. In discussing the family model, Worsley (2013, p. 264) describes the family environment as 'the most open and safe place in which to learn, because it is a place of love'. While this is the ideal, sadly it is not always the experience of young children. In showing prospective parents round my school I often described my school community as operating in the same way as a family. As is customary in a family unit within the setting of a home each member of the family has their own place at the table for meals and in a similar way each child in the school sat in the same place every day to eat their lunch. Teachers knew not only the children in their own class but also all the other children in the school, and as headteacher I knew each child by name and their parents too. We spent our days together, living and learning in an inclusive community with shared Christian values. Everyone was different but everyone was valued and whether children had a faith or not they received the same nurture and hospitality – in short they were treated as model pilgrims. To describe a church school, particularly one catering for the primary age range, as a family is, I believe, appropriate though it cannot be taken for granted that a Christian understanding of the family is the universal experience of all children or adults.

The final model is that of the church school as a 'meeting place'. Within this context hospitality again features as a key aspect of engagement. In the Old Testament the Israelite tent sanctuary was also known as the 'tent of meeting' or Tabernacle. It was the central place of worship, a shrine housing the Ark of the Covenant and as such it was frequently a place of revelation. It represented the visible sign of God's presence among his people Israel. Once constructed it became the place where God communicated with Moses. Throughout the journey from Mount Sinai to the Promised Land the Tabernacle was taken down and it accompanied the people wherever they travelled. Wherever they stopped to make camp the Tabernacle was erected once more so it became a constant feature of their journey. A model therefore deeply rooted in Jewish tradition, it links closely to the concept of the church school as a pilgrim community with its focus on journeying. The Tabernacle was a visual reminder that God was with his people throughout the time they were wandering in the desert. 'As a meeting place, the Church school is clear about its Christian ethos as a place from which it derives its values' (Worsley, 2013, p. 266). Interestingly, as a SIAMS inspector (Statutory Inspection of Anglican and Methodist Schools), I recently inspected a small church school and was customarily given a tour by the head boy and girl. As the tour continued the children took me outside and there in the grounds was a very large tepee. They explained that it was special place within the school where children and adults alike could come to find peace on their journey through the school day. As a meeting place the church school is the embodiment of acceptance rather than tolerance and a place where the incarnate Jesus once more embraces the child as model pilgrim.

Having briefly considered several other models in the light of the church school as pilgrim community it would appear that the notion of life as a journey is a concept that most people would appreciate and be familiar with. For some children and their families part of this journey takes place within the context of a church school and although not a church it is nevertheless a community of faith. As such the church school must fulfil its remit to 'reflect the nature of the Trinity' (Archbishops' Council, 2001, p. 14) which is the supreme example of God who is in relationship. It is my belief that the church school is a pilgrim community in the sense that as Christian educators we are involved in translating Christian practice into Christian pedagogy as we seek to move children from tourists to pilgrims (Woodiwiss, 2011, p. 127).

Discussion Questions

1. Do metaphors have a universal meaning or have they become open to relativist interpretation?
2. To what extent can a church school be a Christian community?
3. In what ways might it be appropriate to think of pupils in a Church of England primary school as pilgrims?
4. Although not a church to what extent is a church school a community of faith?
5. Could the pilgrim model be equally applied to a secondary school?

References

Archbishops' Council, 1988, *Children in the Way: New Directions for the Church's Children*, London: Church House Publishing

Archbishops' Council, 2001, *The Way Ahead: Church of England Schools in the New Millennium*, London: Church House Publishing

Archbishops' Council, 2003, *Sharing the Good News with Children: The Church of England Children's Strategy*, London: Church House Publishing

Archbishops' Council, 2010, *Going for Growth: Transformation of Children, Young People and the Church*, London: Church House Publishing

Archbishops' Council, 2012, *The Church School of the Future Review*, London: Church House Publishing

Archbishops' Council, 2013, *The Evaluation Schedule for the Statutory Inspection of Anglican and Methodist Schools*, London: National Society

Astley, J. and Day, D. (eds), 1992, *The Contours of Christian Education*, Essex: McCrimmons

Astley, J., 2002, 'Church schools and the theology of Christian Education', in *Journal of the Association of Anglican Secondary School Heads*, 10

Department for Children, Schools and Families, 2007, *Faith in the System*, Nottingham: DCSF

Donnelly, D., 1992, 'Pilgrims and Tourists: Conflicting Metaphors for the Christian Journey to God', in *Spirituality Today*, 44.1, pp. 20–36

Fahey, F., 2002, 'Pilgrims or Tourists?', in *The Furrow*, 53.4, pp. 213–218

Fitzmyer, J., 1985, *The Anchor Bible: The Gospel According to Luke 10–24*, New York: Doubleday

Mann, C. S., 1986, *The Anchor Bible – Mark*, New York: Doubleday

Niebuhr, R., 1984, 'Pilgrims and Pioneers', in *Parabola: The Magazine of Myth and Tradition*, Fall: 9.3, pp. 4, 7

Purnell, P., 1995, *Our Faith Story: Its Telling and Sharing*, London: Collins

Smith, D. and Carvill, B., 2000, *The Gift of the Stranger: Faith, Hospitality and Foreign Language Learning*, Grand Rapids, MI: Eerdmans

Smith, D. and Shortt, J., 2002, *The Bible and the Task of Teaching*, Nottingham: The Stapleford Centre

Urry, J., 2002, *The Tourist Gaze*, London: Sage

Woodiwiss, A., 2011, 'From Tourists to Pilgrims: Christian Practices and the First-Year Experience', in Smith, D. and Smith, J. (eds), *Teaching and Christian Practices*, Grand Rapids, MI: Eerdmans, pp. 123–139

Worsley, H. (ed.), 2013, *Anglican Church School Education: Moving Beyond the First Two Hundred Years*, London: Bloomsbury

12

A reflection on decision-making in an inclusive Church of England primary school

JOAN GIBSON

Abstract

The role of primary school headteacher has developed significantly since the 1944 Act with its emphasis on reading, writing and arithmetic. In 2003, *Every Child Matters* (DfE) made the wider role explicit. Staying safe and healthy, active participation and a focus on economic well-being became the core functions of the primary school alongside enjoying learning and achieving well in reading, writing and arithmetic. As school leaders were responding to Lord Lamming's report, the impact of another piece of legislation extended the agenda. The *Denham Report*, a response to riots in 2001, led to schools being required to promote community cohesion. Community cohesion became part of the Ofsted inspection framework. This chapter concerns one school's response to working in this climate. It proposes an inclusive and humble approach to education.

Keywords

Professionalism; humility; community cohesion; faithfulness; accountability

Introduction

In the daily life of a school, the headteacher is faced with translating a vision into operational decisions. There are checks and balances to ensure accountability: the governing body, the Local Authority, the auditors, the Diocesan Board and Ofsted all have their mechanisms for checking up on how things are working out. Perhaps the fiercest critique of this process is made by the headteacher in self-evaluation. This chapter is a reflection on the thinking behind one headteacher's vision for a school community and how it was used to arrive at some of those operational decisions. It starts with a view of professionalism and its impact on the actions of the headteacher and then considers the implications of that headteacher holding a Christian faith in a school with an Anglican foundation. Finally a case study is used to give a contextualized view of what it was like to be part of that community.

Who am I professionally?

The certificate to accredit me with the national professional qualification for headship (NPQH) was signed on 7 September 1999, by the secretary of state for education, David Blunkett. I was part of the first cohort of aspiring school leaders to take this qualification and felt very proud and empowered by the experience. The emphasis of the training course, leading to accreditation for the post, was on the importance of establishing a strategic vision in order to clarify the rationale for implementing operational decisions. In essence, my passion was to create an inclusive community where every child knew that they were members of the school family, that we would all aspire to learn together and we would support each other along the way according to our particular strengths. I have an image of my time in headship as a book: *The Headteacher Standards and Diocesan Expectations* could be seen as the contents page of the book announcing that it was about some children, some teachers, some families, their community and the legislation written to shape the activity. The title of the book was our agreed vision, the author the headteacher. The book is a novel, not a primer, as that is how the headteacher wrote it. The children were responsible for the twists and turns in the plot as they arrived into the story with such an amazing array of mini sagas to be fitted into the title, the vision. The strength of having an agreed vision or ethos within a school lies in being able to meet the various initiatives for change and using them to develop the vision rather than being buffeted by them. The Headteacher Standards interpreted by NPQH and diocesan expectations were a starting point for me in my first headship in 1999 but there was bound to be new legislation to supplement, refocus and contradict them. Change is an accepted norm within the world of education. 'Schools are like litmus paper, reflecting the state of society, and this places teachers in a highly vulnerable position. There is great temptation for them to draw back from changes that might endanger their fragile position' (Watson and Ashton, 1995, p. 11). The hope was that, in establishing a strong sense of purpose within the school community, demands made by central government for change could be accommodated. The school community would have a clear sense of the local context and its priorities and would be able to fit the tidal wave of new initiatives to the school community rather than being overwhelmed and reactive.

In putting a case for seeing the role of headteacher as one holding professional status, the assumption is not wholly uncontroversial. As an occupational group within a particular political landscape, professionalization of teaching can be understood as a political project (Whitty, 2003). Public perceptions of the profession are varied: 'The status of teachers, in the public eye, was more commonly deemed equivalent to that of social workers rather than doctors, although 10 per cent of the sample likened primary and secondary headteachers to doctors in social status' (DfES Research Report RS 755). The case for the professionalization of teachers in the UK in the early 2000s is not the focus of the argument but sets the scene for the operational dilemma to be considered. The assumptions being made in this chapter align with the case made by Hoyle (1995) in seeing professionalization as a hypothetical continuum dependent on the government of the day and the context of a particular culture. My understanding of the role of headteacher as part of a profession was derived from the particular landscape forming the backdrop to my career. The introduction of the NPQH was part of the policy landscape which formed that view. Furthermore, the perspective being considered is a personal one, which considers professionalism as a moral dilemma (Carr, 2000), a set of standards of behaviour (Helsby, 1995), which form a rationale to defend operational decisions in the workplace.

In reflecting on the way that an understanding of professionalism shapes operational decisions, Hoyle's view of the professional resonates with me: 'I take the view that one of the defining characteristics of members of a profession is the ability to function effectively in uncertain and indeterminate situations' (Hoyle, 2008, p. 285). Those 'indeterminate situations' are placed in a particular context which draws upon specific cultural references. I have accepted a post, which entails providing 'professional leadership'. The nature of professionalism and the public perception of it are subject to the context of time, culture and political policy. If I can establish a sense of my own professional identity, at least those around me will know who is leading them and whether they wish to be part of the particular journey. Perhaps knowledge of that identity will enable us to decide what the loaves and stones look like.

During the period that I was in post, the level of autonomy over operational decisions seemed relatively great. Within the last decade the move towards a culture of performativity (Ball, 2003) is reflected in the syllabus of NPQH where raising standards is given much higher priority. One is able to calculate the precise penalty, in terms of data and consequent Ofsted grade, for taking a decision to admit a child/children into school when they are likely to struggle to deliver particular levels of attainment and/or progress in reading, writing and arithmetic. In terms of diocesan inspections, there is a formula, related to attainment data, which limits the grade given to a school for its Christian character. The repercussions of this are considered in the case study.

The revised Ofsted framework in 2014 changed the relationship between schools and central government in its single-minded focus on a particular data set of results derived from testing children in National Curriculum years 2 and 6. This could arguably be seen as a move towards what Helsby (1995) describes as proletarianization of the role of school leader. Less flexibility and autonomy is given to school leaders as the state institutes powers to take control of schools that do not conform to the revised inspection framework. This framework accords greater weight to progress data in English and mathematics than was previously the case when schools were working towards the 5 Outcomes of *Every Child Matters* (DfE, 2003). If the proportion of children who do not conform to national expectations in terms of attainment data exceeds a particular threshold, state intervention in the form of a move to compulsory academy status results. The mechanism for this intervention is clear. However, the mechanism for professionals to evaluate both the educational value for the actual children within the school and the professionalism of the leaders is much less clearly defined. A new dilemma emerges. Times change. Attainment data has assumed a new importance. School priorities can be seen as more the domain of the state than the school.

In shifting the focus firmly onto attainment, the revision of the Teachers' Standards had an impact on the scope of decisions that school leaders could take and modified the level of professional autonomy within the school. Bryan (2012) identifies the heritage of the revision to two historical stories: the standards and accountability movement and a shift towards a post secular state. The standards movement has its genesis, claims Bryan, in James Callaghan's speech at Ruskin College in 1976 where the concept of educational standards first made its appearance in the public domain. The problematic nature of defining and maintaining standards in a 'post-modern condition of pluralism and moral relativism, has given rise to the perceived need by the state to take control of the education system' (Bryan, 2012, p. 220). Alongside the standards agenda, Bryan puts a case for, 'the New Teacher Standards [being] constructed from a post secular perspective, where the relationship between values, religion, faith and teachers' work has been recast' (Bryan, 2012, p. 222).

The revised inspection framework emphasizes a level of rigour over attainment in mathematics and English which will not always sit comfortably with some school leaders' understanding of British values. Some tensions arise which will be illustrated in the case study.

Who am I spiritually?

He has shown you, O mortal, what is good.
And what does the Lord require of you?
To act justly and
To love mercy and
To walk humbly with your God.
Micah 6.8

Within the school's Anglican foundation, how will we fulfil our mission so that, 'Every child should be enabled to flourish in their potential as a child of God, as a sign and expression of the Kingdom'? (National Society, *A framework for inspection and self-evaluation of Church of England and Methodist schools*, revised version, November 2012).

Earlier, I suggested a metaphor of school life as a novel where the mission of the community was the title and the scope of the content was a combination of the headteacher standards and diocesan expectations. Let me extend the fanciful notion and think of allowing the children to take charge of the twists and turns of the story. I, or at least headteacher me, will claim authorship of the tale. It will be a work of fiction and not a primer because the book is about the fascinating process of educating children, their childish anecdotes, their future careers, their growing confidence to manipulate words and numbers, paint and ideas. The genre of the novel is values based. Both the diocesan expectations and the push towards promoting values in the revision of the teacher standards support the notion that values are an inherent part of the role of school leaders: 'I have no difficulty in accepting that all study, whether of the humanities or of the pure and applied sciences, must take place in a values context' (Kenworthy, 1995, Foreword).

I propose using humility as an appropriate vehicle to demonstrate that the school is distinctively and recognizably Christian. The choice of humility arises from a combination of professional self-reflection and a consideration of my understanding of faithfulness. The practical implications of the choice will be seen in the case study. The proposal is not without its problems as Hare articulates: 'Until very recently, modern virtue ethics in the secular tradition was largely indifferent to or even hostile to the character disposition of humility' (Hare, 1996, p. 235).

Hare outlines the philosophical problems describing a potential paradox when considering humility as a virtue. Humility will strongly affirm the equal moral worth of all and yet people vary in their moral ability with some being described as morally superior. The attraction to humility as a virtue in leadership is the sense of perspective it can offer. Teacher Standards and Ofsted frameworks will be revised but the belief that all children are equal before God is a less shifting notion that a Christian leader can rely upon. It does not help to resolve curriculum planning issues or negate the commitment to teaching children to be the most fluent, engaged readers they can be but, and it is a big but for me, it puts academic attainment into perspective. To overemphasize the worth of getting a particular number of marks in a test when a child is six years old seems to me to be giving them a stone when bread is required.

A problematic area in considering humility as a virtue is the possibility that the person regarding themselves to be humble may also regard themselves as having a superior sense of what matters and become contemptuous of the values of others (Hare, 1996). This accords strongly with some of the tensions I felt during some school inspections where the balance between elements of school life was difficult to reconcile with the aims of our inclusive school, 'Or perhaps humility is not a disposition to compare oneself with others at all, but rather a disposition to take a very modest view of oneself simply in relation to some transcendent and super-personal standard, such as God or some ideal' (Hare, 1996, p. 237).

The potential dichotomy between humility and vanity, in assuming moral superiority, has had a strong resonance for me at many points in school leadership. Kellenberger (2010) discusses the many negative elements of humility pointing out that Aristotle, if he acknowledged it at all, regarded humility as a vice. Nevertheless, Kellenberger goes on to discuss humility and religion and notes that: 'In the theistic traditions, religious humility is understood to have within itself an *awareness* of God, as well as oneself as one is and of oneself in relation to God. Given this awareness, humility on the part of those with it is not only proper, being a virtue, but realistic' (Kellenberger, 2010, p. 333).

Kellenberger gives an example of a rock climber looking up at the mountain in awe and humility. This is a realistic view. Similarly, for a Christian leader, humility in the face of the task before God, is realistic: 'Perhaps religious humility is also pragmatic, useful and fulfilling. Whether it is or not, from the standpoint of the self-understanding of the religious (or those who aspire to religious humility), religious humility is realistic, and if its internal awareness is true awareness, then those with religious humility ultimately are truly realistic' (Kellenberger, 2010, p. 333).

This is the touching point for me between a view of professionalism and the desire to fulfil a professional role as a Christian. When operational decisions need to be taken, there is no exemplar script available, but to seek to answer humbly within the professional landscape of one's current school culture gives a sense of strength. It is highly likely that self-doubt and challenge from external agencies such as Ofsted will form part of the landscape, but in terms of aiming towards demonstrating a distinctively Christian school environment, there is a thread of consistency.

A case study

How does professional, Christian me, walk the walk?

A parent of an eight-year-old child (let's call her Mary) has made an appointment to see me. Mum is an articulate woman with a background in the health service, which supports her in her parenting skills. She is very anxious about her daughter as she is not attending school having been taken out of her local primary school and removed from an independent school in a nearby city. The Local Authority is suggesting a place in a pupil referral unit for children with hard-to-manage behaviours but this does not seem like a sensible option to Mum. First, there is a view from a psychologist that Mary is exhibiting some challenging behaviour, possibly as a result of early childhood trauma preceding her adoption, and that a sensible course of action is to show her plenty of firm but fair and consistent love to help her on her way. Second, there is an inconsistency in Mary's behaviour; in some settings, Mary is compliant, sweet natured and helpful; in others she is aggressive, both physically and verbally.

Will we accept Mary into our school?
What goes through the mind of the headteacher?
Our school takes eight-year-olds . . .

Here is an eight-year-old in a supportive family. There are a number of reasons that could explain Mary's current predicament. Once her initial school placement started to go awry, a steady spiral of negative events may have reinforced the inappropriate behaviour. When this was followed by attendance at a very structured setting where there were very high expectations, it is possible that Mary could not meet them . . .

The ethos in our school aims to support all learners and we have a lot of expertise between us in helping children who have come unstuck.

Oh, and let's be honest, I'd love a chance to work with such an intriguing young lady.

But . . .

Mary's contribution to our measurable data such as attainment in mathematics and English at the end of Key Stage Two is highly likely to be negative.

The family live out of the county so we are by no means the nearest school of our designation. Mary is already at the end of year 4 (two years is not long to make an impact and Ofsted require Mary to make progress over an observed lesson). Mary has no label to explain her current failure, no funding will be available and this child is certain to be high maintenance both in terms of cash and professional sense of humour.

And yet . . . this child is a child. There are not many options available to her and her family and I have the possibility of giving it a try . . . so . . . that is how Mary came to be part of the team. Night terrors: is critical realism self-serving? Do Ofsted represent The Truth? Am I giving bread? Removing the plank from my eye? Using my still, small voice?

Mary's story is both particular and illustrative of an approach to leadership. There is a series of conflicts running through my mind as I decide whether to recommend to our governing body the acceptance of this child. In deciding whether a school can meet the needs of a particular child, there are a variety of rules but they are all open to interpretation by the headteacher in consultation with the governing body. In this case, Mary does not have a statement of Special Educational Needs (SEN) so the protocols around the code of practice are limited. There are rules about catchment areas and planned admission numbers but essentially, Mary's mother is looking for advice: do I recommend to our governing body that we admit Mary and having admitted Mary, how do I anticipate squaring the circle around resources and her potential impact on the school community?

The dilemma can be summed up thus: I believe that our school can improve Mary's chances of staying within her locality to access an education among her peers. The title of our story can be paraphrased as, 'We will all learn together'. I am convinced that admitting her will make it more challenging to meet the Ofsted criteria for a Good school and may rule out any hope of

Outstanding. The Standards for headteachers give a conflicting message: 'high standards' with 'personalized learning to realize the potential of all pupils' (National Standards for Headteachers DfES/0083/2004). I have been teaching for long enough to see the challenge here! The background to the *Denham Report* (Home Office, 2001) requiring schools to promote community cohesion was concerned with racial tensions, but the context of our school community makes me wonder whether we would be acting within the spirit of the legislation to turn our backs on Mary. Her alternative place in school would be in a large city well away from her rural neighbours. She has already become socially isolated according to her parents. Do we have the opportunity to rebuild her confidence within the local community? Could the other pupils in the school benefit from learning that we can all live and work together? Would this be an opportunity to build community cohesion and 'establish a culture that promotes excellence, equality and high expectations of all pupils'? At the heart of our Anglican foundation is the imperative that, 'Every child should be enabled to flourish in their potential as a child of God, as a sign and expression of the Kingdom.' Is Mary one of 'our' children? The parable of the Good Samaritan flashes through my mind.

Is my professional duty to organize the school to meet the rigorous data standards set down by Ofsted? (Mary is not looking such a great asset.)

Is it within my professional gift to justify the urge to involve Mary in our school community to satisfy accountability of a different kind? What, if any, is the impact of my professional duty to set these decisions within the ethos of our Anglican foundation?

The decision to embrace Mary into the school community was taken. I suspect that, at least in part, it was an instinctive decision but there is a case for regarding the decision as arising from my professional self-knowledge. I was acting in a way which I believed to be consistent with who I saw myself to be as a professional Christian. Clearly the decision depended on more than my view; it was considered by the governing body, the leadership team and the potential class teacher, not to mention Mary's parents. As the headteacher, however, I had been appointed on a particular mandate and had set up the climate where staff and governors had the opportunity over the years to join the story, challenge it or move on. Who would we be to turn Mary away? Here was a child very hungry for bread; another rejection seemed like a very hard stone indeed. Were we all sure that offering a place to Mary would be a positive move? Certainly not. Did we have the humility to give it our very best try? Or was there an arrogance involved?

The decision was culturally embedded. It was taken at a time when the governing body, staff and wider school community were aligned in their view of school priorities. The school set out its vision as an inclusive school that aimed to support children with diverse strengths and weaknesses. The school community understood the possible consequences of such a decision and had spent time considering the implications in general terms before the specific request to admit Mary arose. In Helsby's (1995) terms, the action was more typical of an English than a French understanding of professionalism, being a semi-autonomous decision rather than an action, which promotes the national agenda. Professionalism takes account of cultural context. The decision may have been different in another school, in a different time or another place, with a different headteacher, albeit one working professionally in a distinctively Christian school. This decision was typical of the particular school at that particular time as it was flavoured by the identity of those involved who had, in turn, been shaped by the policy landscape and their own beliefs.

The inspection framework, which was revised in January 2015, emphasizes the culture of performativity: 'Inspectors focus sharply on those aspects of schools' work that have the greatest impact on raising achievement' (Ofsted 2015, p. 5). Admitting Mary is likely to cause tension. Within school, the duty to strive to teach Mary to read and write and calculate was never in question. It would have been wildly optimistic, however, to imagine that the time scale of this process would conform to Ofsted's view of what constitutes a good school. There was a position to defend as the school data would not conform to national expectations. A case study would be required to justify the action to the Inspectorate. The study would need to show that Mary was an exception to a rule which demands that children attain results in line with or better than national expectations. In my view, some of the difficulties for Mary, and many children, is that once they are viewed as an exception there is a tendency to subscribe to a deficit model along the lines of national expectations minus x per cent. Raising numerical data as the overriding indicator of success or failure of a school to educate children is not a subtle vehicle. I have not heard any serious argument against this data being used, but an overdependency on its value creates tensions for some children who may be seen as unhelpful to the success of the school.

Raising standards can seem to be in conflict with taking a broader view of what constitutes bread or a stone for a particular child. The two aims are not, of course, mutually exclusive but the acceptance of children who don't currently fit the desired data pattern adds a tension when the parent walks through the door and a decision is required. Within the ethos and vision at that moment in history in that school, the headteacher was clear about the proper answer despite the knowledge of the pressure from inspection. The new Teacher Standards could be seen to support the stance: 'This article argues that the new Teachers' Standards situates the teacher within a post secular context. Furthermore, the articulation of teacher work as "values work" moves from a "competency model" of teaching towards a deeper engagement with the possibilities of a liberating pedagogy' (Bryan, 2012, p. 227). There is an empowerment to act to promote a cohesive society, which could be read as an imperative to keep Mary within the locality of her own home and peer group.

It took until year 7 to secure Mary a statement of SEN, just two terms after she would have been expected to move on to secondary school, but we chose to keep her on as the secondary school that needed Mary was not immediately obvious. Happily, she went on to become settled and happy in a Special school. Should she have been admitted to a Special school instead of being admitted to our school? No. The inclusion debate is not within the remit of this chapter but the benefits for Mary and her peers are beyond question to me. During the time Mary was part of our school community she made brilliant progress: she ran the tuck shop, she made us laugh, she laughed with us and she showed massive potential as a child of God. Some of her peers went on to gain very distinguished academic results, some were brilliant at sport or music or were simply brilliant at being themselves but each of them had the opportunity to work and play together in a cohesive community where they knew that they were valued and were expected to value each other.

Conclusion

School leaders are called to translate a vision into operational decisions. There are many tensions created by the competing demands in the policy landscape, the particular culture and the moment in history of a school. As a headteacher, an understanding of one's professional identity and core values is a powerful vehicle for ensuring that decisions are coherent. This does not necessarily answer the demands of all the potential masters, particularly in this case the revised inspection framework, but it enables a level of self-critical respect.

It is impossible for children to tell their stories if they are not in the book. Mary was not a censored chapter. The children who accepted Mary into their community gained a new knowledge of how to live and learn in a cohesive community. They baked her bread when it was required.

Discussion Questions

1. How do school leaders decide which pupils to include?
2. What does professionalism mean to school leaders?
3. Is humility an acceptable/helpful virtue in leadership?

References

Ball, Stephen J., 2003, 'The teacher's soul and the terrors of performativity', in *Journal of Education Policy*, 18.2, pp. 215–228

Bryan, H., 2012, 'Reconstructing the teacher as a post secular pedagogue: a consideration of the new Researchers' Standards', in *Journal of Beliefs and Values*, 33.2, pp. 217–228

The Home Office, 2001, *Building Cohesive Communities, A Report of the Ministerial Group on Public Order and Community Cohesion*, London: THO

Carr, D., 2000, *Professionalism and Ethics in Teaching*, London: Routledge

Department for Education, 2003, *Every Child Matters*, London: TSO

Department for Education and Skills, 2006, *The Status of Teachers and the Teaching Profession: Views from Inside and Outside the Profession*, Research Report No. 755, Nottingham: DfES Publications

Hare, S., 1996, 'The Paradox of Moral Humility', in *American Philosophical Quarterly*, 33.2, pp. 235–241

Helsby, G., 1995, 'Teachers' Construction of Professionalism in England in the 1990s', in *Journal of Education for Teaching: International research and pedagogy*, 21.3, pp. 317–332

Hoyle, E., 1995, 'Changing Conceptions of a Profession', in Busher H. and Saran R. (eds), *Managing Teachers as Professionals in Schools*, London: Kogan Page

Hoyle, E., 2008, 'Changing Conceptions of Teaching as a Profession: Personal Reflections', in Johnson, D. and Maclean, R. (eds) *Teaching Professionalization, Developing Leadership*, New York: Springer, pp. 285–312

Kellenberger, J., 2010, 'Humility', in *American Philosophical Quarterly*, 47.4, pp. 321–336

Kenworthy, J. M., 1995, Foreword in Watson B. and Ashton E., *Education, Assumptions and Values*, London: David Fulton

OfSTED, 2015, *The framework for school inspection*, Manchester: OfSTED

National Society, 2012, *A framework for inspection and self-evaluation of Church of England and Methodist schools*, www.churchofengland.org/media/1585094/siamsinspectionframeworknovember2012., pdf [accessed 7 July 2015]

Watson, B. and Ashton, E., 1995, *Education, Assumptions and Values*, London: David Fulton

Whitty, G., 2003, *Making Sense of Education Policy*, London: Sage

13

What does the metaphor of the good shepherd have to say about school leadership?

SUSAN THOMPSON

Abstract

The Bible uses the metaphor of the good shepherd to refer to leaders of Israel, Jesus and God. Like shepherds of the past, school leaders are not necessarily the most highly regarded members of society yet they contribute towards the future. To fulfil this role the *Framework for excellence* (National College for School Leadership, 2012) states that school leaders in church schools ought to lead with spiritual intelligence, a sense of vocation, demonstrating personal authenticity and modelling the fruit of the Spirit: 'love, joy, peace, patience, kindness, generosity, faithfulness, gentleness, and self-control' (Galatians 5.22–23). In this chapter I have reflected on what the metaphor of the Good Shepherd might suggest for school leaders today. Many shepherds in the Bible demonstrate a sense of vocation and the application of the fruit of the Spirit, as described in the National College document. What can be meaningfully learned from the metaphor of the Good Shepherd in relation to school leadership?

Keywords

Good shepherd, leadership, framework for excellence, fruit of the Spirit (Galatians 5.22–23)

Introduction

Headteachers work within a frame of accountability entitled the National Standards of Excellence for Headteachers (2015). This requires leaders to be skilled in many areas, from personnel, health and safety, to financial prowess and teaching and learning with the aim of improving the life chances of those in their care. It is an awesome list of skills to hone in a context of significant pressures from politicians and increasing accountability measures. School leaders have to ride the changes in education policy, assessment procedures and curriculum content while meeting the physical, emotional, psychological and spiritual needs of those in their community. This contrasts significantly to education before the 1988 Education Act when headteachers determined the curriculum by responding to the local situation and accountability was less prevalent.

The shepherd: multiple layers of meaning

A shepherd spends years learning the trade from other shepherds, giving him or her the experience to face ever-changing scenarios. The dictionary defines the term shepherd as 'a person who herds, tends, and guards sheep' or 'a person who protects, guides, or watches over a person or group of people'. They are skilled in tending a particular breed, knowing the dangers of the terrain and the local predators. The first part of the definition is reflected in references to shepherds throughout the Bible, the first being Adam's son Abel (Genesis 4.2), who was a keeper of sheep. The Old Testament exemplifies how sheep produced wealth for the owner by giving meat (1 Samuel 14.32), milk (Isaiah 7.21–22), clothing (Job 31.20), or as a sacrifice (Exodus 20.24). Hence, originally the role was well regarded but fell from favour as arable crops became more important and the task was then often left to the youngest son or a hireling, concerned only for a day's pay and easily distracted from the task (see the painting by William Holman Hunt, *The Hireling Shepherd*, painted in 1851). The second definition, 'a person who protects, guides or watches over a person or group of people' is also found in the Bible. Both Joseph (Genesis 37.2) and David (Ezekiel 34.23) gained experience as shepherds prior to fulfilling a leadership role for the Hebrew people, the former as administrator (Genesis 39.2), the latter as king (2 Samuel 2).

The word 'shepherd' is used metaphorically numerous times throughout the Bible giving the word multiple layers of meaning. In the Old Testament the term was used of God (Psalm 23.1; Isaiah 40.11), Israel's kings (2 Samuel 5.2) and leaders (Jeremiah 23.1; Ezekiel 34.1) when authority and care were combined. Turning to the New Testament, shepherds are first mentioned in Luke 2.8–20 as Jesus' first visitors. Jesus himself used the term 'good shepherd' (John 10.7–18) and the writer of Hebrews used the term 'great shepherd' (Hebrews 13.20) of Jesus, who cares for and watches over his people. Paul described the Church and its leaders as the flock with their shepherd (Acts 20.28) (see Holman Bible Dictionary). The link between this role and the second definition of guiding the sheep might suggest the role includes the support and development of those in their care. Before looking at this we will turn to some biblical examples in greater depth.

The good shepherd: the biblical metaphor

The shepherd discerns the needs of the sheep. Without the healing and support cited in Exodus 15 and Psalm 23, the challenge would be immense and some may find it insurmountable. The psalmist, David, had an intimate knowledge of shepherding. In writing Psalm 23 he knew, as Henry wrote (1994a, p. 258), what 'kindness it was to them [the sheep] to have one that was skilful and faithful'. The sheep who follow the instruction of the shepherd will be kept safe and will be revived by water. So too will David be revived by the good shepherd who heals the sick, as it says in Exodus 15.26, 'for I am the Lord who heals you'. That the sheep 'shall not want' (Psalm 23.1) implies the supply of whatever the sheep, or in this case the psalmist needed. To this end the sheep would need to be free from parasites, hunger, predators and terror of other sheep. Underlying this is an acknowledgement that needs would be met only if it were perceived to be the right time to meet that need (Henry, 1994a).

On a practical level, referring to Matthew 18, Barclay (1997) informs us that two or three shepherds worked together to care for the sheep owned by the village, although due to the distance from each other they often led a fairly solitary life. They often worked alone in hostile terrain and facing hazards and predators unique to that particular country. Sheep have a tendency to wander and fall into difficult situations, such as down ravines. Nonetheless all are of value and will be searched out. When the shepherd realized a sheep was missing he would not wait for it to return but would look everywhere to find it, risking his own life to save the sheep. The villagers would look out for a shepherd's return and rejoice, hopeful that the shepherd brought back all the sheep alive or, failing that, the fleece or bones to show the village of the sheep's death. They will always be watched, although not necessarily supported by the villagers in this task. The shepherd is held to account by those with business investments in the sheep, the villagers, the farm owner or investors.

The sheepfold (John 10.1) is the term used to describe an area exposed to the sky but with thick walls, acting as a barrier to storms, wild animals and thieves. David's reassurance, 'I fear no evil' (Psalm 23.4) recognizes God as the shepherd whose presence is with him and will care for him, just as a shepherd would take the sheep into the fold. John 10.3 reminds us that Jesus is the shepherd, the master of the sheepfold, 'The gatekeeper opens the gate for him, and the sheep hear his voice. He calls his own sheep by name and leads them out.' Trust develops as the shepherd leaves the fold first to deal with any danger and to show the sheep the way (Henry, 1994c). As the shepherd, Jesus takes notice of each sheep individually, knowing and calling each by name and the sheep respond to his voice.

The above are examples of good shepherds; however, not all illustrations in the Old Testament are of shepherds who fulfil their roles effectively. If the shepherds (the leaders) of Israel did not provide for their flocks but sought only to make themselves rich, great, fat and well clothed (Ezekiel 34.11–16) then God would step in, rescue the sheep and provide them with good pasture (Ezekiel 34.14). Without care or instruction, without the guidance of a shepherd, the sheep will lose their way. This would be a breach of the duty that they held; a betrayal of God's trust which would be answered for on judgement day (Hebrews 13.17) (Henry, 1994b).

What attributes of a shepherd can be paralleled with a school leader?

Atkinson and Field, (1995, p. 544) define leaders as being 'characterized by high tolerance of ambiguity, skill in differentiating, a clear self-concept, energy, standards which are moderately high, and the giving of feedback'. Like shepherds, they are people who create trust and identity in the organization. Their total focus on the vision and continuous reinforcement of the message aid success. Leadership implies power: the ability to reward, the power to punish, possessing expertise, recognized as having authority, inspiring others and having the ability to raise others' self-esteem. It follows that shepherds share many of these attributes, although whether sheep have self-esteem is a question for another time. If a shepherd were to dominate his sheep they would be stressed and unhappy. The fruit of the Spirit (Galatians 5) are a sign of maturity and essential to a leader whose focus is on service, not domination. Furthermore, Atkinson and Field (1995) suggest that all authority is delegated from God, and those exercising it are answerable to him. As a shepherd is answerable to the village, so a leader in school is answerable to the governors and Local Authority or other body (depending on the type of school) to use public resources to enable all to flourish. From a Christian perspective, both are also accountable to God; Barclay suggests God equips people to fulfil this role (Barclay, 1997, p. 186):

God is a protecting love which saves a man for the service of his fellow-men, a love which makes the wanderer wise, the weak strong, the sinner pure, the captive of sin the free man of holiness, and the vanquished by temptation its conqueror.

Leaders should exhibit the highest standards of spirituality, emotional maturity and conduct in family and public life (National College for School Leadership, 2012). They should lead by example and model themselves on Christ (see Luke 22.26). Leaders need to recognize the gifts of others and make disciples by teaching, pasturing, orchestrating the gifts of all to reach maturity and thus empowering others, not just encouraging participation. Empowered by the Holy Spirit, leaders are to serve not dominate. This is one description of leadership which is reflected in the Headteachers' Standards (2015) in that it encourages the gifts of others. Leaders devolve leadership. Be that as it may, this is not the only model of leadership; headteachers who have a more autocratic or domineering leadership style may be less in tune with the model of the good shepherd. This style could be seen as conflicting with the National Teachers Standards (2015) which promotes team building. Others might perceive that headteachers were not permitted to fulfil the role due to the performative context (Luckcock, 2010).

The Royal Military Academy, Sandhurst motto is 'Serve to lead'. Although a potentially uncomfortable parallel, the motto is exemplified in the life of Jesus and in the words of Paul (2 Corinthians 11) who subverts the pagan view of leadership with a new Christian form in which persecution, hardship and service are to the fore. Tom Wright (Taunt, 2008) said leadership is to train others to catch the vision of servant leadership so 'thus you will know them by their fruits' (Matthew 7.20). The Holy Spirit works within hearts to draw them to God; helps to overcome fears and helps Christian school leaders to show leadership as an act of service (NCSL, 2012). In school, it is through consistency and continuity of this leadership that members of the school become forged into a community. Peters (1988) compared the characteristics of the headteachers of six high schools in the USA with the characteristics found in business leaders. He found that the traits of a school leader included doing acts of service (for example, weeding the lawns, picking up rubbish), speaking to each child by name about their results, and paying attention to physical surroundings to reinforce the ethos and to work towards the positive outcomes being sought.

Many school leaders work tirelessly for the benefit of their school community, focusing primarily on meeting the physical, psychological and emotional needs of the children in their care. Sometimes this can seem a thankless task and it is always an exhausting one. So too do shepherds continue to care for their flock despite the long, cold nights or through the storms of winter, despite great fatigue (Genesis 31.40). Yet they know the importance of continuing with their duties otherwise the safety and well-being of the flock are at stake. The Headteacher Standards (DfE 2015) are explicit about the headteachers' duty to ensure that the school is a place of safety, an enormous role on its own. Domain three (p. 6) says headteachers 'provide a safe, calm and well-ordered environment for all pupils and staff, focused on safeguarding pupils'. This encompasses ensuring the testing of the water temperature to prevent Legionnaires' disease through to ensuring that relationships are positive and respectful. As a school leader I have found myself undertaking a range of tasks that I would not have considered to be part of the role; from removing broken door handles allowing children to leave a classroom to picking up litter (or worse!). It is necessary to take steps to keep the community functioning smoothly and safely. School leaders provide safety in the school, with secure physical and emotional boundaries, just as shepherds provide for their sheep the safety of a sheepfold (Psalm 23). The school 'sheepfold' gives the children rest, food, leisure, friendship and learning opportunities about what is safe and good: a place to build up their understanding of themselves. While shepherds only allow entry (John 10.2–3) to those whom they know by name, so in a school the community can be assured that only those with permission can enter to ensure the safety of all within. In God's kingdom real power looks like service, not tyranny. Perhaps the tasks that a school leader undertakes could be seen as being part of the journey of sanctification through which Christians are enabled to become more Christ-like and do good works every day. Based on Calvin's theology of the imitation of Christ (Atkinson and Field, 1995), it is the work of God to transform us into the image of Christ through using our gifts to God's glory. Seeking to understand, unlike the disciples in Mark 10.36 (Taunt, 2008), that it is through serving others and meeting their needs that the kingdom of God is seen on earth.

A shepherd announces his arrival to his sheep: so as not to startle them he knocks on the door of sheepfold to let them know he is there (Keller, 1993). In a similar way Christ comes with peaceful intentions to wilful people to bring peace. It is the Holy Spirit who gives peace to people (Galatians 5.22) to be demonstrated in their lives. Children are often wilful and are learning how to live their lives. For instance, when an autistic child became over stimulated by their surroundings and started to skid down the corridor in his socks he was brought to a place of safety and peace, then he curled up on the pillows under a duvet with his thumb in his mouth and went to sleep, cuddling a teddy. It was only by approaching him in peace that a calm and safe outcome resulted. Some 'insist on having our own way, indulging our own desires, doing our own things, going our own way with our wishes always paramount' (Keller, 1993, p. 160) in their interactions with others or with God. It can be difficult to respond appropriately when the prevailing culture is self-centred, negative or self-enhancing. Jesus doesn't force himself on people, nor does the shepherd force himself on his sheep. Neither does the school leader force themselves on the school community but leaves the way open for an approach to be made and for the relationship to develop, through 'authenticity and integrity that will generate trust among all types of people' (NCSL, 2012, p. 5).

The sheep will run to the shepherd knowing that he always acts in their best interests, speaks positively and does not hold grudges against any who have wandered. The shepherd has patience with the sheep: so too do school leaders need the 'fruit' of patience (Galatians 5.22) to fulfil their role. Members of the school community need to know that, even if they have strayed or not made the best choice or bring with them issues from outside school, they will find 'endless mercy' as Stuart Townsend's version of Psalm 23 states, 'For your endless mercy follows me, Your goodness will lead me home.' This sense of security will help a school to be a healthy place, corresponding to the findings of Melinsky (1973, p. 37) regarding the communities formed by battalions: 'Health grew with morale, and morale grew from such factors as a shared sense of security and a shared sense of purpose.' It is the commanding officer and not the medical officer who can right the poor health of a unit by addressing issues of morale, like the shepherd who tends the needs of his sheep and sets the tone for their feelings of security (Keller, 1993). Melinsky (1973) says it is the function of the people of God to be the means of health and holiness for others which results in high morale and low sickness rates. They make the fullness of life available to others, as the shepherd makes the fullness of life available for his sheep.

While the dangers of tyranny or chaos should be avoided, Philippians 2 and Mark 10 (Taunt, 2008) remind us that the Bible's model of leadership upends the world's model of leadership. Taunt (2008, p. 17) suggests that 'leaders following Jesus need to have their eyes on the new creation', becoming genuinely human and reflecting God's wise and ordered stewardship. This does not mean keeping things as they were, new things can be introduced that bring benefit in a framework of renewal, like the shepherd who rebuilds the sheepfold using new techniques or treats illness with new treatments. School leaders are required to build, energize and develop opportunities for the future benefit of those in the school community (NCSL, 2012). As Jesus was wounded for us, so his followers working as school leaders respond to the humanity of people in the school community bearing the needs of those people, having a 'commitment to the well-being of self and others; understanding well-being as it is understood in the full meaning of the term shalom' (NCSL, 2012, p. 5).

Jesus' leadership is not a copy model; it was a one-off example where his power was different to the Roman world of the sword. However, he does provide an example of how to lead as the good shepherd together with other examples which inspire leaders to be, as Taunt (2008, p. 17) describes, 'leaders who will take us forward into the exciting, innovative world of experimentation and uncertainty'. For Christian school leaders they can do this in the knowledge that, just as the shepherd is faithful to his sheep, God is faithful to those who follow him. As the famous hymn says, 'Great is thy faithfulness, O God my Father' (Thomas O. Chisholm, 1866–1960). So a school leader should endeavour to remain faithful to the children, to the school community and to God regardless of what hazards beset them, such as sickness or crises in the community, or predators who may be perceived to be moderators, or inspectors who exert pressure on a school. Thus they would bear the fruit of faithfulness (Galatians 5.22).

How is the metaphor of the good shepherd unhelpful for school leaders?

The good shepherd is a model of leadership which raises a number of questions. First, in using this metaphor there could be the assumption that the sheep are the children. However, a school leader is not only working with children but with the other members of the school community. Humans, whether children or not, are not the same as sheep: as Melinsky (1973, p. 36) points out, sheep follow whether or not their master knows where they are going, but people ask questions and have free will. Sheep need a person's care and provide a service for humans (1 Corinthians 9.7), however neither children nor adults in a school provide a 'service' for the school leader like sheep do, notwithstanding that the adults are working for and with the leader. Take a moment to consider the hustle and bustle of a school playground. Henry (1994d, p. 830) says:

> Good men, as new creatures, have the good qualities of sheep, harmless and inoffensive as sheep; meek and quiet, without noise; patient as sheep under the hand both of the shearer and of the butcher; useful and profitable, tame and tractable, to the shepherd and sociable one with another.

Not many of these things can (or should) be said of children!

Second, the good shepherd would give his life for his sheep (Acts 20.28), but this is not so, in a literal sense, for the school leader, although some might argue that the hours and pressures might make it feel as if they are giving up their life. If the school leader is not like the shepherd, are they more akin to the hireling, the person employed to look after sheep or in this case the school? The school leader is trained to be a leader. A shepherd is trained through a long apprenticeship to become a shepherd; however a hireling is not prepared and does not have the same investment in the flock. The Bible identifies hirelings fleeing when the wolf gives rise to danger. Their work may be judged by the villagers and the market place, in a similar way that the headteacher is judged for the work they do. Some leaders find this thought too much and do not wish to face the ongoing and changing pressures of accountability.

Third, the school community is not offered as a sacrifice for the sins of the shepherd (Henry, 1994c). Conversely the New Testament reminds all who follow the good shepherd to offer themselves as a living sacrifice (Romans 12.1; 1 Peter 2.5). However, the school does offer a place of safety, even if not in an eternal sense, for those who enter the sheepfold and it is from here that the shepherd protects his sheep and leads them to appropriate pastures just as the school leader provides space for the physical, emotional, psychological and spiritual well-being of all the members of the school community. Or, as the *Framework for excellence* (NCSL, 2012) states, 'Constantly seeking to take the learning of pupils and staff to deeper levels; focusing on the equal importance of physical, moral, emotional and spiritual development.' This implies that any school consists of members who have a variety of needs that the staff seek to provide for, just as different sheep breeds require different food sources or habitats in order to flourish.

Shepherds had to give account of the flock to the village if anything happened; school leaders are held to account for their school standards by the appropriate authorities and the inspection systems. Ezekiel 34 warns shepherds (Henry, 1994a) to watch and work as those who will be called to give account for their flock on judgement day. Questions arise as to whether the metaphor of shepherd is limited to one particular leadership style and whether in a context of performativity the metaphor has value; given that the metaphor is pastoral and that in education a professional's performance is judged against the Teachers Standards (Teachers Standards, 2015) or Headteachers Standards (2015) respectively. If a teacher is unable to meet the needs of the children or does not ensure they make progress then it is the duty of the school leader to develop a 'strong sense of accountability in staff for the impact of their work on pupils' outcomes' (Headteachers Standards, 2015, p. 6) and 'rigorous, fair and transparent systems and measures for managing the performance of all staff' (ibid., p. 6).

Finally, in a society where the understanding and influence of Christian teaching could be said to be reducing, is it appropriate to draw inspiration from teachings over 2,000 years old? The work of a shepherd may be familiar to a few communities in this country but overall there is little practical understanding or knowledge about shepherding today. Jesus used examples that people of his time were familiar with to help them to understand his message, so would a different analogy today be more useful? Is there a more appropriate metaphor about school leadership that would be more easily understood in today's society?

Conclusion

It is problematic to take this metaphor too literally; some elements of the metaphor work effectively and some do not function at all, even verging on the blasphemous if a school leader is equated to the good shepherd. This chapter has assumed the shepherd is the school leader; the flock are members of the school community, and the wolf represents the inspectorate system, progress data and sometimes external consultants. If this is the case then it is important to recognize that shepherds have to treat different breeds differently, just as not all children can be treated the same. This is particularly true when recognizing the diversity of needs in a school where all children are supposed to be making six points progress a year whatever their vulnerabilities. Unlike a shepherd however, there is no expendability clause, there is no acceptable death rate. Hopefully the school leader does not feel they are working alone but facing the hazards together with other professionals to provide the best possible environment for the children to grow, learn and develop safely. Keeping this goal in sight, they bring years of training and experience to lead the team, manage the environment and external demands in order to give the greatest possibility of the highest yield for the children. That is to say, provide the most rounded development opportunities that bring wholeness and success, just as a shepherd does for his sheep.

Despite the imperfections of the metaphor in this context, as a Christian in school leadership I would say a resounding yes, it must be appropriate to look to the example of Jesus for inspiration and guidance in undertaking the role. As it is said in John 20.21, 'As the Father has sent me, so I send you', it is through the strength and wisdom given through God and the bounty of the Holy Spirit in giving the fruit of the Spirit (Galatians 5.22) that the school leader can undertake the task, equipped through God's gifts. The role encompasses supporting the people on the margins, working with those in the community, telling stories that teach and inspire, and embodying the light of Christ as his steward and agent in today's world. In this way the Christian school leader will start on the journey of meeting the requirements set out for school leadership in the *Framework for excellence* (NCSL, 2012) and use the metaphor of the Good Shepherd as a source of inspiration and challenge.

Discussion Questions

1. What is your response to the metaphor of the good shepherd?
2. What is the relationship between ontology and function of the school leader?

3. Would another metaphor of leadership be more helpful and relevant in the twenty-first century?

4. If school leaders have a role as 'shepherds', what implications, if any, does this have for the church in supporting the school leader?

5. If the metaphor of the good shepherd is used for school leaders, what does this say about the sheep?

References

Atkinson, D. J. and Field, D. H. (eds), 1995, *New Dictionary of Christian Ethics and Pastoral Theology*, Leicester: IVP

Barclay, W., 1997, *The Daily Study Bible: The Gospel of Matthew II*, Edinburgh: St Andrew Press

Henry, M., 1994a, *Matthew Henry's Commentary on the whole Bible*, III – *Job to Song of Solomon*, Peabody, MA: Hendrickson

Henry, M., 1994b, *Matthew Henry's Commentary on the whole Bible*, IV – *Isaiah to Malachi*, Peabody, MA: Hendrickson

Henry, M., 1994c, *Matthew Henry's Commentary on the whole Bible*, V – *Matthew to John*, Peabody, MA: Hendrickson

Henry, M., 1994d, *Matthew Henry's Commentary on the whole Bible*, VI – *Acts to Revelation*, Peabody, MA: Hendrickson

Holman Bible Dictionary, www.studylight.org/dictionaries/hbd/view.cgi?number=T5746 [accessed 18 August 2014]

Holman Hunt, William, 1851, painting, *The Hireling Shepherd*, www.ask.com/web?qsrc=1ando=2802andl=dirandq=The+Hireling+Shepherd [accessed 7 March 2015]

Keller, P. (1993) *A Shepherd Looks at Psalm 23*, New York: Inspirational

Luckcock, T., 2010, 'Spirited Leadership and the Struggle for the Soul of Headteachers: Differentiating and Balancing Nine Types of Engagement', in *Educational Management Administration and Leadership*, 38.1, pp. 405–422

Melinsky, M. A. H., 1973, 'Some Theological Considerations', in *Learning for Living: A Journal for Christian Education*, XII 3, pp. 36–38

National College for School Leadership (NCSL), 2012, *A framework for excellence in the leadership of church schools and academies qualities and behaviours*, London: DfE

National Standards of Excellence for Headteachers, 2015, www.gov.uk/government/publications/national-standards-of-excellence-for-headteachers [accessed 18 February 2015]

Peters, T., 1988, *A Passion for Excellence. The Leadership Difference*, Glasgow: William Collins Sons and Co. Ltd

Royal Military Academy, Sandhurst motto, www.army.mod.uk/documents/general/history_of_rmas.pdf [accessed 18 August 2014]

Taunt, N., 2008, 'Notes on Bishop Tom Wright's address at the September 2007 Conference', in *The Journal of the Association of Anglican Secondary School Heads*, XX, pp. 17–18

Teachers Standards, 2013, www.gov.uk/government/collections/teachers-standards [accessed 18 February 2015]

United Nations Convention on the Rights of a child, 1989, www.unicef.org.uk/UNICEFs-Work/UN-Convention/ [accessed 7 March 2015]

14

Spam Ed storytelling for
year 13 students

ROBERT JACKSON

Abstract

This chapter attempts to account for the emergence of didactic storytelling as a key tool in the delivery of Spam Ed (Spiritual and Moral Education). The introduction explains the emergence of Spam Ed and its aims. It also confirms that this storytelling approach, which was, in this case, the result of an evolutionary process, is not only academically sustainable as a technique, but stands a good chance of being effective in practice. The story that ensues should speak for itself . . . as all stories must.

Keywords

Storytelling, Spiritual and Moral Education, year 13, philosophy, Descartes

Introduction

I'm a storyteller . . . but I haven't always been one. It all started when I found myself teaching others, initially as a curate. I would find myself looking for ways to illustrate points and, while real life examples worked, I found that stories could be particularly effective. When I became a school chaplain, this tendency developed and found its most refined expression in the Spam Ed lessons I used to teach to year 13 students.

That I developed as a storyteller is also linked to the task I set myself in the classroom, namely to educate the character. Alasdair MacIntyre, in his book, *After Virtue* (2007) presses the case for the Aristotelian demand to teach virtue, as does Tom Wright in his more readable and no less learned book, *Virtue Reborn* (2010).

In September 2010, Professors Ann Hodgson and Ken Spours of the Institute of Education at the University of London, produced a report commissioned by the Headmasters' and Headmistresses' Conference (HMC). This being a consultative document, they sent questionnaires to 68 HMC schools and then arranged gatherings at six of them to which the representatives from the others were invited. Pupils from the six hosting schools were also questioned. The result was aspirational and reflected a fairly universal desire to have a broad curriculum that was not beholden to public examinations. On the other hand, it was also pessimistic about this happening:

> Despite the desire to pursue broad educational aims and purposes, participants felt under considerable pressure from parents and students to deliver the best possible examination results in a highly competitive market. They perceived that this was exacerbated by the actions of the 'top universities', who not only demand high grades at A Levels but also use GCSE A* grades as selection tools for certain courses, such as medicine, dentistry and law. (Hodgson and Spours, 2010, p. 4)

The Ed. D course, among other things, introduced me to Lev Semyonovich Vygotsky. I really enjoyed what I read and found myself drawn to him for two reasons. First, his concept of the Zone of Proximal Development seemed to offer a penetrating critique of teaching for exams, not least because the demands of the examiners are insensitive to the needs of individual pupils. Second, I started to realize that what Vygotsky was describing was pretty much how Jesus related to his disciples. He bothered to get to know them and he acknowledged their individual traits for he was about to shake them up and overturn their paradigms. Crucially, he would do so gently, beginning with where they were, as individuals, and leading them forward, stage by stage, to the point where, ultimately, a group mostly of artisans from unprivileged families, would be responsible for laying the foundations of the Christian Church.

So, I started with a general lesson on the big questions of life . . . what I call the religious questions. These are the questions that need to be answered in order to do more than merely exist, but they also resist dogmatic certainty and require faith. I condensed them to just two, 'Who are you and what do you want?' We then spent the next few months looking at the ways in which people have addressed this kind of question, ending up in the often confused postmodern state we find ourselves in today. Over the course of 14 years, I discovered I was emulating Jesus as I told stories aimed at helping the pupils to grasp some of these philosophical concepts. Philosophy, like life, is a dialectical process and I simply found that making up stories, often based on an aspect of the life of a key figure, was a way of engendering an understanding of a principle, or even a key phrase. Perhaps more importantly though, telling a story is a gracious act that offers the listener the space to react subjectively, for the impact of a story is as much to do with the heart of listener as the skill of the teller.

Descartes in a car

It's strange, isn't it, how the most benign of habits, when interrupted, can rebel to the point where it lays bare the very roots of a person's identity.

It was a Wednesday morning in late September and, as he had done for the past three years, Martin Rossiter gulped the last inch of tea in the bottom of his mug, kissed Elizabeth, his wife, on the left cheek, smiled at Chandos, their five-year-old Labrador, walked through the hall, shouted goodbye up the stairs to Ruth and Daniel, his children, and headed through the front door to his

Austin 10 that sat at the top of the drive. As he approached it, he saw that Neville had, as he always did, timed his arrival to perfection and was waiting for him by the passenger door. He reached into his right hand jacket pocket and felt for the key that would unlock the car. Extracting it, he approached the nearside door and as he did so, she who was about to interrupt his habit arrived at his side breathing slightly heavily, the result of mild exertion.

Ever since moving to Nosebury in the autumn of 1940, such had been the daily pattern of Martin's departure to work. Martin had met Neville in the summer of 1940 at a physics symposium in Oxford and had been invited to be considered for a job working as a boffin for the government. Martin had jumped at the idea because for some time he had been dreading receiving the call-up letter for, as a happily married father of two, he had no desire whatsoever to risk his life on a battlefield somewhere. The recent crushing of the Allied armies in France had convinced him it was only a matter of time before the letter arrived, so he was delighted that an appointment to a hush-hush outfit ensued, even if it meant the family having to up sticks and head south to a small Buckinghamshire village.

Neville lived next door and together, they would drive each day to Bicester where they worked. This was as well because north Bucks was brand new to Martin and the complete absence of road signs meant that had it not been for Neville, he would never have made it to work. From the outset, Neville had proved to be an excellent guide and it meant that Martin had not had to think about where he was headed, he merely had to listen to Neville's soft authoritative voice and follow his instructions. 'Turn left here.' 'Straight across at the crossroads and then take the right fork,' etc. If Neville was absent, Martin was able to get to work but if truth be told, he never really understood his route in relation to its destination, he simply knew what option to take whenever he encountered a junction. If you'd shown him an unmarked map of the area, he would have been incapable of pointing Bicester out.

And so in the autumn of 1943, had you asked Martin how his life was, he would have been unable to articulate more than the odd minor concern, for he was most content with his lot. He could therefore be excused for not anticipating the life-changing impact of the woman who was now standing beside him as he unlocked the car on that particular Wednesday morning.

Fiona Skelding was a lively, single woman who lived with two others in digs three doors down from Martin and his family. They had moved in during the spring of that year and Fiona had struck up a friendship with the Rossiter children. Like Martin and Neville, Fiona and her friends worked in Bicester but they tended to leave later in a car driven by one of the housemates. They worked for the military but Martin didn't know in what capacity, nor was he likely to find out, for such details were never shared with others. Even so, given that Bicester was not a large town, Martin thought it odd that they had yet to bump into each other.

Anyway, Fiona had knocked on their door at 6.22 pm on Monday evening which was seven minutes after the Rossiters sat down for supper and Martin had been irritated to have to get up from the table to answer the door. Fiona and her housemates had been planning to head to Birmingham for a day out on Wednesday but something had cropped up at work for Fiona and because her friends were still going to go to Birmingham, she had come to beg a lift. Martin had readily agreed and had told her to be there for 7.40 am prompt. On Tuesday, Martin had been surprised by Neville's awkward reaction when he had told him that Fiona would be joining them on the morrow and as Fiona waited for the door to be unlocked, it was clear that there was something amiss, for his cheerful charm had been replaced by an uncustomary silence. Martin inserted the ignition key, withdrew the choke and pressed the start button. The engine turned over for a few seconds before coming to life and after checking to the rear, he depressed the clutch, selected first gear and drove to the end of the lane. Even as Neville intoned the instruction to turn left, Martin was indicating left.

'Don't you mean right?' came a female voice from behind.

'Eh?' said Martin 'no, it's left here.'

'But surely Bicester is to the right,' responded Fiona.

'Absolutely not!' interjected Neville. 'We've been travelling to work together for almost three years and we always turn left.'

'But turning left takes you off towards Bletchley. You need to turn right if you want to go to Bicester.' Fiona was sounding quite insistent.

'Don't talk such rubbish – what do you know? You've only lived here for a few months.' Neville's voice was rising in volume.

'Well, I want to go to Bicester and to get to Bicester, you have to turn right.' Fiona sounded exasperated.

'It's left for Bicester, it always has been and always will be!' shouted Neville.

'I promise you, Martin, I don't know where you think you've been going to, but if you've been turning left here, you've not been going to Bicester and if you insist on going left, could you please let me out because I need to get to Bicester.'

Martin had been taken aback by this unexpected altercation. Instinct told him that he ought to go left because he had always gone left, but why was this his instinct? If he thought about it, which he was now doing with a clarity that surprised him, Neville, the obvious source of this instinct, was, for the first time, not the charming individual he had come to know. Just how well did he know this man who had played such a major role in his life over the past few years? Which way should he turn?

Unable to come to a reasoned decision, Martin submitted to his initial instinct, turned left and immediately pulled over. An exasperated Fiona got out and wished them an interesting onward journey to somewhere other than Bicester. By the time the door had slammed shut, Neville had already collected himself and gently confirmed Martin in his decision but in spite of this, Martin began to think the unthinkable: that Fiona Skelding, in all her spontaneous innocence, bore the truth and that Neville had been deceiving him all this time.

Martin kept these thoughts to himself and a hectic morning left no space to dwell on the curious events of the journey to work, but come lunchtime, he turned right when he exited the hut (instead of left which would have taken him to the NAAFI canteen) and set out into the grounds of the large stately home which housed the outfit he was working for. There, he found a small depression in a little dell, spread his overcoat on the ground, and sat down to ponder.

What had begun as a simple question of who was telling the truth, Neville or Fiona, was fast growing out of hand and Martin felt himself beginning to be confronted by a crisis that went right to the heart of his very existence.

Martin had discovered early on in his life that he was a coward who had a craven desire to avoid conflict at all costs. As a result, he would avoid making up his mind lest he found himself in conflict with those individuals who he increasingly allowed to order his life – he had become a master in acquiescence. As an approach to life, it worked spectacularly well, such that over time he had ceased to recognize that this was his modus operandi. Neville's quiet authority in the matter of his recruitment had been more than he could have wished for and it had made him good to be around on a daily basis.

But right here, right now, while Neville's authority was not in question, Neville's integrity very much was. Fiona had challenged it and so this morning, Martin had had to do something that he had assiduously avoided for so much of his life . . . he had had to make a decision in the face of two conflicting truths. But what truth? The truth of which way to turn at a junction? The truth of where this stately home was? The truth of who he was working for? The truth of where he lived? The truth of who he lived with? What about the truth of his marriage?

These thoughts were hugely unsettling because they seemed to be subject to no authority other than his own mind, but was this actually the case? How could he know if what he was thinking now was no more than the product of something his mother might have said to him about Elizabeth, not because it was the truth, but simply because, as a widow of the Great War, she had not wanted to lose her only son to another woman? And as that thought and others assailed him, he saw the full impact of the implications. How could he know anything at all with any degree of assurance since all his opinions were clearly built upon years and years of input from others whose reliability in the matter of authenticity he could no longer accept. So, Martin decided to try to head back to the beginning of knowledge, to start again from scratch, to attempt to reconstruct his outlook on the basis of what he alone could accept as the truth. And this is where I come into the picture.

Let me introduce myself. My name is Geoff Rossiter. Martin is my grandfather, or should I say he was my grandfather for he died last Wednesday aged 99. I was very close to Grandad Martin and we had always hit it off. I think this was because he saw a lot of himself in me, but whatever the reason, he poked me via Facebook half a year ago saying that he wanted to have a chat. We sorted out a date and I arranged with the nursing home to take him out for 24 hours. By this stage, the growth on his left lung had been declared malignant and Grandad had decided to seek palliative care rather than opt for invasive procedures that might have squeezed an extra year out of his weary body. At this point though, he was still relatively fit.

Grandad had wanted to go to Nosebury and since it was quite a drive from Preston, I had booked overnight accommodation in a Bicester hotel . . . the real Bicester that is, and at his suggestion, we were driving to Nosebury to have lunch in a pub that he had frequented during the war. It seems that this had been the moment he had been waiting for and he had launched into the account that I have just related, and up to this point in the story, it had been a simple case of him telling the tale, quite a bit of which, I already knew.

'What do you mean by start again Grandad?' (How could I call him anything else, in spite of being well into my fifth decade.)

'Well you know how it is, so much of what we think is the case is no more than what we have been brought up to believe, and even when we question those beliefs, we often do so because of what someone else has said, and how do we know if this challenge to our belief presents the truth of the matter or not? I decided that I would systematically doubt anything and everything that I ever thought I knew, and to accept only those things that I considered to be beyond doubt.'

'Go on,' I said.

'Well, that's what suddenly struck me so forcefully that day – Neville, who I had come to rely on as a source of truthful authority had suddenly had his 'truth' challenged. Fiona had challenged him but was she being truthful, and I realized that I had to decide which of them was offering me the truth and after that, it all got out of hand. Maybe it was the intensity of the job I was performing, who knows, but whatever it was, it became an increasingly distressing experience for I was terrified of where it was leading me and yet I felt compelled to proceed.'

'But surely,' I countered, 'you could, for instance, trust the truth of the war.'

'But why? The war was remote for me, going on elsewhere and only conveyed to me through precisely the kind of second and third parties that I was discovering that I couldn't necessarily trust.'

'What about all those bombers that flew over you on their way to bomb Europe?'

'Not only did I have to accept another's word that that was what they were up to, but Geoff, have your eyes ever deceived you?'

This was an unexpected question . . . 'What do you mean?'

'One of the ways in which we engage with the world around us is through our senses and I found myself questioning their reliability. I know that sounds mad but believe me, I was in a very strange place as I began to query the reliability of my senses. If, in the night, I could hear things, or for that matter see things, that demonstrably weren't there, or if I could feel as though my flesh was being tickled even though nothing was tickling it, then it was clear that my senses were not reliable when it came to the truth of the physical world around me.

'Knowledge of myself, I reasoned, came from two sources. First, humans reacted to me and acknowledged my existence but I had learned that none of them could be completely trusted. Second, the physical world reacted to my actions in a way that my senses detected but if I couldn't trust my senses, where did that leave me? You can see that I was becoming genuinely lost in every sense of that word and I was even coming to doubt my very existence.'

'So what happened? How did it resolve itself?'

By this stage, I was so engrossed that I could no longer focus on driving so I pulled over into a layby . . . I was desperate to hear how Grandad had managed to climb out of the pit he had dug himself into.

'Well, it was magnificently simple, as so many things in life are. I realized that my doubt was the solution.'

I was taken aback. What on earth could he mean?

'I realized,' he continued, 'that I couldn't doubt myself if I didn't exist to doubt myself in the first place. In order to doubt, I had to exist to doubt. I remember vividly the lunchtime that this realization struck me. It was fabulous because now that I was finally certain that I existed, I could begin the task of reconstructing my world by working things out for myself. In fact I later realized I was, in my own way, following René Descartes on his journey of self-discovery. His journey had emerged at a time when the Church's absolute authority had been destroyed by the Reformation – there were now two competing Churches offering conflicting truths, just like Neville and Fiona. *Cogito ergo sum – I think therefore I am* could have been my very words!'

I can honestly say that I felt a real thrill at this point. Yes, Descartes' saying was well known to me, not that I had ever grasped its meaning. Now, for the first time, I understood its significance and it was so neat and so profound.

'But how did you go about this task of reconstruction?' I asked.

'Well it was like this. Having taken the decision to doubt everything, I effectively emptied my mind till all that was left was the logic of Descartes' *Cogito ergo sum*. In a sense therefore, I had kind of formatted my brain, as one might do with a computer's hard drive, and I was now free to reprogram it except that now, anything that went into it had to be passed by my own readiness to accept it as being true. I realized, for instance, that my senses were, by and large, reliable, not least because I seemed to know when they were playing tricks on me. People also, I realized, were thinking agents . . . they existed exactly as I did, and so while I didn't necessarily trust them as before, I did allow them to contribute to my understanding of life.'

This seemed to make complete sense to me, so much so that what he said next completely threw me.

'. . . and you wouldn't believe the problems that accompanied this new, exhilarating approach to life.'

'What do you mean?' I asked, incredulously.

'I know it all sounds terribly neat and compact and indeed at the time, that is exactly how it felt, but as the war reached its conclusion, I began to fear the consequences of a world in which everyone relied on their reason alone to establish the truth . . . '

I loved my Grandad: there was so much to him, and right now, he had my complete attention.

'. . . and just like Descartes, on the surface, there was not much that marked the shift of focus in my life, save for the fact that I became more self-confident. By that, I mean that the basic outlook on life that informed the way I conducted myself remained largely intact, just as Descartes had been a Christian both before and after his personal journey. But like me, Descartes had flipped things round. At the start of his journey, Descartes' "given" was God. *In the beginning, God* as the Torah has it. He knew he existed because God had created him. By the end of the journey however, his "given" was no longer God but himself, and now, significantly, God's existence was something that had to be reasoned. In other words, had he decided that belief in the existence of God was unreasonable, he would have become an atheist, rather as many do today. Whether this happens or not, the final arbiter in all matters has become reason, a person's ability to work things out logically based on facts. At first, such a problem was a million miles from where I found myself in what was one of the most stimulating periods in my life. Not only had I grown in confidence but I had also helped to defeat Germany. I even came to see that my cowardice was irrelevant and that it didn't matter that I hadn't risked my life for I knew the significance of the part I had played in beating Hitler.'

'So what was it that made you question your discovery?'

'It was confronting the reasonable arguments that the Germans had presented for eugenics . . . their programme of selective sterilization of the disabled that led to the killing of disabled babies at birth, and then to the selective euthanasia of the mentally disabled. This eventually culminated in an industry dedicated to killing "ethnically disabled" humans, as quickly and as efficiently as possible. Hitler believed, I read recently, that future generations would thank the German people for having had the courage to undertake this unpleasant business of purging the human race of its dross. I found it particularly chilling that initially the Nazis never sought to conceal the truth from their people, and that even when they were killing thousands a day, they encountered little resistance from those working in the "industry". I even discovered that in the 1930s, there was a eugenics movement in the US that proposed the sterilization of certain disabled individuals. The rationale was compelling – to accelerate the process of human evolution by removing defective genes from the human gene pool. The ugly truth was that human reason was capable of plumbing unspeakable depths and it terrified me as one who was in the process of committing everything to the test of my own reason.'

I had read a little about this and what Grandad said made sense but it left a big question . . . what was the alternative? I was curious to find out how he had dealt with this dilemma and I didn't have to prompt him.

'I decided that in any culture where human reason is the only source of truth, a problem will inevitably arise due to its ultimate subjectivity. Not only that but I realized that as I reached this conclusion, not everyone would agree with me, and this only confirmed my deepening conviction that reason alone could never form the basis of a genuine community. You see I was using my reason to reflect on the impact of appealing to reason to sort out the problems of life, and reaching a conclusion that varied from others who were claiming to be employing reason in an identical fashion. At the end of the day though, there was one issue that dominated all others.'

I can say with absolute certainty that I was by this stage hanging on every single word that was issuing forth from my grandfather's mouth. After the war, he had returned to teaching and had taught through to retirement. Physics had been his passion and he found it hard to take when he had been obliged to retire at 60.

He therefore got more involved in the life of his synagogue and he set up a team to host school trips where children would learn about Jewish life and religious practices in the UK. It was hugely successful and rarely did a week go by when a coach did not bring a cohort of youngsters to be entertained and educated by a jolly bunch of elderly Jews.

'And what was that, Grandad?' I asked.

'Purpose! Yes, just a single simple word, but of massive consequence when applied in a particular context. Our brother, Viktor Frankl, had discovered its importance in the death camps – that those who survived were the ones who had a purpose to live for, and he had observed that when a person lost his purpose, he rapidly wasted away and died.

'The problem with having to work out the truth for yourself is that you then have to work out your purpose. It also reduces the idea of a common purpose to being, at best, a happy coincidence but at worst, the product of coercion, whether by force or persuasion. I headed back to the scriptures and to the Torah and began reading once again that which I had become embarrassed by as I progressed through university. At the time, I judged it to fall well short of the exacting challenges presented by modern scientific discoveries. Upon revisiting it, I found myself sinking deep into its account of origins, not as a scientist might, but rather as one reconnecting with God who had somehow, in my mind, been separated from his creation. As Jews, our identity is dependent on the belief that we are a chosen race, chosen by God himself. I believed he created the universe, but as a scientist, I had completely ignored this belief. As I reread the accounts of creation, I connected with it in a completely fresh way and found myself marvelling at a piece of ancient wisdom that not only proclaimed God as the creator, but explained that there was a purpose to creation, not one that was dependent on me to work out, but one that began with the words *Go forth and multiply. Fill the earth and subdue it.*'

Grandad paused and drew breath. The pause lengthened and it wasn't long before I realized that he had finished what he had to say.

'We can go now,' he said.

'Bicester here we come!' I intoned cheerfully as I started the engine and pulled back onto the road.

'You'll need to turn right at the next junction then,' instructed Martin Rossiter with more than a hint of irony in his voice.

'Are you sure?' I asked

'I'm sure.' And with that, he looked out of the window and I indicated right.

The End . . .

In class, I ended the story at the observation that Descartes had changed the given in his life from God to himself, and we then discussed the implications of this. In this written version, I have allowed Martin to describe the course our discussions generally took. Did I lead them? Yes, I guess I did, but then I see that as the role of a teacher, and at least they knew where I was coming from. My overarching objective was to inculcate Christian virtue by encouraging them to think for themselves about the issues as they actually are, and to ensure that they heard a voice that offered a perspective at variance to that of the clamouring voices of the secular media.

Discussion Questions

1. Is it possible to teach spirituality?
2. Can one teach morality and if so, whose morality?
3. Is it legitimate for a Christian teacher to offer a Christian understanding of a topic under discussion?
4. In a nation where a clear majority of the population accepts the existence of a divine power, can the secular demand to keep God out of the classroom be justified?
5. Did I waste 19 years of my life trying to teach virtue, and how will I ever know?

References

Hodgson, A. and Spours, K., 2010, The 13–19 Education in HMC Schools, *Developing a Curriculum for the Future*, Market Harborough: IOS London and HMC

MacIntyre, A., 2007, *After Virtue*, London: Bloomsbury

Wright, N. T., 2010, *Virtue Reborn*, London: SPCK

15

A reflection on using the work
of Michel Foucault in Christian
educational research

Thomas German

Abstract

This chapter will focus on the work of the philosopher Michel
Foucault, more specifically his two works, *Discipline and
Punish* and *Madness and Civilization*. It will attempt to place
these works within a general philosophical context and provide not merely a description of these works but also extend
the explanation to their theoretical implications in relation to
education. In the second part of the chapter I will attempt to
apply this to the specific area of Christian educational research,
and investigate the possibilities of using this secular philosophy in faith-based research. I will then attempt to show how
Christian theology can provide an alternative to current secular
educational theory.

Keywords

Postmodernism; surveillance; social; institution; panopticon

Introduction

The past 30 years have seen many interesting changes in education
policy, that reflect wider changes in social policy. As someone who

comes from a teaching family this was brought home to me on a daily basis, as my parents taught throughout the 1990s when perhaps the most rapid change was occurring. These changes were reinforced for me when I began teacher training in 2010. Whereas my parents had been taught to teach at a time when there was an intense focus on the philosophical and ethical underpinnings of education, when I began training there was an emphasis on both the practicalities of teaching as well as the personal reflection and development of the individual teacher. There seemed to be little comment on the ideology of different education policies.

As I entered into the teaching profession, I became aware of how statistically-driven the college I worked in was. I was fairly sure that there is a link between the training I received and the ethos of the further education sector, but I lacked a structure to analyse this process. It was then that I discovered the French philosopher, Michel Foucault.

Michel Foucault was a philosopher and historian who operated most productively from the 1960s to the 1980s. Central to Foucault's intellectual project was a forensic examination of the episteme (Cousins, 1990), the 'given' truths of any era. Key to this was a technique of examining the minutiae of the functioning of a chosen area (such as manuals of discipline in the military) and observing how this might reflect subtle changes in the view of the human being. In this sense Foucault analyses the macrocosm in light of the microcosm. An example of this in education might be looking at classroom layouts in a particular era, and what that might say about attitudes to children at the time.

Foucault viewed this process of the identification of minutiae as being a neutral process, and always used terms such as archaeology or genealogy to describe his work (Donnelly, 1982, chapter 2). So we can imagine Foucault as a nineteenth century scientist sifting through samples in a museum. This forensic approach can provide the reader with some startling insights into the human condition in modern society.

Madness and Civilization

Within this work Foucault charts in painstaking detail the different conceptions of madness that have existed in Western culture. In true Foucauldian fashion, this takes the form of studying a diverse range of sources from medical manuals to art. The central theme of his analysis of medieval madness is both the treatment of lepers, and also the 'Ship of Fools' (Foucault, 1988), especially Hieronymous Bosch's artistic depiction of this fourteenth century institution. Foucault describes how, in the medieval period, the mad, alongside lepers, were excommunicated from society but, in this move, accepted in their 'otherness'. In their very partitioning from society they were established as a separate entity guided by their own laws, embodied in the metaphor and actualization in the Ship of Fools, a separate domain of the damned. Here is Foucault describing this phenomenon: 'Madmen then led an easy wandering existence. The towns drove them outside their limits; they were allowed to wander in the open countryside' (Foucault, 1988, p. 8).

In this binary separation, a separation which was undoubtedly cruel, we also find a curious source of amazement for the medieval mind, a source of inspiration and the divine. In the medieval era, as with the creation of leper colonies, the separation of the mad from society represents, for Foucault, the acknowledgement on the part of the ruling class of alternate domains to conventional society – lands where different gods and different laws ruled. Here Foucault describes the dual nature of medieval exclusion: 'What matters is that the vagabond madmen, the act of driving them away, their departure and embarkation do not assume their entire significance on the plane of social utility or security. Other meanings much closer to rite are certainly present' (Foucault, 1988, p. 10).

What changes, therefore, in the classical era is that a more effective, if different, solution to the practical problem is used, and there is a change in the symbolic meaning as well. First, the classical period introduces internal confinement. Whereas in the medieval period the mad were excluded and set free, now they are internally confined. Foucault also discusses the way in which medical language and new labels are devised to justify these changes. Another aspect that developed in attitudes towards madness in the classical period is a moral attitude towards madness. The new institutes of madness became not just holding or confinement areas, but places of correction, places where the individual is modified. An eccentric example of this is the 'tea parties' staged in asylums, where the mad were coerced into engaging in tea parties dressed as ladies and gentlemen:

> Curiously, this rite is not one of intimacy, of dialogue, of mutual acquaintance; it is the organization around the madman of a world where everything would be like and near him, but in which he himself would remain a stranger, the stranger par excellence, who is judged not only by appearances but by all that they may betray and reveal in spite of themselves. (Foucault, 1988, p. 249)

How does this work relate to educational research? *Madness and Civilization* is a work that deals specifically with madness, those who have been excluded from society. Education, apart from in specialized circumstances, doesn't tend to function at the margins of the social order. In this sense, the 'moral', socializing function of education has historically been linked in to a Christian ethos and agenda, but in a postmodern, secular age informed by corresponding philosophies, there still remains a debate to be had about the role education has to play in the process of socialization, which in turn has implications for Christian research and influence.

First, I believe that Foucault's concept of the subject, that is explored extensively in *Madness and Civilization* and then carried on throughout his philosophical work, is of crucial importance. Foucault constantly focuses on the duality between subject and object. Here is Alec McHoul's description of Foucault's concept of the subject:

In his earlier work on historical construction, Foucault refused to give priority to individual creative subjects. He was much more interested at that time in how particular kinds of subject (the mad, the ill, the sexual pervert, for example) were produced as effects of discursive power relations. (McHoul and Grace, 1993, p. 91)

Here Foucault focuses on the way in which thinking individuals are transformed into docile subjects by society – how we are moulded and formed by the requirements of society, specifically how these requirements embed themselves in the subject, so that they function independently within the subject, without a central guiding force. Foucault's concept of the self is complex, and not fully drawn out in *Madness and Civilization*, but in keeping with postmodernism's decentralization of the self, Foucault drew a picture of the self as a meeting point between the power structures of society and needs of the individual. Here Deleuze discusses Foucault's somewhat amorphous conception of the self:

this is the central chamber, which one need no longer fear since one fills it with oneself. Here one becomes master of one's speed and, relatively speaking, a master of one's molecules and particular features: in the zone of subjectivication: the boat is the interior of the exterior. (Deleuze, 1986, p. 101)

In this sense the object takes on a dual function of two modes having simultaneously, a subjective and an objective mode. An object can be viewed from the subjective viewpoint with all of its associated memories and reflections, in Freudian terms the personal ego, and an objective viewpoint from the perspective of the imagined view of society, in Freudian terms labelled the super-ego, with society's rules internalized into the psyche of the subject, the source in Freudian psychology of repression and guilt. What differentiates Foucault's version of the self from Freud's is that it is far less mechanical and far more amorphous (Freud, 2010).

It must be remembered that this complex notion of the subject situates Foucault within a postmodern view of the self, in which, along with the collapse of the metanarrative (Lyotard, 1984), the idea of a solid ego, or personality, or even the concept of a soul is also disintegrated, leaving the self as a container, more a vessel to be filled than the indestructible kernel or soul of the traditional Christian viewpoint. This ontology of the self – found in Foucault and other postmodern authors – is key to understanding the relation between the institution and the self, as the institution provides the meaning that situates the individual in relation to the reality of the void, the fact that the self actually does not exist. The subject, which in postmodern ontology constitutes a localized site for different discourses, faced with the possibility of its true nothingness, chooses to find its meaning within the institution rather than face itself. Thus the individual knowingly imprisons himself in the comfort of society with its all-encompassing rules.

Pertinent examples of educational research that use Foucault's notion of the subject are J. Morrissey's 'Governing the Academic Subject' (2013) which focuses on the specific topic of the subject in education and 'After Foucault: the Question of Civility' by Roger Mourad (2001) which looks at the link between education and well-being. Both these papers focus on the subject in the education sector, and are just two examples among many of papers which use this approach.

The use of *Madness and Civilization* in educational research is thus twofold. Foucault's emphasis on the decentralized subject, and the power discourses that then fill this empty self, can provide useful insights into the treatment of learners and the effect that education may have in perpetuating power discourses and socializing the subject.

Discipline and Punish

Discipline and Punish is a work that charts, in a similar fashion to *Madness and Civilization*, the treatment of a marginalized underclass, in this case, prisoners from the medieval period to the classical era. What Foucault is attempting is to chart the way in which we view the prisoner, and asking the all-important question: has this changed over the course of history? Was the medieval mindset different in relation to crime and punishment from that of the modern era?

Like many of Foucault's works, *Discipline and Punish*, starts with a vivid description of a real event, which draws out the themes that will become apparent in the work. In this case, the work starts with a description of the execution of Damiens, a regicide who attempted to murder King Louis XV. This is meant to display in graphic terms the way in which punishment prior to the Enlightenment was enacted on the body of the criminal as a reflection of the crime against the body of the king which symbolized the collective social order. A key detail in this case was that the hand that Damiens held the knife in was particularly targeted with burning sulphur, a feature which was prominent in the punishments of those times. Key was the symbolic 'like for like' punishment of divine justice (Foucault, 1991).

Within a monarchy, Foucault observes that punishment was first of the crime, rather than the criminal. If the body of the monarch represents the state in a monarchical structure, then a crime against the state is a crime against the body of the monarch (note that in British law the crime is always against the monarch).

In line with the metaphysical views of the Middle Ages that supported a monarchical structure, justice in the Middle Ages is not something that focuses on aberrance from a social norm, but functions merely as a physical manifestation of divine justice. When a crime is committed it is committed against the abstract concept of the body of the king, and therefore the punishment is there to balance the natural order.

This is in direct contrast to the modern era, in which there is an emphasis upon the correction and modification of the individual to the mould of a social norm. What Foucault then describes is the way in which in a similar fashion to the treatment of the mad, prisons are no longer places of exclusion and death, but places of correction.

Foucault describes, especially in the chapter 'Docile Bodies' (Foucault, 1991), the precise manner in which the bodies of the individual are given prescribed movements and disciplines which they must follow, by the social body. The most vivid example that Foucault gives are the military training manuals for nineteenth-century armies. Foucault again identifies a dual purpose in this training. On the one hand the disciplining of the body is essential for the practical functioning of the army both in war and peacetime, but also it functions symbolically to create a domination of every aspect of the soldier's life:

> By the late eighteenth century, the soldier has become something which can be made; out of a formless clay, an inapt body, the machine required can be constructed; posture is gradually corrected; a calculated constraint runs slowly through each part of the body, mastering it, making it pliable, ready at all times, turning silently into the automatism of habit. (Foucault, 1991, p. 135)

This 'automatism of habit' is applied in the prison, as is displayed by Foucault's contrast between the treatment of Damiens and the timetable of the prison: 'we have then, a public execution and a timetable. They do not punish the same crime or the same type of delinquent. But they each define a certain penal style' (Foucault, 1991, p. 7).

As with *Madness and Civilization*, what Foucault challenges is the notion that this change is due to a humanizing process. So therefore what develops out of changes in the prison system becomes an analogy for society as a whole, and for Foucault the visual analogy for society's new structure is provided by Jeremy Bentham's panopticon. Designed by Jeremy Bentham, the English philosopher, the panopticon was a prison octagonal in shape and split into cells. At the centre of the prison was an elevated observation tower, from which a guard could observe every prisoner detained within. The brilliance of this (an idea which, with the advent of CCTV, has become fairly commonplace) is that the prisoners do not know whether they are being observed or not, and this in turn modifies their behaviour into a total obedience.

While the panopticon was never actually created physically, Foucault presents it to us as a metaphor for the ideas that shaped a time. Panopticism, the idea of the isolated subject naked to the ever present gaze of 'society', manifests itself in several unique ways according to Foucault. The first is referred to as the 'inversion of the disciplines' (Foucault, 1991, p. 210) and concerns the manner in which disciplines such as medicine and law, which employed measures to exclude those not part of the profession, would turn those 'disciplines' on themselves. In other words, disciplines and practices that were designed to exclude others from the profession were turned inwards on behalf of a wider concept of the state. Recent changes in the medical profession illustrate this point, with the last bastion of the old professions (doctors) coming under the scrutiny of Ofsted-style inspections under the new Case Quality Commission framework (2013).

This went hand in hand with the 'swarming of the disciplinary mechanisms' (Foucault, 1991, p. 211) whereby the methods of control, previously unique to an individual profession, would swarm across the system as a whole, forming flexible and universally applicable methods of control. A modern example of this would be the modern reliance upon statistics or inspections which are now used in almost every professional context (Brady and Randle, 1997). These combined mechanisms work in tandem to become the organizing principles of the power structure. In Foucault's words:

> Taken one by one, most of these techniques have a long history behind them. But what was new, in the eighteenth century, was that, by being combined and generalized, they attained a level at which the formation of knowledge and the increase of power regularly reinforce one another in a circular process. (Foucault, 1991, p. 224)

With these disciplinary mechanisms representing the method or set of methods by which the system is maintained, Foucault turns in the final chapter to a description of the system as a whole. Here Foucault describes the dual nature of this carceral system:

It is highly probable that the great carceral continuum, which provides a communication between the power of discipline and the power of the law, and extends without interruption from the smallest coercions to the longest penal detention, constituted the technical and real, immediately material counterpart of that chimerical granting of the right to punish. (Foucault, 1991, p. 303)

This carceral continuum penetrates all layers of society and creates canopies of power maintained by flexible disciplinary techniques that can be applied universally, and also collusion between disciplines. Foucault hyphenates these complex unions between professions, calling them judicio-medical for instance. Here Foucault describes how these technologies of power shape the fabric of society itself, embedding within the individual subject the insidious notion of the 'norm': 'With this new economy of power, the carceral system, which is its basic instrument, permitted the emergence of a new form of "law": a mixture of legality and nature, prescription and constitution, the norm' (Foucault, 1991, p. 304).

A good example of this would be the links between education and social services or the medical profession and education such as in 'Healthy Eating' programmes.

How does this complex work, now almost 40 years old, that concerns the emergence of the prison system 300 years ago, relate to the modern education system?

The use of Foucault since his death in 1984 has become particularly prevalent as there has been a marked increase in state surveillance, especially in the UK where, as of 2013, there are 5.9 million CCTV cameras (Barrett, 2013).

Foucault's concept of Panopticism can be used very effectively when analysing any modern institution, because Foucault's fundamental observation of flexible forms of discipline (such as statistics) and his conclusion that there is more categorization, labelling and organization in the modern state, is undeniable. So Foucault is useful for the analysis of society as a whole (Gane, 2012).

In educational research, it can be argued that the development of education can be linked with the development of both the treatment of the insane and the treatment of prisoners, from Christian beginnings in the Middle Ages to the modern 'mind factories' of the twentieth century. Again we can trace the change from a teleological pursuit of the virtues, education for its own sake, to the utilitarian and routinized education of the modern period. Foucault provides us with a perspective through which we can view this change and analyse its implications.

Two examples of the use of the application of Foucault's philosophy in educational research are 'Panopticism, play and the resistance of surveillance: case studies of the observation of student Internet use in UK schools' by Andrew Hope (2007). In this work Hope uses the localized and specific topic of Internet use in schools and applies Panopticism to it, especially the aspects of Panopticism concerning observation as play. This paper displays the adaptability of Panopticism to a variety of different surveillance issues. Another example is 'The Scarlet P: Plagiarism, Panopticism and the Rhetoric of Academic Integrity' (Zwagerman, 2008), a work that seeks to use Panopticism to interrogate plagiarism-detection systems prevalent in modern universities. These two examples show how an understanding of Panopticism can give insights into a wide range of academic and educational contexts and situations. Furthermore, it is useful to place Foucault's philosophy in a wider intellectual context. One can link Foucault clearly with the rise of postmodernity in society, or what social commentator Zygmunt Baumann calls 'liquid modernity', a stage in which the structures that formed modernity in the early modern era (family, nation, state, religion) dissolve faster than they are formed, and society becomes increasingly less rigid and uniform. This gives rise to fear, described here by Baumann: 'It looks as if our fears have become self-perpetuating and self-reinforcing; as if they have acquired a momentum of their own – and can go on growing by drawing exclusively on their own resources' (Baumann, 2007, p. 9). This fear in turn leads to public acquiescence to ever more draconian laws in order to protect against fear: more Panopticism.

So, to sum up these two works, I believe a 'toolkit' emerges from them that can be applied:

Foucauldian subject – The decentralized subject and the binary nature in which society labels and excludes allows us to look in depth at the way in which society treats the subject.

Panopticism – Panopticism allows us to analyse societies' structures of discipline, and the way in which power over subjects spirals and increases.

The carceral continuum – Foucault shows us the way in which power structures, bolstered by Panoptic techniques form overarching power structures who use similar flexible disciplinary methods and work together.

In the previous sections, I have sought to show how two specific works can inform analysis of current educational systems and policy. I am now going to show how Christian thinking can provide an alternative view to that exposed by Foucault's deconstruction.

First, I am of the opinion that the current models of human development that are used in education are in opposition to Christian models of human development. A good example is the way in which modern education's views on developing a strong sense of individualism and self compare with a Christian model which might teach that links between individuals and society are primary (Hill, 2004, chapter 5) and therefore, that the Christian educator is often at odds with the modern education system (Cooling, 2010).

For the Christian researcher wishing to find an approach for applying theology to the modern world there are two main approaches.

The work that directly addresses this predicament is Hyman's *The Predicament of Postmodern Theology* (2001), a work which displays the two options available to the theologian who wants to confront and encapsulate the postmodern in their work. The first is to pursue a 'radical' approach that demythologizes the biblical narrative and seeks to concede ground to the break-up of the *grand récit* (Christianity can be seen as the prime example of a metanarrative). This approach is especially prevalent in early to mid-twentieth-century theology in the work of a theologian such as Don Cupitt (Cupitt, 1977, chapter 7). The second option is found in radical orthodoxy whereby there is a bold restatement of the Christian narrative, dominant because it is the only narrative that can encapsulate difference, and moreover the only narrative which can ground reality, avoiding the collapse into the void of nihilism (Milbank, 1991). For these approaches, using Foucault's deft approach to power and the subject, as well as the external tools of the identification of the panoptic and the carceral archipelago, can be a useful framework for evaluation.

One aspect of this particular movement which I wish to explore, and which I believe is particularly fruitful for the Christian education researcher, is the work of the 'Radical Orthodox' theological movement. Headed up by John Milbank, Radical Orthodoxy represents the most sustained attempt to engage with the modern philosophical project and provide a viable Christian alternative to secular philosophy (Hyman, 2001). Working on the premise that Christian Orthodoxy (as interpreted through the medieval Thomist tradition) is the most radical philosophy known to man, Radical Orthodoxy seeks to critique the modern world via the lens of both Continental Philosophy and Modern Theology (Milbank, 1991; Shakespeare, 2007). It therefore turns the view, prevalent from the nineteenth century onwards, that religion can and should be critiqued by psychology and sociology.

A second strand of this line of thought is the work of Alasdair MacIntyre, whose work *After Virtue* (2011) seeks to reassert the tradition of virtues as opposed to utilitarianism or 'emotivism' – the idea that there is no 'right' solution to moral conundrums but that the solution to a problem lies in who is best able to express themselves forcefully. This lapse into emotivism is, according to MacIntyre due to the breakdown in the words that govern ethical discourse (MacIntyre, 2011, chapter 1), a phenomenon linked with Lyotard's deconstruction of grand metanarratives. Both these authors' works recognize and choose one side in a particular dilemma facing theology. MacIntyre has become the spearhead of a trend towards a Christian revival of virtue-based education or character-based education.

Indeed, Milbank's treatment of Foucault in *Theology and Social Theory* (1991, p. 278), which simultaneously groups Foucault together with the other 'Nietzscheans', and states that their philosophies are inevitably grounded in an 'ontology of violence,' in the author's opinion, misses the strong moral compass that runs throughout Foucault's work. Foucault, for instance, chose to use the marginalized as his subject of study, something which could be construed as being very Christian. When read from a certain perspective, Foucault's work has a distinctly moral tone, although this is merely one reading of his work, a reading which is hard to elucidate partly due to the elusive nature of Foucault himself (Macey, 1993).

Foucault never approached theology directly. However, while secular philosophers' work on religion has much worth to the theologian as a serious external engagement with the sacred, the work of those who have never made any direct statement may have a clarity of purpose and neutrality useful to the religious academic in those areas touching on the human in relation to society and human institutions. I believe that Foucault is one of these thinkers.

In terms of education, Foucault can provide a rich philosophical framework for evaluating the systems and institutions that govern teaching, however he appears to be uncertain as to what solutions he offers to replace the current system, or, given that his view on human institutions is so cynical, who initiated this state of affairs and why.

This is where I think that Foucault's philosophy can be useful for the Christian educator, as a tool for both understanding and deconstructing modern society. However, having used this tool, Christian theology can then look at rebuilding society on a new model or models, or at least contributing to discussions surrounding these areas. The 'Death of God' theologies, in the author's opinion, don't provide a robust enough structure and are too close to the nihilism inherent in Foucault and postmodernism identified by John Milbank (1991). Therefore, the Radical

Orthodoxy expounded by John Milbank, and also approaches such as Alasdair MacIntyre's allow a re-imagining of Christian orthodoxy in a modern context, and provides a new direction for the individual who wishes to investigate Christian education.

Discussion Questions

1. Is it possible to use secular philosophical ideas in Christian research?
2. Is there a virtue-based approach to education which could have a prominent voice in the current education sector?
3. Is postmodern philosophy inherently nihilistic?
4. Can Foucault be considered a Christian thinker?
5. What possible consequences does the work of Foucault have for education professionals in our treatment of learners?

References

Barrett, David, 2013, www.telegraph.co.uk/technology/10172298/one-surveillance-camera-for-every-11-people-in-Britain-says-CCTV-survey.html

Baumann, Z., 2007, *Liquid Times: Living in an Age of Uncertainty*, 1st edn, London: Polity Press, pp. 1–30

Brady, N. and Randle, K., 1997, 'Managerialism and Professionalism in the "Cinderella Service"', in *Journal of Vocational Education and Training*, 49.1, pp. 121–139

Case Quality Commission, 2013, *A fresh start for the regulation and inspection of GP practices and GP out-of-hours services*, www.cqc.org.uk/sites/default/files/documents/20131211_-_gp_signposting_statement_-_final.pdf [accessed 8 April 2015]

Cooling, T., 2010, *Doing God in Education*, 1st edn, London: Theos

Cousins, M. and Hussain, A., 1990, *Michel Foucault*, Michigan: Macmillan

Cupitt, D., 1977, 'The Christ of Christendom', in Hick, J. (ed.) *The Myth of God Incarnate*, 4th edn, London: SCM Press, pp. 133–147

Deleuze, G., 1986, *Foucault*, London: Continuum

Donnolly, 1982, 'Foucault's genealogy of the human science', in Gane, M. (ed.), *Towards a Critique of Foucault*, Oxford: Routledge and Kegan Paul

Foucault, M., 1991, *Discipline and Punish*, 2nd edn, London: Penguin

Foucault, M., 1988, *Madness and Civilization*, 1st edn, New York: Random House

Freud, S., 2010, *The Ego and the Id*, 1st edn, London: CreateSpace Independent Publishing Platform

Gane, N., 2012, 'The governmentalities of neoliberalism: Panopticism, post-panopticism and beyond', in *Sociological review*, 60.4, pp. 611–634

Hill, B., 2004, *Exploring Religion in School*, 1st edn, Adelaide: Openbook, pp. 44–55

Hope, A., 2007, 'Panopticism, play and the resistance of surveillance: case studies of the observation of student Internet use in UK schools', in *British Journal of Sociology of Education*, 26.3, pp. 359–373

Hyman, G., 2001, *The Predicament of Postmodern Theology*, 1st edn, Westminster: John Knox Press

Lyotard, Jean-François, 1984, *The Postmodern Condition*, 1st edn, Minnesota: University of Minnesota Press

Macey, D., 1993, *The Lives of Michel Foucault*, 1st edn, London: Vintage

MacIntyre, A., 2011, *After Virtue*, 4th edn, London: Bloomsbury

McHoul, A. and Grace, W., 1993, *A Foucault Primer*, 1st edn, New York: UCL Press

Milbank, J., 1991, *Theology and Social Theory*, 2nd edn, Oxford: Blackwell

Morrissey, J., 2013, 'Governing the Academic Subject', in *Oxford Review of Education*, 39.6, pp. 797–810

Mourad, R., 2001, 'After Foucault: The Question of Civility', in *Teachers College Record*, 103.5, pp. 739–759

Shakespeare, S., 2007, *Radical Orthodoxy: A Critical Introduction*, (Kindle edn) London: SPCK, pp. 1–100

Zwagerman, S., 2008, 'The Scarlet P: Plagiarism, Panopticism and the Rhetoric of Academic Integrity', in *College Composition and Communication*, 59.4, pp. 676–710